Addressing Urbanism Challenges With AI and the Internet of Things

Adnène Arbi
University of Carthage, Tunisia

Imene Ouali
University of Sfax, Tunisia

Achraf Wali
University of Sfax, Tunisia

IGI Global
Scientific Publishing
Publishing Tomorrow's Research Today

Vice President of Editorial	Melissa Wagner
Managing Editor of Acquisitions	Mikaela Felty
Managing Editor of Book Development	Jocelynn Hessler
Production Manager	Mike Brehm
Cover Design	Phillip Shickler

Published in the United States of America by
IGI Global Scientific Publishing
701 East Chocolate Avenue
Hershey, PA, 17033, USA
Tel: 717-533-8845
Fax: 717-533-7115
Website: https://www.igi-global.com E-mail: cust@igi-global.com

Library of Congress Cataloging-in-Publication Data

LCCN: 2024053467 (CIP Data Pending)
ISBN13: 9798369381410
EISBN13: 9798369381434

British Cataloguing in Publication Data
A Cataloguing in Publication record for this book is available from the British Library.

Table of Contents

Detailed Table of Contents

In today's data-driven world, organizations across industries are leveraging data science and Business Intelligence (BI) to extract actionable insights from vast amounts of data. This article explores the role of data science and BI in driving informed decision-making, optimizing business processes, and gaining a competitive edge in the digital era. From data collection and preprocessing to advanced analytics and visualization techniques, we delve into the key components of data science and BI and their transformative impact on businesses. Additionally, we examine real-world applications, challenges, and future trends shaping the convergence of data science and BI, paving the way for data-driven innovation and organizational success.

In an era marked by unprecedented volumes of data generated from various sources, the field of Big Data has emerged as a critical enabler of innovation, decision-making, and competitive advantage across industries. This article explores the advancements in Big Data technologies, methodologies, and applications, highlighting their transformative impact on data analytics, business intelligence, and scientific discovery. From data collection and storage to processing and analysis, Big Data solutions offer scalable, efficient, and cost-effective means to unlock actionable insights from complex and heterogeneous datasets. Through case studies and real-world examples, this article demonstrates the value of Big Data in driving informed decision-making, optimizing operations, and driving innovation in diverse domains, including healthcare, finance, marketing, and cybersecurity. Furthermore, it examines emerging trends and future directions in the field, such as machine learning, artificial intelligence, edge computing, and ethical considerations, shaping the evolution of Big Data and its role in shaping the digital economy and society.

Urban areas face numerous challenges related to population growth, resource management, environmental sustainability, and infrastructure efficiency. The integration of Internet of Things (IoT) and Artificial Intelligence (AI) technologies offers innovative solutions to tackle these urbanism problems. This article explores the application of IoT and AI in addressing various urban challenges, including traffic congestion, energy consumption, waste management, public safety, and urban planning. By leveraging real-time data collection, predictive analytics, and autonomous systems, IoT and AI solutions empower cities to optimize resource utilization, enhance service delivery, and improve overall quality of life for residents.

Artificial Intelligence (AI) has emerged as a transformative force in healthcare, revolutionizing the industry through its ability to analyze complex data, optimize processes, and enhance decision-making. This article provides an overview of the applications of AI in healthcare, including disease diagnosis, treatment personalization, predictive analytics, and administrative tasks. Additionally, challenges and opportunities associated with AI implementation in healthcare are discussed, highlighting the potential for AI to improve patient outcomes, reduce costs, and transform the delivery of healthcare services.

This paper provides a concise review of the role of artificial intelligence in the development of autonomous vehicles for sustainable development goals. It highlights the significance of artificial intelligence in enabling autonomous vehicles to achieve sustainable transportation goals such as reduced emissions, improved traffic efficiency, and enhanced safety. The paper discusses the fundamental components of autonomous vehicles and the key artificial intelligence techniques used in perception, decision making, and control system. It also explores the challenges and perspectives associated the use of autonomous vehicles for achieving the sustainable development goals. This review serves as a valuable resource for researchers, and professionals interested in leveraging artificial intelligence for sustainable autonomous vehicles development.

Waste management has turned out to be one of the prime issues over the last few years. Even though municipal corporations and authorities around the world have employed workers to clean and empty out garbage cans of their localities every once in few days, there are days when the garbage overflows lead to spillage of waste which attracts flies and spreads other diseases within the locality. Furthermore, in most of the cases the garbage cans are left unclean or are just washed with water which often leaves a lot of moisture content in the garbage can resulting in the growth of microbes and bacteria. In order to address this issue, we have proposed and elaborated on a smart waste management system which is automated and works using Arduino board and a set of necessary sensors. Furthermore, we have also proposed an additional feature of automated sanitation to the smart waste management system which would make use of a sprinkler mechanism to sanitize the entire garbage can using solvents which are volatile and would dissolve the dirt present in the dustbin easily and evaporate.

key advanced technologies for sustainability and environment, highlighting their potential benefits, challenges, and implications for addressing pressing global environmental issues.

This chapter focuses on building a smart environment that can preserve energy on its own. The proposed model incorporates a bidirectional visitor counter that adjusts power supply based on peoples' presence or absence. In the case of a living room, this system will identify the amount of people in the room and switch on electricity to specified equipment. When the number of individuals within a closed space, the system turns off the power supply. The deployed appliances will be controlled by one or more programmed microcontrollers, which will instruct them to work efficiently based on need, drawing just the necessary amount of electricity and conserving power in the process. The majority of appliances may be handled from a single location, thereby increasing convenience. There will be greater energy efficiency. The intelligent design of interconnected appliances allows the user to remotely manage and monitor their operation even when they are far away from them.

Preface

Urban areas, the epicenters of human activity, are under unprecedented pressure as they adapt to the rapid pace of global urbanization. Cities today face a multitude of challenges: population growth, congestion, environmental degradation, resource scarcity, and aging infrastructure, to name a few. These issues require innovative solutions that go beyond traditional urban planning approaches, leveraging advanced technology to create smarter, more sustainable cities.

In this transformative era, **Artificial Intelligence (AI)** and the **Internet of Things (IoT)** have emerged as cornerstone technologies capable of addressing complex urban challenges. AI, with its ability to analyze and interpret vast data sets, coupled with IoT's capacity to collect real-time information through interconnected devices, presents a powerful synergy. Together, they enable cities to anticipate needs, optimize resources, enhance citizen experiences, and improve overall quality of life.

The inspiration for this book, *Addressing Urbanism Challenges With AI and the Internet of Things*, stems from the growing recognition of AI and IoT's role in urban transformation. It is a curated compilation of research, case studies, and perspectives that highlight the application of these technologies across various urban contexts. From smart traffic systems and sustainable energy grids to AI-powered urban planning and IoT-based environmental monitoring, this book showcases the diverse ways in which technology is shaping the future of cities.

This volume is designed to serve a broad audience, including:

- **Academics and researchers** exploring urbanism, AI, IoT, and smart city dynamics.
- **Policymakers** shaping urban strategies and governance frameworks.
- **Urban planners and city managers** integrating technology into urban operations.
- **Technology developers and engineers** crafting innovative AI and IoT solutions.
- **Students and educators** interested in the intersection of technology and urban studies.
- **Professionals** in architecture, environmental science, and public safety seeking actionable insights.

Our contributors delve into a range of topics, including:

- Innovations in **smart city infrastructure and management**.
- The role of AI in **urban planning and development strategies**.
- IoT applications for **environmental monitoring and sustainability**.
- Predictive analytics for **urban services and utilities optimization**.
- AI and IoT-driven advancements in **public safety and security**.
- Real-world **case studies** demonstrating successful implementations.

The collaborative effort behind this book reflects the interdisciplinary nature of addressing urban challenges with technology. As editors, we extend our gratitude to the contributors whose expertise and insights bring this vision to life.

We hope this book serves as a vital resource for understanding how AI and IoT can redefine urbanism, and as a catalyst for fostering smarter, more resilient cities worldwide. By addressing today's challenges with innovation and foresight, we can pave the way for sustainable urban futures.

Editors

Adnène Arbi

University of Carthage, Tunisia

Imene Ouali

University of Sfax, Tunisia

Achraf Wali

University of Sfax, Tunisia

Acknowledgment

This revolutionary adventure in the advanced technologies related to different urbanism services has not been completed without teamwork, and we are very appreciative of everyone who has made a substantial contribution to this cause.

Above all, we would want to express our sincere gratitude to **Achraf Wali, Imene Ouali and Adnène Arbi**. Your commitment, wisdom, and resolute assistance have been indispensable to the production of this book. Your varied viewpoints and combined experience have enhanced the text, guaranteeing a thorough examination of the topic.

To Achraf Wali, our investigation of the recent technologies used for various urbanism challenges has gained depth and usefulness from your scholarly contributions and abundance of experience. Your knowledge has been crucial in converting abstract ideas into practical that decision makers, governors and mayors can use.

Imène Ouali, this project has a dynamic energy because of your unique approach and original thoughts. Your knowledge of cutting-edge technologies and how they may be used in the urbanism has been crucial in bringing attention to the importance of the addressing urbanism challenges with Artificial Intelligence and the Internet of Things.

Adnène Arbi, the depth and caliber of this book are forever changed by your painstaking attention to detail and dedication to academic rigor. Your input has been crucial in forming the story and improving the content's overall cohesion.

Our heartfelt thanks go to Ms. **Elizabeth Barrantes**, Senior Development Editor, for her invaluable guidance and tireless efforts in helping us refine and submit a high-quality final version. Her keen insights and support have been instrumental in shaping this project in its best possible form.

We would also like to extend our sincere appreciation to Ms. **Jocelynn Hessler**, Managing Editor for Book Development, whose dedication and professionalism greatly facilitated the smooth progression of our work. Furthermore, we are grateful to the entire team at IGI Global Scientific Publishing for their unwavering commitment and exceptional support throughout the publication process.

Lastly, we extend our profound thanks to all the authors and reviewers who contributed chapters to this volume. Their research, dedication, and expertise have enriched this book, making it a comprehensive and impactful resource for the integration of AI and IoT in addressing urbanism challenges.

Thank you all for your valuable contributions, collaboration, and support in bringing this project to fruition.

EDITORIAL ADVISORY BOARD

Chapter 1
Data Science and Business Intelligence Transforming Insights Into Action

Oussama Wali
https://orcid.org/0009-0002-3197-0360
University of Tübingen, Germany

Mohamed Saifeddine Hadj Sassi
IT for Innovative Services Department, Luxembourg Institute of Science and Technology, Luxembourg

ABSTRACT

In today's data-driven world, organizations across industries are leveraging data science and Business Intelligence (BI) to extract actionable insights from vast amounts of data. This article explores the role of data science and BI in driving informed decision-making, optimizing business processes, and gaining a competitive edge in the digital era. From data collection and preprocessing to advanced analytics and visualization techniques, we delve into the key components of data science and BI and their transformative impact on businesses. Additionally, we examine real-world applications, challenges, and future trends shaping the convergence of data science and BI, paving the way for data-driven innovation and

DOI: 10.4018/979-8-3693-8141-0.ch001

organizational success.

1. INTRODUCTION

In an increasingly interconnected and data-rich environment, the ability to harness the power of data has become a strategic imperative for organizations seeking to thrive in today's competitive landscape. Data science and Business Intelligence (BI) play pivotal roles in unlocking the value hidden within vast and complex datasets, enabling organizations to derive actionable insights, drive informed decision-making, and gain a deeper understanding of their customers, operations, and market dynamics.

Data science, which encompasses disciplines such as statistics, machine learning, and data engineering, provides the tools and methodologies needed to extract meaningful patterns and predictions from raw data. It involves the use of advanced analytical techniques to uncover trends, make predictions, and support strategic planning. Through data mining, predictive modeling, and algorithm development, data science transforms raw data into valuable knowledge that can be leveraged across various business functions.

Business intelligence, on the other hand, focuses on the strategic use of data to inform business decisions. It involves the aggregation, analysis, and visualization of data to provide comprehensive insights into business performance. BI tools and platforms enable organizations to monitor Key Performance Indicators (KPIs), identify areas for improvement, and streamline operations. By translating complex data into intuitive visual formats, BI facilitates the interpretation and dissemination of insights across the organization.

The synergy between data science and business intelligence is essential for creating a data-driven culture within organizations. While data science provides the analytical horsepower to process and interpret large datasets, business intelligence ensures that these insights are accessible and actionable for decision-makers. Together, they empower organizations to move from reactive decision-making to proactive strategy development, fostering innovation and competitive advantage.

Moreover, the integration of data science and BI is driving significant transformations across various industries. In healthcare, data-driven insights are enhancing patient care and optimizing resource allocation. In finance, predictive analytics are improving risk management and investment strategies. Retailers are leveraging customer data to personalize marketing and improve customer experiences. Manufacturing firms are optimizing supply chains and improving production efficiency through data-driven insights.

As organizations continue to amass vast amounts of data, the importance of data governance, data quality, and ethical considerations cannot be overstated. Ensuring data accuracy, protecting privacy, and adhering to ethical standards are critical components of successful data science and BI initiatives. Furthermore, the ongoing advancement of technologies such as artificial intelligence, cloud computing, and the Internet of Things (IoT) is expanding the horizons of what data science and BI can achieve.

In this article, we will explore the foundational concepts of data science and business intelligence, examine their applications in various sectors, and discuss the future trends and challenges in this dynamic field. By understanding the transformative potential of data science and BI, organizations can better navigate the complexities of the modern business environment and harness data to drive innovation, efficiency, and growth.

2. THE ROLE OF DATA SCIENCE AND BI

Data science and BI play pivotal roles in modern organizations, empowering them to leverage data assets effectively and drive informed decision-making across all levels of the enterprise. Here, we delve deeper into the multifaceted contributions of data science and BI(LARSON *et al.*,2016):

2.1 Strategic Decision-Making Support

Strategic decision-making is the cornerstone of organizational success, and data science and Business Intelligence (BI) play a critical role in providing decision-makers with the insights they need to navigate complex business landscapes and make informed choices. Here's a closer look at how data science and BI support strategic decision-making:

- **Data-Driven Insights**: Data science and BI enable organizations to transform raw data into meaningful insights that drive strategic decision-making. By aggregating, analyzing, and visualizing data from disparate sources, decision-makers gain a comprehensive understanding of market trends, customer preferences, and competitive landscapes, empowering them to make data-driven decisions with confidence(NIU *et al.,* 2021).
- **Predictive Analytics:** Through the use of advanced analytics techniques such as predictive modeling and machine learning, data science and BI help organizations anticipate future trends and outcomes. By leveraging historical data and statistical algorithms, decision-makers can forecast market demand, identify emerging opportunities, and proactively address potential challenges, positioning their organizations for long-term success.
- **Scenario Analysis:** Data science and BI facilitate scenario analysis, allowing decision-makers to evaluate the potential impact of various strategic options and contingencies. By simulating different scenarios and assessing their outcomes, organizations can identify the most favorable courses of action, mitigate risks, and optimize resource allocation to achieve their strategic objectives effectively(PHILLIPS-WREN*et al.,* 2021).
- **Competitive Intelligence:** Data science and BI enable organizations to gather and analyze competitive intelligence, providing insights into competitors' strategies, market positioning, and performance metrics. By monitoring competitors' activities and benchmarking against industry peers, decision-makers can identify competitive threats and opportunities, refine their own strategies, and maintain a competitive edge in the marketplace(PHILLIPS-WREN*et al.,*2021).
- **Performance Monitoring:** Data science and BI facilitate real-time performance monitoring, allowing decision-makers to track Key Performance Indicators (KPIs), monitor progress against strategic goals, and identify areas for improvement. Through interactive dashboards, scorecards, and reports, decision-makers gain action-

able insights into organizational performance, enabling them to make timely adjustments and course corrections as needed(NIU *et al.*,2021).

In summary, data science and BI empower decision-makers with the insights they need to make strategic decisions that drive organizational growth and success. By leveraging data-driven insights, predictive analytics, scenario analysis, competitive intelligence, and performance monitoring, organizations can navigate uncertainty, capitalize on opportunities, and achieve their strategic objectives effectively in today's dynamic business environment.

2.2 Operational Efficiency and Process Optimization

Operational efficiency and process optimization are paramount for organizations seeking to streamline operations, reduce costs, and maximize productivity. Data science and Business Intelligence (BI) play a crucial role in identifying inefficiencies, automating processes, and optimizing workflows to enhance operational performance. Here's a deeper exploration of how data science and BI contribute to operational efficiency and process optimization:

Data-Driven Insights: Data science and BI enable organizations to gain valuable insights into their operational processes by analyzing vast amounts of data generated from various sources such as sensors, IoT devices, transactional systems, and social media platforms. By leveraging advanced analytics techniques, including descriptive, diagnostic, predictive, and prescriptive analytics, organizations can uncover patterns, trends, and anomalies in their operational data, enabling them to make data-driven decisions to improve efficiency(SIMON *et al.,* 2001).

- **Process Mining:** Process mining is a data-driven approach that involves analyzing event logs and transactional data to discover, monitor, and improve business processes. By visualizing process flows, identifying bottlenecks, and analyzing process variations, organizations can gain a comprehensive understanding of their operational processes and identify opportunities for optimization. Process mining techniques, such as process discovery, conformance checking, and performance analysis, enable organizations to streamline workflows, reduce cycle times, and eliminate inefficiencies(SIMON *et al.,*2001).

- **Predictive Maintenance:** Data science and BI enable organizations to implement predictive maintenance strategies to optimize asset performance and minimize downtime. By analyzing historical maintenance data, sensor data, and equipment telemetry, organizations can predict when equipment is likely to fail and proactively schedule maintenance activities to prevent unplanned downtime and costly repairs. Predictive maintenance techniques, such as machine learning models and condition monitoring algorithms, enable organizations to optimize maintenance schedules, extend asset lifecycles, and reduce operational costs.

- **Supply Chain Optimization:** Data science and BI help organizations optimize their supply chain operations by providing insights into demand forecasting, inventory management, and logistics optimization. By analyzing supply chain data, including sales data, supplier performance metrics, and transportation data, organizations can optimize inventory levels, reduce stockouts, and minimize transportation costs. Advanced analytics techniques, such as demand forecasting models, inventory optimization algorithms, and route optimization algorithms, enable organizations to improve supply chain efficiency and responsiveness to customer demand(GAD-ELRAB, 2021).

- **Robotic Process Automation (RPA):** Data science and BI support the implementation of Robotic Process Automation (RPA) solutions to automate repetitive, rule-based tasks and streamline business processes. By leveraging RPA tools and technologies, organizations can automate manual tasks such as data entry, invoice processing, and customer service inquiries, freeing up human resources to focus on more value-added activities. RPA solutions, coupled with data analytics capabilities, enable organizations to achieve greater operational efficiency, reduce errors, and improve overall productivity(GAD-ELRAB, 2021).

In summary, data science and BI play a pivotal role in driving operational efficiency and process optimization across organizations. By leveraging data-driven insights, process mining techniques, predictive maintenance strategies, supply chain optimization, and robotic process automation, organizations can streamline operations, reduce costs, and enhance productivity, ultimately gaining a competitive advantage in today's dynamic business landscape.

2.3 Customer Understanding and Personalization

Customer understanding and personalization are critical aspects of modern business strategies aimed at enhancing customer satisfaction, loyalty, and retention. Data science and business intelligence (BI) play a crucial role in helping organizations gain deep insights into customer behavior, preferences, and needs, enabling them to deliver personalized experiences and tailored offerings. Here's a closer look at how data science and BI contribute to customer understanding and personalization:

- **Customer Segmentation:** Data science and BI techniques enable organizations to segment their customer base into distinct groups based on demographics, psychographics, purchasing behavior, and other relevant attributes. By clustering customers into homogeneous segments, organizations can better understand their diverse customer base and tailor marketing campaigns, product offerings, and services to meet the unique needs and preferences of each segment. Customer segmentation helps organizations optimize their marketing efforts, improve customer targeting, and enhance overall engagement and satisfaction(ANSHARI *et al.,*2019).
- **Predictive Analytics:** Predictive analytics leverages historical customer data to forecast future behavior and outcomes, enabling organizations to anticipate customer needs, preferences, and churn risk. By applying machine learning algorithms and statistical models to analyze customer data, organizations can predict customer lifetime value, identify high-value customers, and personalize marketing messages and promotions to target specific customer segments effectively. Predictive analytics empowers organizations to proactively address customer needs, enhance customer experiences, and drive customer loyalty and retention.
- **Recommendation Systems:** Recommendation systems leverage data science and machine learning algorithms to provide person-

alized product recommendations and content to customers based on their past behavior, preferences, and interactions. By analyzing customer purchase history, browsing behavior, and feedback, recommendation systems can suggest relevant products, services, and content to customers, increasing cross-selling and upselling opportunities and driving revenue growth. Recommendation systems enhance the customer shopping experience, increase customer engagement, and foster brand loyalty and advocacy(ANNAPURANI *et al.,* 2021).

- **Sentiment Analysis:** Sentiment analysis, also known as opinion mining, involves analyzing textual data such as customer reviews, social media posts, and survey responses to determine customer sentiment and feedback. By applying Natural Language Processing (NLP) techniques and sentiment analysis algorithms, organizations can extract insights from unstructured text data, identify positive and negative sentiment, and understand customer perceptions and opinions about their products, services, and brand. Sentiment analysis helps organizations identify areas for improvement, address customer concerns, and enhance overall customer satisfaction and loyalty(ANNAPURANI *et al.,* 2021).
- **Real-Time Personalization:** Real-time personalization leverages data science and BI capabilities to deliver personalized experiences to customers in real time across various touchpoints, including websites, mobile apps, and customer service interactions. By integrating customer data from multiple sources and applying real-time analytics, organizations can dynamically adjust content, offers, and interactions based on customer behavior and preferences, delivering relevant and contextual experiences that resonate with individual customers. Real-time personalization enhances customer engagement, increases conversion rates, and drives customer loyalty and advocacy(ANNAPURANI *et al.,* 2021).

In summary, data science and BI play a crucial role in enabling organizations to gain deep insights into customer behavior, preferences, and needs, allowing them to deliver personalized experiences and tailored offerings that drive customer satisfaction, loyalty, and retention. By leveraging customer segmentation, predictive analytics, recommendation systems, sentiment analysis, and real-time personalization, organizations can optimize their marketing efforts, enhance customer engagement, and differentiate themselves in today's competitive marketplace.

2.4 Risk Management and Compliance

Risk management and compliance are paramount considerations for businesses operating in today's complex regulatory landscape. Data science and Business Intelligence (BI) tools and techniques play a crucial role in helping organizations identify, assess, and mitigate risks, as well as ensuring compliance with relevant laws, regulations, and industry standards. Here's a deeper dive into how data science and BI contribute to risk management and compliance:

- **Risk Identification and Assessment:** Data science and BI enable organizations to identify and assess various types of risks, including financial, operational, strategic, and reputational risks. By analyzing vast amounts of structured and unstructured data from internal and external sources, organizations can uncover patterns, trends, and anomalies that may indicate potential risks or threats to the business. Advanced analytics techniques, such as predictive modeling and machine learning, help organizations forecast and quantify risks, allowing them to prioritize risk mitigation efforts and allocate resources effectively.
- **Fraud Detection and Prevention:** Data science and BI solutions are instrumental in detecting and preventing fraudulent activities across various business functions, including finance, procurement, sales, and marketing. By analyzing transactional data, user behavior, and other relevant indicators, organizations can identify suspicious patterns and anomalies indicative of fraudulent behavior, such as unauthorized transactions, unusual spending patterns, or account takeovers. Advanced analytics algorithms can flag suspicious activities in real time, enabling organizations to investigate and take corrective action promptly to mitigate financial losses and reputational damage(HADJ SASSI *et al.*,2024).

- **Compliance Monitoring and Reporting: Data** science and BI tools enable organizations to monitor and track compliance with relevant laws, regulations, and industry standards, ensuring adherence to legal and regulatory requirements. By integrating data from multiple sources, including internal systems, external databases, and regulatory agencies, organizations can establish robust compliance monitoring frameworks and automate the process of gathering, analyzing, and reporting compliance-related data. Advanced analytics capabilities, such as Natural Language Processing (NLP) and semantic analysis, facilitate the interpretation of complex regulatory documents and enable organizations to stay abreast of evolving regulatory requirements.
- **Regulatory Risk Assessment:** Data science and BI help organizations assess and manage regulatory risks associated with changes in laws, regulations, and industry standards. By analyzing regulatory trends, enforcement actions, and precedents, organizations can anticipate regulatory developments and assess their potential impact on business operations and compliance obligations. Predictive analytics techniques allow organizations to model various scenarios and assess the likelihood and severity of regulatory risks, enabling proactive risk management and strategic decision-making(SILVA *et al.,* 2018).
- **Internal Controls and Governance:** Data science and BI support the implementation and monitoring of robust internal controls and governance frameworks designed to mitigate risks and ensure accountability and transparency within organizations. By analyzing internal audit findings, control deficiencies, and key risk indicators, organizations can identify weaknesses in their control environment and implement remedial actions to strengthen internal controls and mitigate risks effectively. BI dashboards and reporting tools provide stakeholders with real-time visibility into risk and compliance metrics, enabling informed decision-making and proactive risk management(SILVA *et al.,*2018).

In summary, data science and BI play a critical role in enabling organizations to identify, assess, and mitigate risks, as well as ensuring compliance with relevant laws, regulations, and industry standards. By leveraging advanced analytics techniques and BI tools, organizations can enhance their risk management capabilities, detect and prevent fraud, monitor compliance, assess regulatory risks, and strengthen internal controls and governance frameworks, ultimately safeguarding the organization's reputation and long-term sustainability.

2.5 Innovation and Competitive Advantage

In today's highly competitive business landscape, innovation is a key driver of sustainable growth and competitive advantage. Data science and Business Intelligence (BI) play a pivotal role in fostering innovation and enabling organizations to gain a competitive edge in the market. Here's a closer look at how data science and BI contribute to innovation and competitive advantage:

- **Data-Driven Decision Making: Data** science and BI empower organizations to make informed, data-driven decisions based on insights derived from analyzing large volumes of structured and unstructured data. By leveraging advanced analytics techniques such as predictive modeling, machine learning, and data mining, organizations can uncover hidden patterns, trends, and correlations in their data, enabling them to identify new market opportunities, anticipate customer needs, and develop innovative products and services that meet or exceed customer expectations.
- **Market Intelligence and Trend Analysis**: Data science and BI enable organizations to gain valuable market intelligence and stay abreast of industry trends, competitor activities, and consumer preferences. By analyzing market data, social media sentiment, customer feedback, and other external sources of information, organizations can identify emerging trends, market gaps, and unmet customer needs, providing valuable insights that drive innovation and product development initiatives. BI tools and dashboards facilitate real-time monitoring of market dynamics and competitor per-

formance, enabling organizations to respond quickly to changing market conditions and gain a competitive advantage.

- **Product and Service Innovation:** Data science and BI facilitate product and service innovation by providing organizations with actionable insights into customer behavior, preferences, and purchasing patterns. By analyzing customer data, including demographics, psychographics, and purchase history, organizations can identify opportunities for product and service customization, personalization, and differentiation. Advanced analytics techniques enable organizations to segment their customer base, target specific customer segments with tailored offerings, and optimize product features and pricing strategies to maximize customer satisfaction and loyalty.
- **Operational Efficiency and Process Optimization:** Data science and BI enable organizations to streamline their operations, improve efficiency, and optimize business processes across the value chain. By analyzing operational data, including supply chain, logistics, and manufacturing data, organizations can identify inefficiencies, bottlenecks, and areas for improvement, enabling them to implement data-driven process optimizations and cost-saving initiatives. BI dashboards and performance metrics provide stakeholders with real-time visibility into operational performance, enabling continuous monitoring and improvement of Key Performance Indicators (KPIs) and operational metrics(MEDEIROS*et al.,* 2020).
- **Customer Experience Enhancement:** Data science and BI help organizations enhance the customer experience by providing personalized, timely, and relevant interactions across all touchpoints and channels. By analyzing customer data and behavior, organizations can create targeted marketing campaigns, personalized product recommendations, and customized customer experiences that resonate with individual preferences and needs. BI tools enable organizations to track and measure customer satisfaction, loyalty, and engagement metrics, enabling them to identify areas for improvement and implement strategies to enhance the overall customer experience(MEDEIROS*et al.,* 2020).

In summary, data science and BI play a critical role in driving innovation and enabling organizations to gain a competitive advantage in today's dynamic business environment. By leveraging advanced analytics techniques, market intelligence, customer insights, and operational data, organizations can make data-driven decisions, identify new market opportunities, innovate products and services, optimize business processes, and enhance the overall customer experience, ultimately positioning themselves for long-term success and growth.

2.6 Continuous Improvement and Performance Monitoring

Continuous improvement and performance monitoring are essential aspects of data science and Business Intelligence (BI) initiatives, ensuring that organizations can adapt, evolve, and optimize their strategies and processes over time. Here's a deeper exploration of how these elements contribute to the success of data-driven organizations:

- **Agile Methodologies and Iterative Development:** Data science and BI projects often employ agile methodologies and iterative development processes to facilitate continuous improvement and adaptation. By breaking down large projects into smaller, manageable tasks or sprints, organizations can quickly deliver value and gather feedback from stakeholders, enabling them to make incremental improvements and adjustments based on real-world insights and user feedback. Agile practices such as regular retrospectives, sprint reviews, and continuous integration and deployment foster a culture of continuous improvement and enable organizations to respond rapidly to changing requirements and priorities(MEDEIROS*et al.*, 2020).
- **Key Performance Indicators (KPIs) and Metrics:** Performance monitoring involves the tracking and analysis of Key Performance Indicators (KPIs) and metrics to measure the effectiveness and impact of data science and BI initiatives. Organizations define relevant KPIs and metrics aligned with their strategic objectives and business goals, such as revenue growth, cost reduction, customer satisfaction,

and operational efficiency. BI tools and dashboards provide stakeholders with real-time visibility into KPI performance, enabling them to monitor progress, identify trends, and make data-driven decisions to drive continuous improvement and achieve organizational objectives(MEDEIROS*et al.,* 2020).

- **Root Cause Analysis and Corrective Actions:** Continuous improvement involves identifying areas for improvement, analyzing root causes of issues or challenges, and implementing corrective actions to address underlying problems. Data science and BI enable organizations to conduct root cause analysis by analyzing historical data, identifying patterns, trends, and anomalies, and uncovering factors contributing to performance issues or deviations from expected outcomes. By understanding the root causes of problems, organizations can develop targeted interventions, process improvements, and corrective actions to address underlying issues and drive continuous improvement in performance and outcomes(MEDEIROS*et al.,*2020).
- **Predictive Analytics and Forecasting:** Predictive analytics and forecasting play a crucial role in performance monitoring and continuous improvement by enabling organizations to anticipate future trends, risks, and opportunities. By leveraging historical data, statistical models, and machine learning algorithms, organizations can develop predictive models to forecast future outcomes, trends, and behavior, enabling them to proactively identify potential issues, mitigate risks, and capitalize on emerging opportunities. Predictive analytics enables organizations to make data-driven decisions and take preemptive actions to optimize performance, enhance efficiency, and drive continuous improvement in business operations.
- **Feedback Loops and Stakeholder Engagement:** Effective performance monitoring and continuous improvement require active engagement and collaboration with stakeholders across the organization. Feedback loops enable organizations to gather input, insights, and feedback from stakeholders, including employees, customers, and partners, to identify areas for improvement and prioritize initiatives. Stakeholder engagement fosters a culture of continuous improvement, innovation, and accountability, empowering employees

to contribute ideas, share feedback, and take ownership of improvement initiatives. By soliciting input from diverse perspectives and engaging stakeholders in the improvement process, organizations can drive meaningful change and achieve sustainable performance improvement over time.

In summary, continuous improvement and performance monitoring are integral components of data science and BI initiatives, enabling organizations to adapt, evolve, and optimize their strategies and processes in response to changing business conditions and stakeholder needs. By embracing agile methodologies, defining relevant KPIs and metrics, conducting root cause analysis, leveraging predictive analytics, and engaging stakeholders, organizations can drive continuous improvement, enhance performance, and achieve their strategic objectives and business goals in a dynamic and competitive business environment.

In essence, data science and BI are integral components of modern business operations, enabling organizations to harness the power of data to drive innovation, optimize performance, and achieve sustainable growth in an increasingly competitive and data-driven environment.

3. KEY COMPONENTS OF DATA SCIENCE AND BI

Data science and Business Intelligence (BI) encompass a wide range of methodologies, techniques, and tools aimed at extracting valuable insights from data to support decision-making and drive business success. Here are the key components that form the foundation of data science and BI initiatives:

3. 1. Data Collection and Integration

- Data collection involves gathering raw data from various sources, including internal databases, external sources, sensors, social media, and third-party data providers(SUN *et al.,*2018).

- Data integration combines data from disparate sources into a unified repository or data warehouse, ensuring consistency, accuracy, and accessibility for analysis(SUN *et al.,* 2018).

3. 2. Data Storage and Management

- Data storage involves storing and organizing data in a structured, semi-structured, or unstructured format, depending on its type and characteristics.
- Data management encompasses activities such as data cleansing, transformation, indexing, and archival to maintain data quality, integrity, and usability over time.

3. 3. Data Exploration and Preprocessing

- Data exploration involves examining and visualizing data to understand its structure, patterns, and relationships.
- Data preprocessing includes cleaning, filtering, and transforming raw data to prepare it for analysis, addressing missing values, outliers, and inconsistencies.

3. 4. Descriptive Analytics

- Descriptive analytics focuses on summarizing historical data to provide insights into past performance and trends, answering questions such as "What happened?" and "Why did it happen?"(WANG *et al.,* 2022).
- Techniques such as data aggregation, summarization, and visualization are commonly used to analyze and present descriptive insights(WANG *et al.,* 2022).

3. 5. Diagnostic Analytics

- Diagnostic analytics aims to identify the root causes of past events or outcomes by analyzing historical data and relationships between variables(LARSON *et al.,* 2016).

- Techniques such as regression analysis, correlation analysis, and hypothesis testing help uncover patterns, trends, and relationships in data to explain why certain events occurred(LARSON *et al.*,2016).

3. 6. Predictive Analytics

- Predictive analytics leverages statistical modeling, machine learning algorithms, and data mining techniques to forecast future trends, behaviors, and outcomes based on historical data.
- Predictive models enable organizations to make data-driven predictions, anticipate changes, and proactively address opportunities and risks.

3. 7. Prescriptive Analytics

- Prescriptive analytics goes beyond predicting future outcomes to recommend actions or interventions that optimize decision-making and drive desired outcomes(MEDEIROS *et al.,* 2020).
- By simulating various scenarios and evaluating potential actions, prescriptive analytics helps organizations identify the most effective strategies and courses of action to achieve their goals(MEDEIROS *et al.,*2020).

3. 8. Reporting and Dashboards

- Reporting tools and dashboards provide interactive visualizations and reports that communicate key insights and performance metrics to stakeholders(WANG *et al.,* 2022).
- Customizable dashboards enable users to monitor KPIs, track performance, and gain real-time visibility into business operations(WANG *et al.,* 2022).

3. 9. Data Governance and Security

- Data governance frameworks and security protocols ensure that data is managed, protected, and compliant with regulations and industry standards(WANG *et al.,* 2022).
- Measures such as access controls, encryption, and data masking safeguard sensitive information and mitigate risks of data breaches or unauthorized access(WANG *et al.,*2022).

3. 10. Advanced Analytics and Machine Learning

- Advanced analytics techniques, including machine learning, natural language processing (NLP), and deep learning, enable organizations to derive deeper insights, uncover hidden patterns, and automate decision-making processes(AYANKOYA *et al.,*2014).
- Machine learning algorithms analyze large datasets to identify patterns, make predictions, and generate recommendations, driving innovation and competitive advantage(AYANKOYA *et al.,* 2014).

In summary, data science and BI encompass a comprehensive set of components and methodologies that enable organizations to harness the power of data to gain insights, make informed decisions, and drive business success. By integrating data collection, storage, analysis, and visualization capabilities, organizations can unlock the full potential of their data assets and gain a competitive edge in today's data-driven world.

4. REAL-WORLD APPLICATIONS

Data science and Business Intelligence (BI) have revolutionized decision-making processes and operations across various industries(see Figure 1).

Figure 1. Utilization of Big Data Analytics in Organizational Context: Insights from Evans Data Corporation.

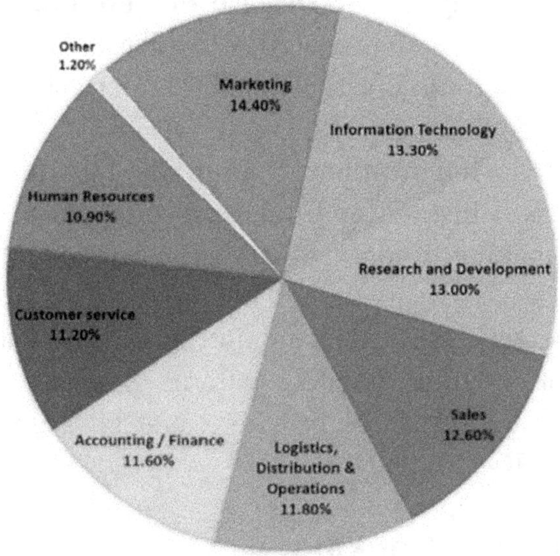

Here are some real-world applications where these technologies are making a significant impact:

4. 1. Retail and E-Commerce

- **Customer Segmentation:** Retailers use data analytics to segment customers based on demographics, purchase history, and behavior, enabling personalized marketing campaigns and product recommendations.
- **Inventory Optimization**: BI tools analyze sales data and inventory levels to optimize stock levels, reduce stockouts, and minimize excess inventory, improving supply chain efficiency.
- **Demand Forecasting**: Predictive analytics models forecast future demand for products, allowing retailers to anticipate trends, adjust pricing strategies, and optimize promotions.

4. 2. Healthcare

- **Predictive Analytics for Disease Prevention:** Healthcare providers leverage predictive analytics to identify individuals at risk of developing chronic diseases, enabling early intervention and preventive care strategies(ARBI *et al.*,2021).
- **Clinical Decision Support:** Data-driven algorithms analyze patient data, medical history, and treatment outcomes to support clinical decision-making, improve diagnosis accuracy, and optimize treatment plans.
- **Fraud Detection:** BI tools monitor healthcare claims data to detect fraudulent activities, identify patterns of abuse, and prevent financial losses for insurance providers and government agencies(ANNAPURANI *et al.*,2021).

4. 3. Finance and Banking

- **Credit Scoring and Risk Assessment:** Banks use machine learning algorithms to assess creditworthiness, predict default risk, and determine loan approval decisions, enhancing lending practices and reducing credit risk(RADMEHR *et al.*, 2017, HAMDI *et al.* 2024).
- **Fraud Detection and Prevention:** Data analytics tools analyze transactional data and detect anomalies or suspicious patterns indicative of fraudulent activities, helping financial institutions prevent fraud and safeguard customer assets(RADMEHR *et al.*, 2017).
- **Algorithmic Trading:** Investment firms employ quantitative models and algorithmic trading strategies to analyze market data, identify profitable opportunities, and execute trades at optimal prices, maximizing returns and minimizing risks(RADMEHR *et al.*,2017).

4. 4. Manufacturing and Supply Chain

- **Predictive Maintenance:** Manufacturing companies utilize IoT sensors and predictive analytics to monitor equipment performance, predict maintenance needs, and prevent costly downtime, optimizing asset utilization and productivity.

- **Supply Chain Optimization:** BI tools analyze supply chain data, including supplier performance, inventory levels, and transportation logistics, to optimize procurement, minimize costs, and improve delivery efficiency(HAZEN *et al.,* 2014).
- **Quality Control:** Data analytics techniques identify patterns and anomalies in production processes, enabling real-time quality monitoring, defect detection, and process improvements to ensure product quality and consistency(HAZEN *et al.,*2014).

4. 5. Telecommunications

- **Customer Churn Prediction:** Telecommunication providers use predictive analytics to forecast customer churn, identify at-risk subscribers, and implement targeted retention strategies, reducing customer attrition and improving loyalty(KRASIC *et al.,* 2021).
- **Network Performance Management:** BI solutions analyze network data and performance metrics to identify bottlenecks, optimize resource allocation, and enhance the reliability and speed of telecommunications networks(KRASIC *et al.,* 2021).
- **Personalized Marketing:** Data-driven segmentation and analysis enable telecom companies to deliver personalized offers, services, and promotions based on individual preferences, driving customer engagement and revenue growth(KRASIC *et al.,*2021).

4. 6. Marketing and Advertising

- Campaign Optimization: Data analytics platforms analyze customer data, engagement metrics, and campaign performance to optimize marketing strategies, allocate budgets effectively, and maximize ROI.
- **Sentiment Analysis:** Natural Language Processing (NLP) techniques analyze social media, customer reviews, and online conversations to understand sentiment, trends, and public opinion, guiding marketing efforts and brand management(CHAUDHARY *et al.,* 2022).

- **Attribution Modeling:** BI tools attribute conversions and sales to specific marketing channels, campaigns, or touchpoints, providing insights into the effectiveness of marketing efforts and informing future investment decisions(CHAUDHARY *et al.*,2022).

These examples illustrate the diverse range of applications where data science and business intelligence play a crucial role in driving innovation, improving decision-making, and delivering value across industries. As organizations continue to leverage data-driven insights and technologies, the potential for transformative impact on business operations and outcomes will only continue to grow(ARBI *et al.*,2024).

5. CHALLENGES AND OPPORTUNITIES

Data science and Business Intelligence (BI) offer immense opportunities for organizations to gain insights, optimize operations, and drive innovation. However, along with these opportunities come several challenges that need to be addressed to fully harness the potential of these technologies. Below are some key challenges and opportunities in the field:

5. 1. Challenges

5. 1. 1. Data Quality and Governance: Ensuring data quality, consistency, and accuracy remains a significant challenge, particularly when dealing with large volumes of disparate data sources. Establishing robust data governance frameworks and implementing data quality management practices are essential to address this challenge(BALACHANDRAN *et al.,* 2017).

5. 1. 2. Data Privacy and Security: With the increasing emphasis on data privacy regulations such as GDPR and CCPA, organizations face challenges in safeguarding sensitive information and ensuring compliance with regulatory requirements. Protecting data against breaches, unauthorized access, and cyber threats requires robust security measures and privacy-enhancing technologies(ARBI,2018).

5. 1. 3. Skill Shortage: There is a shortage of skilled professionals with expertise in data science, machine learning, and advanced analytics. Recruiting and retaining top talent remains a challenge for organizations seeking to build data-driven capabilities and extract actionable insights from data(BALACHANDRAN *et al.,*2017).

5. 1. 4. Integration Complexity: Integrating disparate data sources, systems, and applications to create a unified view of data is often complex and time-consuming. Organizations face challenges in integrating legacy systems with modern data platforms and ensuring seamless interoperability across heterogeneous environments (OUALI *et al.,*2021).

5. 1. 5. Ethical Considerations: As data-driven technologies become more pervasive, ethical considerations surrounding data usage, algorithmic bias, and responsible AI adoption become increasingly important. Organizations must navigate ethical dilemmas and ensure that data-driven decision-making processes are fair, transparent, and unbiased(OUALI *et al.,*2024).

5. 2. Opportunities

5. 2. 1. Advanced Analytics: The proliferation of data science techniques, including machine learning, artificial intelligence, and predictive analytics, presents opportunities for organizations to extract actionable insights, uncover hidden patterns, and drive data-driven decision-making across various business functions.

5. 2. 2. Real-Time Insights: Advances in streaming analytics and real-time data processing enable organizations to gain immediate insights from streaming data sources, allowing for faster decision-making, proactive risk management, and enhanced operational agility.

5. 2. 3. Data Monetization: Organizations can unlock new revenue streams and business opportunities by monetizing data assets through data sharing agreements, subscription-based services, and personalized offerings. Data-driven business models enable organizations to create value from data assets and drive innovation in new markets(LARSON *et al.,* 2016).

5. 2. 4. Personalized Customer Experiences: Leveraging data analytics and AI-driven personalization techniques, organizations can deliver personalized customer experiences, tailored product recommendations, and targeted marketing campaigns, enhancing customer engagement, loyalty, and satisfaction.

5. 2. 5. Operational Efficiency: Data-driven insights enable organizations to optimize processes, streamline operations, and reduce costs across the value chain. From supply chain optimization to resource allocation and workforce management, data analytics drives efficiencies and improves organizational performance.

5. 2. 6. Innovation and Competitive Advantage: Organizations that leverage data science and BI capabilities to innovate, experiment, and iterate faster gain a competitive edge in the market. Data-driven innovation fosters a culture of continuous improvement, agility, and adaptability, positioning organizations for long-term success in a rapidly evolving business landscape(LARSON *et al.,*2016).

By addressing these challenges and embracing these opportunities, organizations can unlock the full potential of data science and business intelligence to drive growth, innovation, and sustainable value creation. As data continues to evolve as a strategic asset, organizations that prioritize data-driven decision-making and invest in data-driven capabilities will thrive in the digital age(ARBI *et al.,*2018).

6. FUTURE TRENDS AND OUTLOOK

As data science and business intelligence (BI) continue to evolve, several emerging trends are shaping the future landscape of the field. Understanding these trends is essential for organizations seeking to stay ahead of the curve and harness the full potential of data-driven technologies. Below are some key future trends and outlooks in data science and BI:

6. 1. Augmented Analytics: Augmented analytics, powered by artificial intelligence and machine learning algorithms, will revolutionize the way organizations derive insights from data. These advanced analytics tools automate data preparation, analysis, and interpretation, enabling business users to make informed decisions faster and more accurately(SABIR *et al.,*2021).

6. 2. Explainable AI: As AI and machine learning models become more complex and pervasive, the need for explainable AI (XAI) becomes increasingly critical. Explainable AI techniques aim to provide transparency and interpretability into the decision-making process of AI algorithms, ensuring accountability, trust, and compliance with regulatory requirements(ULLAH*et al.,* 2024).

6. 3. Data Democratization: Data democratization initiatives will empower employees at all levels of the organization to access, analyze, and leverage data for decision-making purposes. Self-service BI tools, intuitive dashboards, and data literacy programs will enable non-technical users to derive insights from data independently, fostering a data-driven culture across the organization(SASSI *et al.,*2020b).

6. 4. Edge Analytics: With the proliferation of Internet of Things (IoT) devices and edge computing technologies, organizations are increasingly adopting edge analytics solutions to analyze data at the edge of the network in real-time. Edge analytics enables faster decision-making, reduced latency, and improved operational efficiency, particularly in remote or resource-constrained environments(OUALI *et al.,*2022b).

6. 5. Ethical AI and Responsible Data Use: Ethical considerations surrounding AI ethics, data privacy, and responsible data use will continue to gain prominence in the coming years. Organizations will need to prioritize ethical AI principles, such as fairness, transparency, accountability, and bias mitigation, to ensure that AI technologies are developed and deployed in a socially responsible manner(SASSI *et al.,*2019b).

6. 6. Predictive and Prescriptive Analytics: The shift towards predictive and prescriptive analytics will enable organizations to anticipate future trends, identify emerging opportunities, and proactively mitigate risks. Predictive analytics models leverage historical data and machine learning algorithms to forecast future outcomes, while prescriptive analytics algorithms provide actionable recommendations to optimize decision-making processes(SABIR, *et al.*2020).

6.7. Quantum Computing: The advent of quantum computing holds the potential to revolutionize data processing, optimization, and cryptography. Quantum computing technologies will enable organizations to solve complex computational problems that are currently infeasible for classical computers, opening up new frontiers in data science, cryptography, and machine learning(ULLAH*et al.,*2024).

6. 8. Data Ethics and Governance Frameworks: With the increasing scrutiny around data privacy and ethical AI, organizations will need to develop robust data ethics and governance frameworks to ensure compliance with regulatory requirements and industry standards. Data governance initiatives will focus on data quality, integrity, security, and privacy, fostering trust and accountability in data-driven decision-making processes.

6. 9. Hyperautomation and Intelligent Process Automation (IP-A): Hyperautomation, powered by AI, machine learning, and Robotic Process Automation (RPA), will automate and optimize business processes across the organization. Intelligent Process Automation (IPA) solutions will combine RPA with cognitive capabilities, Natural Language Processing (NLP), and machine learning to automate complex, cognitive tasks traditionally performed by humans(OUALI *et al.,*2022c).

6. 10. Data Collaboration and Ecosystems: Collaborative data ecosystems and data sharing initiatives will enable organizations to leverage external data sources, partnerships, and ecosystem networks to drive innovation, co-create value, and address complex business challenges collaboratively. Data collaboration platforms and federated learning approaches will facilitate secure, decentralized data sharing while preserving data privacy and confidentiality(SASSI et al., 2019a).

By embracing these future trends and outlooks, organizations can position themselves for success in the data-driven era and unlock new opportunities for innovation, growth, and competitive differentiation. As data science and business intelligence continue to evolve, organizations that proactively adapt to these trends and invest in emerging technologies will emerge as leaders in their respective industries, driving positive impact and sustainable value creation(OUALI *et al.,*2023a).

7. CONCLUSION

In conclusion, data science and business intelligence are indispensable tools for organizations seeking to thrive in the digital age. By harnessing the power of data, organizations can gain a competitive edge, drive innovation, and create value for stakeholders. The integration of advanced analytics and insightful data visualization allows businesses to uncover hidden patterns, make informed decisions, and implement strategies that are both proactive and responsive to market demands(SASSI *et al.,*2019c).

As data science and BI continue to evolve, organizations must embrace emerging trends, address challenges, and cultivate a data-driven culture to realize the full potential of data-driven decision-making. This involves staying abreast of technological advancements, such as artificial intelligence, machine learning, and big data platforms, which are reshaping the landscape of data analytics. It also requires a commitment to ongoing education and skill development for employees to effectively leverage these tools and methodologies.

Moreover, the ethical considerations surrounding data usage cannot be overlooked. Organizations must ensure the integrity, security, and privacy of their data to build trust with customers and comply with regulatory requirements. Developing robust data governance frameworks is crucial for maintaining data quality and ensuring ethical standards are met(OUALI *et al.,*2023b).

The future of data science and BI promises even greater integration and application across industries. With the rise of the Internet of Things (IoT), organizations will have access to real-time data from a multitude of sources, further enhancing their ability to make timely and impactful decisions. Predictive analytics and automation will continue to streamline operations, reduce costs, and improve customer experiences(OUALI et al., 2022a).

In summary, data science and business intelligence represent the cornerstone of modern business operations, enabling organizations to navigate complexity, drive innovation, and achieve sustainable growth in an increasingly data-driven world. By embracing these disciplines and fostering a culture that values data-driven insights, organizations can position themselves for long-term success and resilience in the face of rapid technological change and competitive pressures. The strategic use of data not only enhances operational efficiency but also empowers organizations to anticipate and adapt to future challenges, ensuring they remain at the forefront of their respective industries(GUO *et al.*,2022).

REFERENCES

Annapurani, . (2021). Healthcare Data Analytics Using Business Intelligence Tool. In *Machine Learning and Analytics in Healthcare Systems* (pp. 191–212). CRC Press. DOI: 10.1201/9781003185246-10

Anshari, , Almunawar, M. N., Lim, S. A., & Al-Mudimigh, A. (2019). Customer relationship management and big data enabled: Personalization & customization of services. *Applied Computing and Informatics*, *15*(2), 94–101. DOI: 10.1016/j.aci.2018.05.004

Arbi, , Cao, J., & Alsaedi, A. (2018). Improved synchronization analysis of competitive neural networks with time-varying delays. *Nonlinear Analysis (Vilnius)*, *23*(1), 82–107. DOI: 10.15388/NA.2018.1.7

Arbi, , Guo, Y., & Cao, J. (2021). Convergence analysis on time scales for HOBAM neural networks in the Stepanov-like weighted pseudo almost automorphic space. *Neural Computing & Applications*, *33*(8), 3567–3581. DOI: 10.1007/s00521-020-05183-0

Arbi, , & Tahri, N. (2024). Synchronization analysis of novel delayed dynamical Clifford-valued neural networks on timescales. *Journal of Algorithms & Computational Technology*, *18*, 17483026241241492. DOI: 10.1177/17483026241241492

Arbi, A. (2018). Dynamics of BAM neural networks with mixed delays and leakage time-varying delays in the weighted pseudo–almost periodic on time-space scales. *Mathematical Methods in the Applied Sciences*, *41*(3), 1230–1255. DOI: 10.1002/mma.4661

Ayankoya, . (2014),Intrinsic relations between data science, big data, business analytics and datafication. In: *Proceedings of the Southern African Institute for Computer Scientist and Information Technologists Annual Conference 2014 on SAICSIT 2014 Empowered by Technology*. p. 192-198. DOI: 10.1145/2664591.2664619

Balachandran, , & Prasad, S. (2017). Challenges and benefits of deploying big data analytics in the cloud for business intelligence. *Procedia Computer Science*, *112*, 1112–1122. DOI: 10.1016/j.procs.2017.08.138

Chaudhary, . (2022). *Big data analytics: applications in business and marketing*. Auerbach Publications. DOI: 10.1201/9781003307761

Gad-Elrab, A. A. (2021). Modern business intelligence: Big data analytics and artificial intelligence for creating the data-driven value. In *E-Business-Higher Education and Intelligence Applications*. IntechOpen.

Guo, , Ge, S. S., & Arbi, A. (2022). Stability of traveling waves solutions for nonlinear cellular neural networks with distributed delays. *Journal of Systems Science and Complexity*, *35*(1), 18–31. DOI: 10.1007/s11424-021-0180-7

Hadj Sassi, M. S., & Chaari Fourati, L. (2024). Design cognitive IoT architecture framework for immersive visual technologies of air quality monitoring systems. *Multimedia Tools and Applications*, *83*(17), 51615–51646.

Hamdi, , Mestiri, S., & Arbi, A. (2024). Artificial intelligence techniques for bankruptcy prediction of tunisian companies: An application of machine learning and deep learning-based models. *Journal of Risk and Financial Management*, *17*(4), 132. DOI: 10.3390/jrfm17040132

Hazen, , Boone, C. A., Ezell, J. D., & Jones-Farmer, L. A. (2014). Data quality for data science, predictive analytics, and big data in supply chain management: An introduction to the problem and suggestions for research and applications. *International Journal of Production Economics*, *154*, 72–80. DOI: 10.1016/j.ijpe.2014.04.018

Krasic., ... (2021), Big data and business intelligence: research and challenges in telecom industry. In: *Annals of DAAAM and Proceedings of the International DAAAM Symposium*, p. 339-348. DOI: 10.2507/32nd.daaam.proceedings.050

Larson, , & Chang, V. (2016). A review and future direction of agile, business intelligence, analytics and data science. *International Journal of Information Management*, *36*(5), 700–710. DOI: 10.1016/j.ijinfomgt.2016.04.013

Medeiros, , Hoppen, N., & Maçada, A. C. G. (2020). Data science for business: Benefits, challenges and opportunities. *The Bottom Line (New York, N.Y.)*, *33*(2), 149–163. DOI: 10.1108/BL-12-2019-0132

Niu, Y., Ying, L., Yang, J., Bao, M., & Sivaparthipan, C. B. (2021). Organizational business intelligence and decision making using big data analytics. *Information Processing & Management, 58*(6), 102725. DOI: 10.1016/j.ipm.2021.102725

Ouali, . (2021), Architecture for real-time visualizing arabic words with diacritics using augmented reality for visually impaired people. In: *International conference on advanced information networking and applications*. Cham: Springer International Publishing, p. 285-296. DOI: 10.1007/978-3-030-75100-5_25

Ouali, . (2022a), Text detection and recognition using augmented reality and deep learning. In: *International conference on advanced information networking and applications*. Cham: Springer International Publishing, p. 13-23. DOI: 10.1007/978-3-030-99584-3_2

Ouali, . (2022b). *Real-time application for recognition and visualization of arabic words with vowels based dl and ar. In: 2022 International Wireless Communications and Mobile Computing (IWCMC)*. IEEE. DOI: 10.1109/IWCMC55113.2022.9825089

Ouali., ... (2023b), A novel method for arabic text detection with interactive visualization. In: *2023 IEEE Symposium on Computers and Communications (ISCC)*. IEEE, 2023. p. 1046-1050. DOI: 10.1109/ISCC58397.2023.10218141

Ouali, , Ben Halima, M., Masmoudi, N., Ayadi, M., Almuqren, L., & Wali, A. (2024). Text recuperated using ontology with stable marriage optimization technique and text visualization using AR. *Multimedia Tools and Applications, 83*(41), 1–28. DOI: 10.1007/s11042-024-18795-8

Ouali, , Halima, M. B., & Wali, A. (2023a). An augmented reality for an arabic text reading and visualization assistant for the visually impaired. *Multimedia Tools and Applications, 82*(28), 43569–43597. DOI: 10.1007/s11042-023-14880-6

Ouali, , Halima, M. B. E. N., & Wali, A. (2022c). Augmented reality for scene text recognition, visualization and reading to assist visually impaired people. *Procedia Computer Science, 207*, 158–167. DOI: 10.1016/j.procs.2022.09.048

Phillips-Wren, G., Daly, M., & Burstein, F. (2021). Reconciling business intelligence, analytics and decision support systems: More data, deeper insight. *Decision Support Systems*, *146*, 113560. DOI: 10.1016/j.dss.2021.113560

Radmehr, E., & Bazmara, M. (2017). A Survey of Business Intelligence Solutions in Banking Industry and Big Data Applications.

Sabir, , Raja, M. A. Z., Arbi, A., Altamirano, G. C., & Cao, J. (2021). Neuro-swarms intelligent computing using Gudermannian kernel for solving a class of second order Lane-Emden singular nonlinear model. *AIMS Mathematics*, *6*(3), 2468–2485. DOI: 10.3934/math.2021150

Sabir, , Saoud, S., Raja, M. A. Z., Wahab, H. A., & Arbi, A. (2020). Heuristic computing technique for numerical solutions of nonlinear fourth order Emden–Fowler equation. *Mathematics and Computers in Simulation*, *178*, 534–548. DOI: 10.1016/j.matcom.2020.06.021

Sassi, . (2019a). *Computer-aided software engineering (CASE) tool for big data and IoT architecture. In: 2019 15th International wireless communications & mobile computing conference (IWCMC).* IEEE.

Sassi, . (2019b). *Business information architecture for big data and Internet of Things. In: 2019 15th International Wireless Communications & Mobile Computing Conference (IWCMC).* IEEE.

Sassi., ... (2019c), Multi-Oriented Real-Time Arabic Scene Text Detection with Deep Fully Convolutional Networks. In: *2019 IEEE/ACS 16th International Conference on Computer Systems and Applications (AICCSA).* IEEE, 2019. p. 1-6. DOI: 10.1109/AICCSA47632.2019.9035340

Sassi, . (2020b). *Investigation on deep learning methods for privacy and security challenges of cognitive IoV. In: 2020 International Wireless Communications and Mobile Computing (IWCMC).* IEEE. DOI: 10.1109/IWCMC48107.2020.9148417

Silva, . (2018). Analytical intelligence in processes: Data science for business. *Revista IEEE América Latina*, *16*(8), 2240–2247. DOI: 10.1109/TLA.2018.8528241

Simon., ... (2001),*Data warehousing and business intelligence for e-commerce*. Elsevier, 2001.

Sun, , Sun, L., & Strang, K. (2018). Big data analytics services for enhancing business intelligence. *Journal of Computer Information Systems*, *58*(2), 162–169. DOI: 10.1080/08874417.2016.1220239

Ullah, I., Adhikari, D., Su, X., Palmieri, F., Wu, C., & Choi, C. (2024). Integration of data science with the intelligent IoT (IIoT): Current challenges and future perspectives. *Digital Communications and Networks*.

Wang, , Omar, A. H., Alotaibi, F. M., Daradkeh, Y. I., & Althubiti, S. A. (2022). Business intelligence ability to enhance organizational performance and performance evaluation capabilities by improving data mining systems for competitive advantage. *Information Processing & Management*, *59*(6), 103075. DOI: 10.1016/j.ipm.2022.103075

Chapter 2
Advancements in Big Data Transforming Data Into Insights

Achraf Wali
https://orcid.org/0009-0001-2071-0136
FSGS, Tunisia

Imene Ouali
https://orcid.org/0000-0001-5176-5482
ENIS, Tunisia

Adnène Arbi
https://orcid.org/0000-0002-2834-0248
Polytechnic School of Tunisia, Tunisia

ABSTRACT

In an era marked by unprecedented volumes of data generated from various sources, the field of Big Data has emerged as a critical enabler of innovation, decision-making, and competitive advantage across industries. This article explores the advancements in Big Data technologies, methodologies, and applications, highlighting their transformative impact on data analytics, business intelligence, and scientific discovery. From data collection and storage to processing and analysis, Big Data solutions

DOI: 10.4018/979-8-3693-8141-0.ch002

offer scalable, efficient, and cost-effective means to unlock actionable insights from complex and heterogeneous datasets. Through case studies and real-world examples, this article demonstrates the value of Big Data in driving informed decision-making, optimizing operations, and driving innovation in diverse domains, including healthcare, finance, marketing, and cybersecurity. Furthermore, it examines emerging trends and future directions in the field, such as machine learning, artificial intelligence, edge computing, and ethical considerations, shaping the evolution of Big Data and its role in shaping the digital economy and society.

1. INTRODUCTION

In today's digital age, the proliferation of digital devices, online platforms, and sensor networks has led to an explosion of data, commonly referred to as Big Data. This wealth of information presents both opportunities and challenges for organizations seeking to extract actionable insights and derive value from their data assets. The field of Big Data encompasses a wide range of technologies, methodologies, and practices aimed at collecting, storing, processing, and analyzing large and complex datasets to uncover patterns, trends, and correlations that can inform decision-making and drive innovation.

As businesses and industries increasingly rely on data-driven strategies, the ability to harness Big Data has become a critical competitive advantage. Predictive analytics, for example, allows companies to anticipate market trends and customer behavior, leading to more informed strategic planning and improved customer experiences. Machine learning algorithms can identify hidden patterns within data, enabling businesses to optimize operations, reduce costs, and innovate product offerings. Real-time data processing facilitates immediate decision-making, which is crucial in dynamic environments such as finance (HAMDI et al. 2024), healthcare, and logistics.

Furthermore, Big Data is revolutionizing how governments operate and deliver services. Data-driven governance can enhance public services, improve policy-making, and foster transparency and accountability. By leveraging Big Data, governments can address urban planning challenges, monitor public health trends, and respond more effectively to crises and disasters.

From a societal perspective, Big Data holds the potential to address some of the most pressing global issues, such as climate change, healthcare disparities, and social inequality. By analyzing large datasets, researchers can gain deeper insights into these complex problems and develop more effective interventions.

However, the journey from data to insights is fraught with challenges. The sheer volume, variety, and velocity of Big Data demand robust infrastructure and sophisticated analytical tools. Data privacy and security concerns are paramount, as the misuse of data can have severe implications for individuals and organizations. Moreover, the ethical use of data and ensuring equitable access to Big Data technologies are critical considerations that must be addressed.

This article provides an overview of the advancements in Big Data and their implications for businesses, governments, and society at large. We will explore the latest technologies and methodologies driving the Big Data revolution, examine case studies of successful Big Data implementations, and discuss the future directions and challenges in this rapidly evolving field.

2. EVOLUTION OF BIG DATA TECHNOLOGIES

The evolution of Big Data technologies has been characterized by continuous innovation and adaptation to meet the ever-growing demands of data-driven enterprises. Initially, traditional Relational DataBaseManagement Systems (RDBMS) were the primary means of storing and processing structured data. However, with the advent of the internet and the proliferation of digital devices, data began to grow at an exponential rate, surpassing the capabilities of traditional database systems(see Figure 1).

To address the challenges posed by the volume, velocity, and variety of data, new technologies and paradigms emerged, leading to the development of distributed storage and processing frameworks. Apache Hadoop, an open-source framework inspired by Google's MapReduce and Google

File System (GFS), revolutionized Big Data analytics by enabling distributed processing of large datasets across clusters of commodity hardware. Hadoop's Distributed File System (HDFS) provided fault tolerance and scalability, allowing organizations to store and analyze petabytes of data efficiently(EREVELLES et al., 2016).

Subsequently, Apache Spark emerged as a powerful alternative to Hadoop, offering in-memory processing capabilities and a more expressive programming model. Spark's ability to perform iterative and interactive analytics in memory accelerated the processing of large-scale datasets, making it well-suited for real-time and interactive applications(EREVELLESet al., 2016).

In addition to distributed storage and processing frameworks, the rise of cloud computing has democratized access to Big Data infrastructure, enabling organizations to provision and scale resources on-demand. Cloud-based platforms, such as Amazon Web Services (AWS), Microsoft Azure, and Google Cloud Platform (GCP), offer a wide range of Big Data services, including managed Hadoop and Spark clusters, data lakes, and serverless computing, empowering organizations to leverage the benefits of Big Data without the need for upfront infrastructure investments(EREVELLESet al., 2016).

Figure 1. Exploring the Resource-Based View: Big Data's Influence on Competitive Advantage.

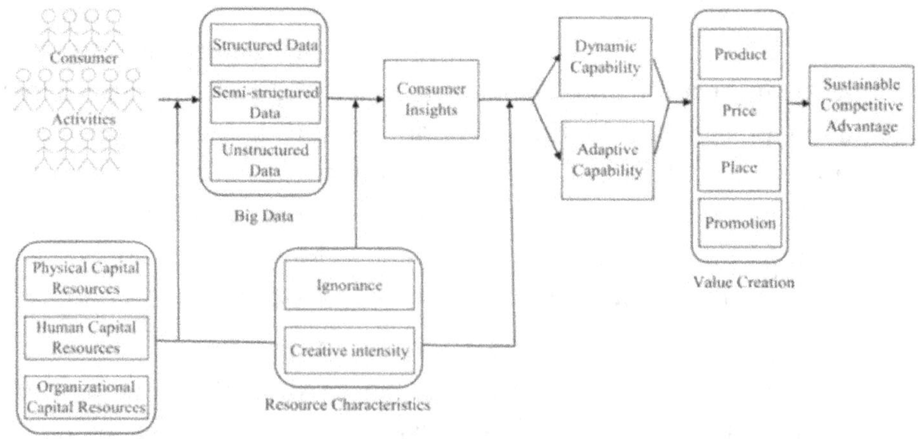

Furthermore, the emergence of NoSQL databases, such as MongoDB, Cassandra, and Couchbase, addressed the need for flexible and scalable solutions for storing and querying unstructured and semi-structured data. Unlike traditional relational databases, NoSQL databases are schema-less and horizontally scalable, making them ideal for handling diverse data types, such as social media feeds, sensor data, and log files(SEDKAOUI and Khelfaoui, 2019).

Moreover, advancements in streaming data processing technologies, such as Apache Kafka and Apache Flink, have enabled organizations to analyze real-time data streams and derive insights from high-velocity data sources, such as IoT devices, social media platforms, and clickstream data(SEDKAOUI and Khelfaoui, 2019).

Overall, the evolution of Big Data technologies has transformed the way organizations store, process, and analyze data, empowering them to extract actionable insights and derive value from their data assets at scale. As the Big Data landscape continues to evolve, organizations must stay abreast of emerging trends and technologies to remain competitive in today's data-driven economy.

3. METHODOLOGIES AND BEST PRACTICES IN BIG DATA ANALYTICS

In the realm of Big Data analytics, the methodologies and best practices play a pivotal role in ensuring the efficiency, accuracy, and reliability of data-driven decision-making processes(see Figure 2).

Figure 2. Framework of a Big Data Analytics Platform.

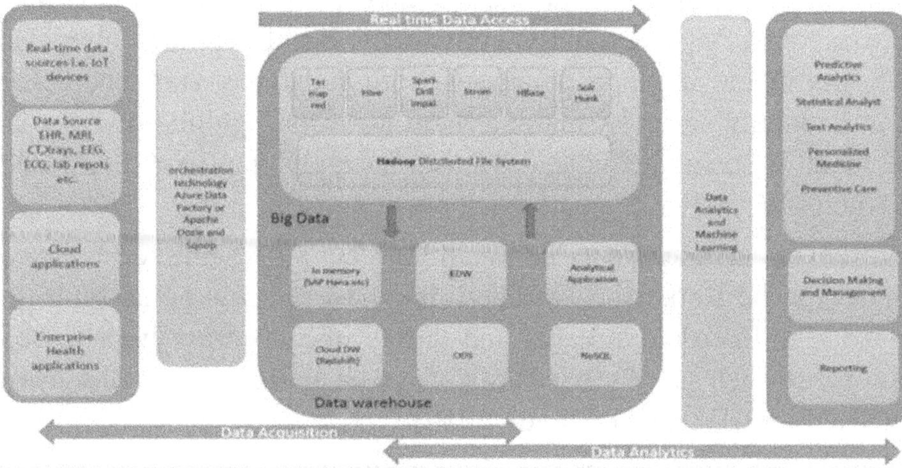

Here, we delve into various methodologies and best practices that are instrumental in harnessing the power of Big Data analytics:

3.1 Data Collection and Integration

Data collection and integration are foundational steps in the big data analytics process. This subsection focuses on the various methods, technologies, and best practices involved in collecting and integrating diverse data sources to form a unified dataset for analysis.

Data Sources: Big data analytics often involves collecting data from a myriad of sources, including structured and unstructured data from internal and external sources such as enterprise databases, sensors, social media platforms, web logs, and IoT devices. This subsection explores different data sources and the challenges associated with integrating heterogeneous data types (Russom, 2011).

Data Acquisition Techniques: It discusses the techniques and tools used for data acquisition, such as data scraping, web crawling, API integration, and real-time data streaming. Emphasis is placed on the importance of data quality, completeness, and consistency during the acquisition process to ensure the integrity and reliability of the dataset.

Data Preprocessing: Data preprocessing steps, including data cleaning, transformation, and normalization, are crucial for preparing raw data for analysis. This subsection discusses preprocessing techniques to handle missing values, outliers, duplicates, and inconsistencies, ensuring that the data is suitable for analysis.

Data Integration Technologies: It explores various data integration technologies and approaches, such as Extract, Transform, Load (ETL) processes, data virtualization, and data federation. These technologies enable organizations to combine data from disparate sources into a unified, coherent dataset for analysis, providing a holistic view of the business types (Russom, 2011).

Data Governance and Security: Data governance and security considerations are paramount in the data collection and integration process. This subsection discusses best practices for ensuring data privacy, security, and compliance with regulatory requirements, such as General Data Protection Regulation (GDPR) and Health Insurance Portability and Accountability Act (HIPAA), throughout the data lifecycle types (Russom, 2011).

Scalability and Performance: As data volumes continue to grow exponentially, scalability and performance become critical considerations in data collection and integration. This subsection explores scalable data integration architectures, distributed processing frameworks, and cloud-based solutions to handle large-scale data processing tasks efficiently.

Case Studies and Use Cases: Real-world case studies and use cases demonstrate how organizations leverage advanced data collection and integration techniques to derive actionable insights and drive business value. Examples include customer segmentation, predictive maintenance, fraud detection, and personalized marketing campaigns types (Russom, 2011).

By addressing the challenges and adopting best practices outlined in this subsection, organizations can establish a robust foundation for their big data analytics initiatives, enabling them to harness the full potential of their data assets and gain a competitive edge in today's data-driven marketplace.

3.2 Data Preprocessing and Cleaning

Data preprocessing and cleaning are crucial stages in the data analytics pipeline, where raw data is transformed and refined to improve its quality and prepare it for analysis. This subsection explores the methodologies, techniques, and best practices involved in data preprocessing and cleaning, highlighting their significance in ensuring the accuracy, consistency, and reliability of analytical results.

Data Quality Assessment: Before proceeding with any analysis, it is essential to assess the quality of the raw data. This involves identifying and addressing various data quality issues, such as missing values, outliers, duplicates, and inconsistencies. Techniques for data profiling and quality assessment are discussed, including summary statistics, data visualization, and anomaly detection algorithms.

Missing Data Handling: Missing data is a common issue in real-world datasets, which can adversely affect the accuracy and reliability of analytical models. This subsection explores different approaches for handling missing data, such as deletion, imputation, and advanced machine learning-based methods. Strategies for selecting the most appropriate imputation technique based on data characteristics and analysis objectives are discussed.

Outlier Detection and Treatment: Outliers, or anomalous data points, can significantly impact the performance of analytical models and distort the interpretation of results. Techniques for detecting outliers, including statistical methods, clustering algorithms, and proximity-based approaches, are examined. Strategies for handling outliers, such as removal, transformation, or adjustment, are discussed to mitigate their influence on analytical outcomes.

Data Transformation and Normalization: Data transformation and normalization techniques are applied to standardize the scale, distribution, and format of the data, making it suitable for analysis. This subsection explores various transformation techniques, such as log transformation, power transformation, and z-score normalization, along with their implications for different types of data distributions and analytical tasks.

Feature Engineering: Feature engineering involves creating new features or transforming existing features to improve the performance of machine learning models. This subsection discusses common feature engineering techniques, such as binning, encoding, scaling, and dimensionality reduction. Strategies for selecting relevant features, reducing dimensionality, and addressing multicollinearity are explored to enhance model interpretability and predictive accuracy.

Data Cleaning Pipelines: Data preprocessing and cleaning pipelines automate the process of transforming raw data into analysis-ready datasets. This subsection examines the design principles and implementation considerations for building effective data cleaning pipelines, including workflow orchestration, version control, error handling, and scalability. Tools and frameworks for building and deploying data cleaning pipelines, such as Apache Spark, TensorFlow Data Validation, and scikit-learn, are discussed.

Case Studies and Use Cases: Real-world case studies and use cases illustrate the importance of data preprocessing and cleaning in various domains, such as healthcare, finance, retail, and manufacturing. Examples include fraud detection, customer churn prediction, sentiment analysis, and predictive maintenance, demonstrating how effective data preprocessing and cleaning can drive actionable insights and decision-making.

By incorporating the methodologies and best practices outlined in this subsection into their data analytics workflows, organizations can ensure the reliability, accuracy, and integrity of their analytical results, ultimately leading to better-informed decisions and improved business outcomes. (Russom, 2011).

3.3 Exploratory Data Analysis (EDA)

Exploratory Data Analysis (EDA) is a critical phase in the data analytics process that focuses on gaining insights and understanding the underlying patterns, trends, and relationships within the dataset. This subsection delves into the methodologies, techniques, and best practices involved in conducting EDA, highlighting its importance in uncovering valuable information and guiding subsequent analysis and decision-making processes(SASSI et al., 2019b).

Descriptive Statistics: Descriptive statistics provide a summary overview of the dataset's key characteristics, including measures of central tendency, dispersion, and distribution. This subsection explores common descriptive statistics techniques, such as mean, median, mode, standard deviation, range, and percentiles, and discusses their application in understanding the dataset's structure and properties(HADJ SASSI et al., 2024).

Data Visualization: Data visualization techniques play a crucial role in EDA by transforming raw data into visual representations that are intuitive and easy to interpret. This subsection examines various data visualization methods, including histograms, box plots, scatter plots, line charts, and heatmaps, and discusses their utility in identifying patterns, trends, and outliers within the dataset.

Correlation Analysis: Correlation analysis measures the strength and direction of relationships between variables in the dataset. This subsection explores correlation techniques, such as Pearson correlation coefficient, Spearman rank correlation coefficient, and Kendall tau rank correlation coefficient, and discusses their application in identifying linear and non-linear dependencies between variables.

Dimensionality Reduction: Dimensionality reduction techniques aim to reduce the number of features or variables in the dataset while preserving its essential information and structure. This subsection examines common dimensionality reduction methods, such as Principal Component Analysis (PCA), t-distributed Stochastic Neighbor Embedding (t-SNE), and Linear Discriminant Analysis (LDA), and discusses their role in visualizing high-dimensional data and identifying meaningful patterns.

Cluster Analysis: Cluster analysis techniques partition the dataset into groups or clusters based on similarity or distance measures between data points. This subsection explores clustering algorithms, such as K-means clustering, hierarchical clustering, and DBSCAN (Density-Based Spatial Clustering of Applications with Noise), and discusses their application in identifying natural groupings and patterns within the dataset.

Association Rule Mining: Association rule mining techniques identify frequent patterns, correlations, and associations between variables or items in transactional datasets. This subsection examines association rule mining algorithms, such as Apriori and FP-growth, and discusses their application in market basket analysis, recommendation systems, and sequential pattern mining (Arbi et al., 2018).

Interactive Data Exploration: Interactive data exploration tools and platforms empower users to interactively explore and analyze large and complex datasets through intuitive interfaces and visualizations. This subsection discusses the importance of interactive data exploration in facilitating collaboration, hypothesis generation, and knowledge discovery, and highlights emerging tools and technologies in this space.

Case Studies and Use Cases: Real-world case studies and use cases demonstrate the application of exploratory data analysis techniques in various domains, such as healthcare, finance, marketing, and social media analytics. Examples include customer segmentation, anomaly detection, sentiment analysis, and predictive maintenance, illustrating how EDA can uncover actionable insights and drive data-driven decision-making.

By incorporating the methodologies and best practices outlined in this subsection into their data analytics workflows, organizations can leverage exploratory data analysis to gain valuable insights, identify opportunities, and make informed decisions that drive business success (Russom, 2011).

3.4 Feature Engineering

Feature engineering is a crucial aspect of the data preprocessing phase in big data analytics, focusing on transforming raw data into informative features that enhance the performance of machine learning models and predictive algorithms. This subsection explores the methodologies, techniques, and best practices involved in feature engineering, highlighting its importance in extracting relevant information and improving the accuracy and effectiveness of data analysis and prediction tasks.

Feature Extraction: Feature extraction techniques involve deriving new features or representations from raw data sources to capture meaningful information and patterns. This subsection discusses common feature extraction methods, such as text mining, image processing, signal processing, and time-series analysis, and explores their application in converting unstructured or high-dimensional data into structured and actionable features (Ouali et al., 2021).

Feature Selection: Feature selection techniques aim to identify the most relevant and discriminative features from the dataset while discarding irrelevant or redundant ones. This subsection examines feature selection methods, such as filter methods (e.g., correlation-based feature selection), wrapper methods (e.g., recursive feature elimination), and embedded methods (e.g., LASSO regression), and discusses their role in improving model performance, reducing overfitting, and enhancing interpretability (Arbi et al., 2021).

Feature Transformation: Feature transformation techniques involve modifying the scale, distribution, or representation of features to make them more suitable for modeling and analysis. This subsection explores feature transformation methods, such as normalization, standardization, logarithmic transformation, and polynomial transformation, and discusses their application in addressing issues related to data skewness, heteroscedasticity, and nonlinearity.

Feature Encoding: Feature encoding techniques convert categorical or textual features into numerical representations that can be processed by machine learning algorithms. This subsection examines feature encoding methods, such as one-hot encoding, label encoding, target encoding, and binary encoding, and discusses their utility in handling categorical variables, preserving ordinality, and reducing dimensionality.

Feature Scaling: Feature scaling techniques standardize or normalize the scale of numerical features to ensure that they have a consistent range and distribution. This subsection explores feature scaling methods, such as min-max scaling, z-score normalization, robust scaling, and log transformation, and discusses their role in improving model convergence, stability, and performance.

Feature Construction: Feature construction techniques involve creating new features by combining or aggregating existing ones to capture higher-order interactions or domain-specific relationships. This subsection examines feature construction methods, such as polynomial features, interaction terms, and domain-specific transformations, and discusses their application in enriching the feature space and capturing complex patterns and relationships.

Automatic Feature Engineering: Automatic feature engineering approaches leverage machine learning algorithms and optimization techniques to automatically generate relevant features from raw data sources. This subsection explores automatic feature engineering frameworks, such as featuretools and auto-sklearn, and discusses their potential in automating the feature engineering process and accelerating model development.

Case Studies and Use Cases: Real-world case studies and use cases demonstrate the application of feature engineering techniques in various domains, such as predictive modeling, fraud detection, customer segmentation, and recommendation systems. Examples include churn prediction, credit risk assessment, sentiment analysis, and product recommendation, illustrating how feature engineering can enhance predictive accuracy and drive actionable insights(SASSI et al., 2020b).

By incorporating the methodologies and best practices outlined in this subsection into their data preprocessing and modeling pipelines, organizations can leverage feature engineering to extract relevant information, improve model performance, and derive actionable insights from their data assets (Morabito, 2015).

3.5 Model Selection and Evaluation

Model selection and evaluation play a pivotal role in the success of big data analytics projects by identifying the most suitable algorithms and assessing their performance on unseen data. This subsection delves into the methodologies, techniques, and best practices involved in model selection and evaluation, encompassing the entire lifecycle of machine learning model development and deployment.

Algorithm Selection: Algorithm selection involves choosing the most appropriate machine learning algorithms or models based on the characteristics of the dataset, the nature of the problem, and the desired outcomes. This subsection discusses common algorithm families, such as supervised learning (e.g., regression, classification), unsupervised learning (e.g., clustering, dimensionality reduction), and semi-supervised learning, and explores their strengths, weaknesses, and suitability for different types of tasks and datasets(see Figure 3).

Figure 3. Advanced Deep Learning Architecture for Big Data Analytics.

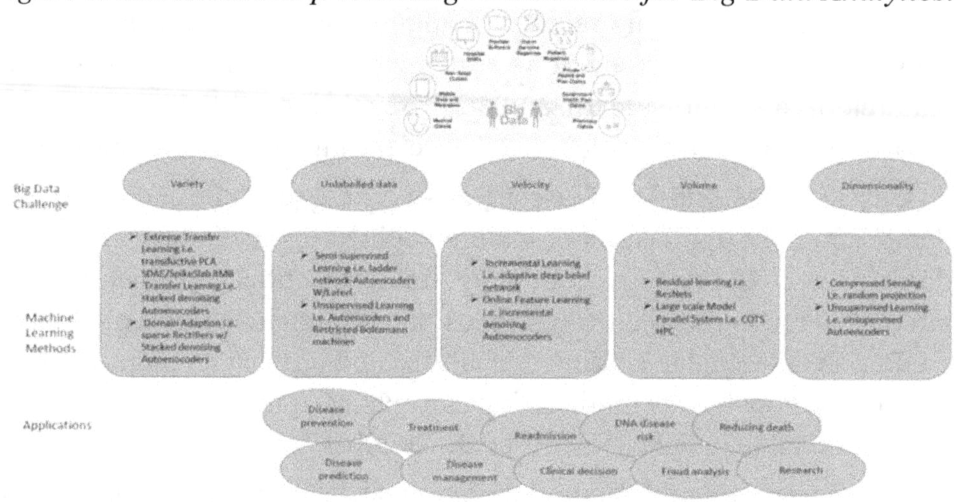

Hyperparameter Tuning: Hyperparameter tuning aims to optimize the performance of machine learning models by fine-tuning the hyper-parameters that govern their behavior and complexity. This subsection examines hyperparameter tuning techniques, such as grid search, random search, Bayesian optimization, and genetic algorithms, and discusses their role in optimizing model performance, improving generalization, and mitigating overfitting.

Cross-Validation: Cross-validation is a resampling technique used to assess the generalization performance of machine learning models by partitioning the dataset into multiple subsets and training/testing the model on different combinations of these subsets. This subsection explores cross-validation strategies, such as k-fold cross-validation, stratified cross-validation, and leave-one-out cross-validation, and discusses their utility in estimating model performance, reducing bias/variance, and detecting overfitting.

Model Evaluation Metrics: Model evaluation metrics quantify the performance of machine learning models by measuring their predictive accuracy, reliability, and effectiveness on unseen data. This subsection examines common evaluation metrics, such as accuracy, precision, recall, F1-score, ROC AUC, Mean Squared Error (MSE), and Mean Absolute Error (MAE), and discusses their interpretation, trade-offs, and applicability to different types of tasks and domains (Arbi and Tahri, 2024).

Model Interpretability and Explainability: Model interpretability and explainability techniques aim to elucidate the underlying mechanisms and decision-making processes of machine learning models, particularly in complex or opaque models such as deep learning neural networks. This subsection explores interpretability methods, such as feature importance analysis, partial dependence plots, SHAP (SHapley Additive exPlanations) values, and LIME (Local Interpretable Model-agnostic Explanations), and discusses their role in enhancing model transparency, trustworthiness, and regulatory compliance.

Ensemble Learning: Ensemble learning techniques combine multiple base models or algorithms to create a stronger and more robust predictive model that outperforms individual models. This subsection examines ensemble learning methods, such as bagging, boosting, stacking, and random forests, and discusses their advantages, trade-offs, and applications in improving predictive accuracy, reducing variance, and handling complex datasets and tasks.

Model Deployment and Monitoring: Model deployment and monitoring involve deploying trained machine learning models into production environments and continuously monitoring their performance and behavior to ensure they remain effective and reliable over time. This subsection explores deployment strategies, such as batch processing, real-time scoring, and containerization, and discusses monitoring techniques, such as drift detection, anomaly detection, and model retraining, and their role in maintaining model integrity, scalability, and compliance.

Case Studies and Use Cases: Real-world case studies and use cases illustrate the application of model selection and evaluation techniques in various domains, such as healthcare, finance, e-commerce, and cybersecurity. Examples include fraud detection, sentiment analysis, recommendation systems, and predictive maintenance, showcasing how model selection and evaluation can drive actionable insights, optimize business processes, and enhance decision-making.

By integrating the methodologies and best practices outlined in this subsection into their machine learning workflow, organizations can streamline the model development process, improve model performance, and derive actionable insights from their data assets, ultimately driving innovation, efficiency, and competitive advantage (Morabito, 2015).

3.6 Scalability and Performance Optimization

Scalability and performance optimization are paramount considerations in big data analytics, especially when dealing with large-scale datasets, complex algorithms, and resource-intensive computations. This subsection explores the methodologies, techniques, and strategies employed to enhance the scalability, efficiency, and performance of big data analytics systems and applications.

Distributed Computing Paradigms: Distributed computing paradigms, such as MapReduce, Apache Hadoop, Apache Spark, and Apache Flink, enable the processing of large-scale datasets across distributed clusters of computers, thereby improving computational efficiency and scalability. This subsection delves into the architecture, components, and workflow of distributed computing frameworks and discusses their role in parallelizing data processing tasks, handling fault tolerance, and enabling horizontal scalability.

Parallelization and Concurrency: Parallelization and concurrency techniques aim to maximize computational throughput and resource utilization by executing multiple tasks concurrently across distributed computing nodes or processor cores. This subsection explores parallel computing models, such as shared-memory parallelism, distributed-memory parallelism, task parallelism, and data parallelism, and discusses their applicability to different types of analytics workloads, such as batch processing, stream processing, and iterative processing.

Data Partitioning and Sharding: Data partitioning and sharding strategies involve dividing large datasets into smaller, more manageable partitions or shards and distributing them across distributed storage systems or computing nodes. This subsection examines data partitioning techniques, such as range partitioning, hash partitioning, and round-robin partitioning, and discusses their role in improving data locality, minimizing data transfer overhead, and enhancing query performance in distributed computing environments.

Cluster Management and Resource Allocation: Cluster management and resource allocation techniques aim to optimize resource utilization and allocation across distributed computing clusters by dynamically provisioning, scaling, and scheduling computing resources based on workload demands and performance requirements. This subsection explores cluster management systems, such as Apache YARN, Kubernetes, and Apache Mesos, and discusses their capabilities in resource scheduling, workload isolation, and fault tolerance.

Data Compression and Serialization: Data compression and serialization techniques aim to reduce data storage and transmission overhead by encoding data in a compact and efficient format and compressing it using lossless or lossy compression algorithms. This subsection examines data compression algorithms, such as gzip, Snappy, and LZ4, and serialization formats, such as Apache Avro, Protocol Buffers, and Apache Parquet, and discusses their role in minimizing disk I/O, network bandwidth, and memory footprint in big data processing pipelines.

Cache Optimization and Memory Management: Cache optimization and memory management techniques aim to exploit memory hierarchies and caching mechanisms to minimize data access latency, maximize cache hit rates, and improve overall system performance. This subsection explores caching strategies, such as block caching, query caching, and result caching, and memory management techniques, such as garbage collection, memory pooling, and memory mapping, and discusses their impact on query performance, data processing throughput, and system stability.

Data Partitioning and Indexing: Data partitioning and indexing techniques aim to organize and structure data in distributed storage systems or databases to facilitate efficient data retrieval, filtering, and aggregation operations. This subsection examines indexing techniques, such as B-tree, hash index, and bitmap index, and partitioning strategies, such as range partitioning, list partitioning, and composite partitioning, and discusses their role in improving query performance, reducing data access latency, and enabling parallel query execution.

Optimized Algorithms and Data Structures: Optimized algorithms and data structures are tailored to the characteristics and constraints of big data analytics environments, such as distributed computing clusters, memory-constrained systems, and high-throughput processing pipelines. This subsection explores algorithmic optimizations, such as algorithmic complexity analysis, algorithmic parallelization, and algorithmic approximation, and data structure optimizations, such as Bloom filters, inverted indexes, and sparse matrices, and discusses their role in accelerating data processing tasks, minimizing resource consumption, and enabling real-time analytics (Ouali et al., 2024).

Case Studies and Use Cases: Real-world case studies and use cases illustrate the application of scalability and performance optimization techniques in various domains, such as web-scale analytics, real-time streaming, and large-scale graph processing. Examples include web search engines, social media analytics platforms, and financial trading systems, showcasing how scalability and performance optimization can drive agility, resilience, and competitiveness in data-driven organizations.

By incorporating the scalability and performance optimization strategies outlined in this subsection into their big data analytics workflows, organizations can enhance the efficiency, reliability, and agility of their analytics infrastructure, enabling them to derive actionable insights, make informed decisions, and capitalize on new business opportunities in today's data-driven world (Morabito, 2015).

3.7 Data Privacy and Security

Data privacy and security are critical considerations in big data analytics to ensure the confidentiality, integrity, and availability of sensitive information and to comply with regulatory requirements and industry standards. This subsection explores the methodologies, technologies, and best practices employed to protect data privacy and enhance data security in big data analytics environments.

Encryption and Cryptography: Encryption and cryptography techniques are used to secure data at rest and in transit by encrypting data using cryptographic algorithms and keys. This subsection examines encryption methods, such as symmetric encryption, asymmetric encryption, and homomorphic encryption, and cryptographic protocols, such as SSL/TLS, AES, RSA, and SHA, and discusses their role in protecting data confidentiality, preventing unauthorized access, and mitigating data breaches.

Access Control and Authorization: Access control and authorization mechanisms are used to enforce policies and permissions governing data access and usage by authenticating users, authorizing actions, and auditing activities. This subsection explores access control models, such as Role-Based Access Control (RBAC), Attribute-Based Access Control (ABAC), and Mandatory Access Control (MAC), and authorization frameworks, such as OAuth, OpenID Connect, and SAML, and discusses their role in managing access privileges, enforcing data governance, and ensuring regulatory compliance.

Anonymization and Pseudonymization: Anonymization and pseudonymization techniques are used to de-identify and obfuscate Personally Identifiable Information (PII) and sensitive data to protect individual privacy and comply with data protection regulations, such as GDPR and HIPAA. This subsection examines anonymization methods, such as k-anonymity, l-diversity, and t-closeness, and pseudonymization techniques, such as tokenization, hashing, and masking, and discusses their role in preserving data privacy, minimizing privacy risks, and enabling lawful data processing.

Data Masking and Redaction: Data masking and redaction methods are used to conceal sensitive information and mask confidential data fields to prevent unauthorized access and disclosure. This subsection explores data masking techniques, such as Format-Preserving Encryption (FPE), randomization, and substitution, and redaction approaches, such as full redaction, partial redaction, and dynamic redaction, and discusses their role in safeguarding sensitive data, protecting data subjects' privacy, and ensuring regulatory compliance.

Secure Data Transmission and Storage: Secure data transmission and storage protocols and mechanisms are used to encrypt data in transit and at rest, authenticate data sources and recipients, and ensure data integrity and confidentiality. This subsection examines secure communication protocols, such as HTTPS, SSH, and VPN, and secure storage solutions, such as encrypted databases, secure file systems, and cloud storage encryption, and discusses their role in preventing eavesdropping, tampering, and data leakage.

Auditing and Logging: Auditing and logging mechanisms are used to track and record data access, usage, and modifications for accountability, transparency, and compliance purposes. This subsection explores auditing frameworks, such as syslog, SNMP, and ELK stack, and logging standards, such as ISO 27001, NIST SP 800-53, and PCI DSS, and discusses their role in detecting security incidents, investigating breaches, and demonstrating regulatory compliance.

Threat Detection and Incident Response: Threat detection and incident response strategies are used to identify, mitigate, and remediate security threats and incidents in real-time to minimize the impact on data assets and business operations. This subsection examines threat detection techniques, such as anomaly detection, behavior analytics, and Intrusion Detection Systems (IDS), and incident response frameworks, such as NIST Cybersecurity Framework, SANS Incident Handling, and CERT-CC Incident Response, and discusses their role in proactively detecting security breaches, containing incidents, and restoring normal operations.

Data Governance and Compliance: Data governance and compliance frameworks are used to establish policies, procedures, and controls for managing data assets, ensuring data quality, and complying with legal and regulatory requirements. This subsection explores data governance models, such as DAMA-DMBOK, COBIT, and GDPR, and compliance standards, such as HIPAA, PCI DSS, and SOX, and discusses their role in establishing accountability, transparency, and trust in data-driven organizations.

Privacy-Preserving Analytics: Privacy-preserving analytics techniques enable data analysis and mining while preserving individual privacy and confidentiality. This subsection examines privacy-enhancing technologies, such as differential privacy, federated learning, and secure Multi-Party Computation (MPC), and discusses their role in enabling collaborative analytics, data sharing, and knowledge discovery without compromising data privacy and security.

Ethical Considerations and Social Implications: Ethical considerations and social implications of data privacy and security are essential to address the ethical, legal, and societal implications of big data analytics, such as algorithmic bias, discrimination, and privacy violations. This subsection explores ethical frameworks, such as IEEE Ethically Aligned Design, ACM Code of Ethics, and Belmont Report, and discusses their role in promoting responsible data stewardship, fairness, and transparency in the use of big data technologies.

By incorporating the data privacy and security strategies outlined in this subsection into their big data analytics workflows, organizations can mitigate privacy risks, enhance data protection, and foster trust and confidence in their data-driven initiatives, thereby unlocking the full potential of big data while respecting individual privacy rights and regulatory requirements.

In summary, adopting sound methodologies and best practices in Big Data analytics is essential for unlocking the full potential of data assets and driving informed decision-making in today's data-driven enterprises. By adhering to rigorous data management, analysis, and security standards, organizations can harness the power of Big Data to gain actionable insights, optimize operations, and gain a competitive edge in the digital economy (Ouali et al., 2022a).

4. APPLICATIONS OF BIG DATA ACROSS INDUSTRIES

The application of Big Data analytics spans across various industries, revolutionizing business processes, enhancing decision-making, and driving innovation. Here, we explore some of the key industries and their use cases where Big Data analytics has made significant strides (Chen & Zhang, 2014):

4. 1. Healthcare

- **Clinical Decision Support:** Big Data analytics enables healthcare professionals to make data-driven clinical decisions by analyzing large volumes of patient data, Electronic Health Records (EHRs), and medical imaging data (Rehman et al., 2022).
- **Disease Surveillance and Outbreak Detection:** Big Data analytics facilitates the early detection and monitoring of infectious diseases, such as COVID-19, by analyzing real-time health data, epidemiological patterns, and social media sentiment analysis (Rehman et al., 2022).
- **Personalized Medicine:** Big Data analytics enables the development of personalized treatment plans and precision medicine approaches by analyzing patient genomics, medical history, and lifestyle data to tailor therapies to individual patients(see Figure 4).

Figure 4. Comprehensive Workflow of Real-time Healthcare Data Streaming.

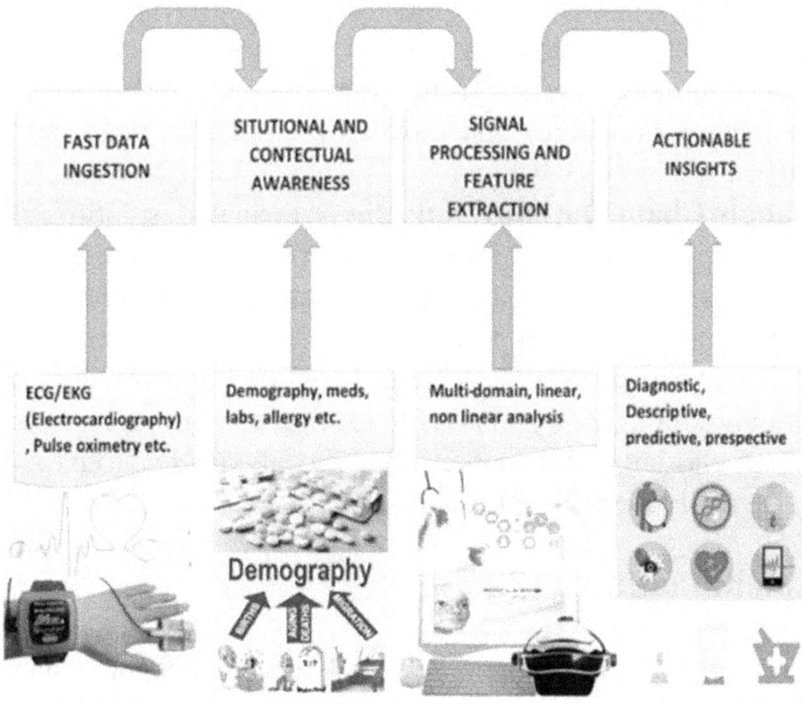

4. 2. Finance

- **Fraud Detection and Prevention:** Big Data analytics helps financial institutions detect and prevent fraudulent activities by analyzing transactional data, customer behavior patterns, and anomaly detection algorithms(SETH et al., 2015).
- **Risk Management:** Big Data analytics enables banks and insurance companies to assess and mitigate risks by analyzing market data, credit scores, and macroeconomic indicators to optimize lending and investment decisions(SETH et al., 2015).
- **Algorithmic Trading:** Big Data analytics powers algorithmic trading strategies by analyzing large-scale financial data, market trends, and sentiment analysis to execute high-frequency trades and optimize investment portfolios(SETH et al., 2015).

4. 3. Retail and E-commerce

- **Customer Segmentation and Targeting:** Big Data analytics enables retailers to segment customers based on their shopping behavior, preferences, and demographics, allowing for personalized marketing campaigns and targeted promotions (Akter & Wamba, 2016).
- **Supply Chain Optimization:** Big Data analytics optimizes supply chain operations by analyzing inventory levels, demand forecasts, and logistics data to streamline procurement, inventory management, and distribution processes (Akter & Wamba, 2016).
- **Price Optimization:** Big Data analytics helps retailers optimize pricing strategies by analyzing competitor pricing, customer demand elasticity, and market trends to maximize profits and minimize markdowns(SABIR et al., 2021).

4. 4. Manufacturing

- **Predictive Maintenance:** Big Data analytics enables manufacturers to implement predictive maintenance strategies by analyzing sensor data, equipment performance metrics, and historical maintenance records to identify potential equipment failures and minimize downtime (Belhadi et al., 2019).
- **Quality Control:** Big Data analytics improves product quality and defect detection by analyzing manufacturing process data, sensor readings, and image analysis techniques to identify anomalies and deviations from quality standards (Belhadi et al., 2019).
- **Supply Chain Visibility:** Big Data analytics enhances supply chain visibility by analyzing production data, supplier performance metrics, and transportation logistics to optimize inventory levels, reduce lead times, and improve order fulfilment (Belhadi et al., 2019).

4. 5. Telecommunications

- **Customer Churn Prediction:** Big Data analytics helps telecom companies predict and reduce customer churn by analyzing customer usage patterns, network performance data, and customer service interactions to identify at-risk customers and implement retention strategies (Keshavarz et al., 2021).

- **Network Optimization:** Big Data analytics optimizes network performance and capacity planning by analyzing network traffic data, Call Detail Records (CDRs), and Location-Based Services (LBS) data to optimize network infrastructure and improve service quality (Keshavarz et al., 2021).
- **Predictive Maintenance:** Big Data analytics enables telecom operators to perform predictive maintenance on network equipment by analyzing telemetry data, fault logs, and performance metrics to proactively identify and address network issues before they escalate (Keshavarz et al., 2021).

These are just a few examples of how Big Data analytics is transforming industries across the globe. From healthcare and finance (HAMDI et al. 2024) to retail and manufacturing, organizations are leveraging the power of Big Data to gain actionable insights, drive operational efficiency, and deliver enhanced value to customers. As technology continues to evolve, the potential applications of Big Data analytics will only continue to expand, revolutionizing business processes and driving innovation across diverse sectors (Ouali et al., 2022b).

5. CHALLENGES AND FUTURE DIRECTIONS

Despite the immense potential of Big Data analytics, several challenges persist, hindering its widespread adoption and effectiveness. Addressing these challenges and charting future directions are crucial for realizing the full benefits of Big Data analytics. Here, we delve into some of the key challenges and propose future directions for advancing the field (Luan et al., 2020):

5. 1. Data Privacy and Security

- **Challenge:** Ensuring the privacy and security of sensitive data poses a significant challenge, particularly in industries like healthcare and finance where strict regulatory compliance is essential (Bhattarai et al., 2019).
- **Future Directions:** Developing robust encryption techniques, implementing data anonymization methods, and adopting advanced cybersecurity measures can help mitigate privacy and security risks associated with Big Data analytics (Bhattarai et al., 2019).

5. 2. Data Quality and Integration

- **Challenge:** Ensuring the quality, accuracy, and consistency of data from disparate sources is a major challenge, as data may be incomplete, inconsistent, or outdated, leading to erroneous insights(SABIR, *et al.* 2020).
- **Future Directions:** Investing in data quality management tools, establishing data governance frameworks, and implementing data integration platforms can enhance data quality and facilitate seamless integration of heterogeneous data sources (Bhattarai et al., 2019).

5. 3. Scalability and Performance

- **Challenge:** Processing and analyzing massive volumes of data in real-time pose scalability and performance challenges, particularly with traditional computing infrastructures (Chen & Zhang, 2014).
- **Future Directions:** Embracing distributed computing technologies such as Hadoop, Spark, and Apache Flink, leveraging cloud computing resources, and adopting parallel processing techniques can improve scalability and performance of Big Data analytics platforms (Chen & Zhang, 2014).

5. 4. Skills Gap and Talent Shortage

- **Challenge:** The shortage of skilled data scientists, analysts, and engineers with expertise in Big Data technologies poses a significant barrier to harnessing the full potential of Big Data analytics(GUO et al., 2022).
- **Future Directions:** Investing in data science education and training programs, upskilling existing workforce, and fostering collaboration between academia and industry can address the skills gap and cultivate a talent pool capable of driving Big Data innovation (Chen & Zhang, 2014).

5. 5. Ethical and Societal Implications

- **Challenge:** Big Data analytics raise ethical concerns related to data privacy, bias, discrimination, and unintended consequences, necessitating ethical frameworks and guidelines for responsible data usage (Luan et al., 2020).
- **Future Directions:** Developing ethical guidelines and regulations, promoting transparency and accountability in algorithmic decision-making, and fostering public dialogue on the ethical implications of Big Data analytics are essential for addressing ethical and societal concerns (Luan et al., 2020).

5. 6. Interpretability and Explainability

- **Challenge:** Black-box algorithms used in Big Data analytics may lack interpretability, making it challenging to understand and explain the rationale behind the insights and decisions generated.
- **Future Directions:** Advancing explainable AI techniques, developing interpretable machine learning models, and incorporating human-centric design principles can enhance the interpretability and explainability of Big Data analytics systems, fostering trust and transparency (Luan et al., 2020).

5. 7. Integration with Emerging Technologies

- **Challenge:** Integrating Big Data analytics with emerging technologies such as artificial intelligence, Internet of Things (IoT), and blockchain presents integration and interoperability challenges.
- **Future Directions:** Embracing interoperability standards, developing seamless integration frameworks, and fostering cross-disciplinary collaboration can facilitate the integration of Big Data analytics with emerging technologies, unlocking new opportunities for innovation and synergy (Bibrim 2018).

5. 8. Sustainability and Environmental Impact

- **Challenge:** The energy consumption and environmental footprint of Big Data infrastructure and computing resources raise sustainability concerns, necessitating energy-efficient and eco-friendly solutions.
- **Future Directions:** Designing energy-efficient data centers, optimizing data processing algorithms for minimal energy consumption, and leveraging renewable energy sources can mitigate the environmental impact of Big Data analytics and promote sustainability (Bibri, 2018).

Addressing these challenges and embracing future directions will be pivotal in advancing the field of Big Data analytics, unlocking new opportunities for innovation, driving socio-economic growth, and addressing pressing societal challenges in the digital age. By overcoming these hurdles and charting a course for the future, we can harness the transformative power of Big Data analytics to create a brighter and more sustainable future for all (Ouali et al., 2023b).

6. CONCLUSION

In conclusion, the advancements in Big Data technologies and analytics hold immense promise for organizations seeking to unlock the value of their data assets and drive innovation in an increasingly data-driven world.

By leveraging scalable and efficient data storage, processing, and analysis tools, and adopting best practices in data governance, organizations can harness the power of Big Data to gain actionable insights, optimize operations, and create value for their stakeholders (Ouali et al., 2023a).

The transformative potential of Big Data extends beyond business optimization. In healthcare, predictive analytics can lead to early diagnosis and personalized treatment plans, improving patient outcomes and reducing costs. In urban planning, Big Data can enhance smart city initiatives, improving traffic management, resource allocation, and public safety. The integration of Big Data in environmental monitoring allows for better management of natural resources and more effective responses to climate change challenges (Ouali et al., 2022c).

Moreover, by addressing the challenges and embracing the opportunities presented by Big Data, organizations can position themselves for success in the digital economy and contribute to sustainable growth, societal well-being, and environmental stewardship. Ensuring robust data privacy and security measures is crucial to maintaining public trust and protecting sensitive information. Additionally, fostering a culture of data literacy within organizations empowers employees to utilize data effectively and make informed decisions (Arbi, 2018).

As we embark on this journey of data-driven transformation, it is essential to adopt a holistic and responsible approach to Big Data, guided by ethical principles, transparency, and accountability. This involves recognizing and mitigating biases in data and algorithms, ensuring equitable access to Big Data technologies, and promoting policies that safeguard individual rights. By doing so, we can ensure that the benefits of Big Data are realized equitably and ethically for the benefit of all(SASSI et al., 2019c).

The future of Big Data is bright, with continuous advancements promising even greater capabilities and applications. As organizations, governments, and societies adapt to this new paradigm, collaboration and innovation will be key to overcoming challenges and maximizing the potential of Big Data. Together, we can harness the power of data to create a more informed, efficient, and equitable world(SASSI et al., 2019a).

REFERENCES

Akter, S., & Wamba, S. F. (2016). Big data analytics in E-commerce: A systematic review and agenda for future research. *Electronic Markets*, *26*(2), 173–194. DOI: 10.1007/s12525-016-0219-0

Arbi, A. (2018). Dynamics of BAM neural networks with mixed delays and leakage time-varying delays in the weighted pseudo–almost periodic on time-space scales. *Mathematical Methods in the Applied Sciences*, *41*(3), 1230–1255.

Arbi, A., Cao, J., & Alsaedi, A. (2018). Improved synchronization analysis of competitive neural networks with time-varying delays. *Nonlinear Analysis (Vilnius)*, *23*(1), 82–107. DOI: 10.15388/NA.2018.1.7

Arbi, A., Guo, Y., & Cao, J. (2021). Convergence analysis on time scales for HOBAM neural networks in the Stepanov-like weighted pseudo almost automorphic space. *Neural Computing & Applications*, *33*(8), 3567–3581. DOI: 10.1007/s00521-020-05183-0

Arbi, A., & Tahri, N. (2024). Synchronization analysis of novel delayed dynamical Clifford-valued neural networks on timescales. *Journal of Algorithms & Computational Technology*, *18*, 17483026241241492.

Belhadi, A., Zkik, K., Cherrafi, A., & Sha'ri, M. Y. (2019). Understanding big data analytics for manufacturing processes: Insights from literature review and multiple case studies. *Computers & Industrial Engineering*, *137*, 106099. DOI: 10.1016/j.cie.2019.106099

Bhattarai, B. P., Paudyal, S., Luo, Y., Mohanpurkar, M., Cheung, K., Tonkoski, R., Hovsapian, R., Myers, K. S., Zhang, R., Zhao, P., Manic, M., Zhang, S., & Zhang, X. (2019). Big data analytics in smart grids: State-of-the-art, challenges, opportunities, and future directions. *IET Smart Grid*, *2*(2), 141–154. DOI: 10.1049/iet-stg.2018.0261

Bibri, S. E. (2018). The IoT for smart sustainable cities of the future: An analytical framework for sensor-based big data applications for environmental sustainability. *Sustainable Cities and Society*, *38*, 230–253. DOI: 10.1016/j.scs.2017.12.034

Chen, C. P., & Zhang, C. Y. (2014). Data-intensive applications, challenges, techniques and technologies: A survey on Big Data. *Information Sciences*, *275*, 314–347. DOI: 10.1016/j.ins.2014.01.015

Erevelles, S., Fukawa, N., & Swayne, L. (2016). Big Data consumer analytics and the transformation of marketing. *Journal of Business Research*, *69*(2), 897–904. DOI: 10.1016/j.jbusres.2015.07.001

Guo, Y., Ge, S. S., & Arbi, A. (2022). Stability of traveling waves solutions for nonlinear cellular neural networks with distributed delays. *Journal of Systems Science and Complexity*, *35*(1), 18–31. DOI: 10.1007/s11424-021-0180-7

Hadj Sassi, M. S., & Chaari Fourati, L. (2024). Design cognitive IoT architecture framework for immersive visual technologies of air quality monitoring systems. *Multimedia Tools and Applications*, *83*(17), 51615–51646.

Hamdi, M., Mestiri, S., & Arbi, A. (2024). Artificial intelligence techniques for bankruptcy prediction of tunisian companies: An application of machine learning and deep learning-based models. *Journal of Risk and Financial Management*, *17*(4), 132. DOI: 10.3390/jrfm17040132

Keshavarz, H., Mahdzir, A. M., Talebian, H., Jalaliyoon, N., & Ohshima, N. (2021). The value of big data analytics pillars in telecommunication industry. *Sustainability (Basel)*, *13*(13), 7160. DOI: 10.3390/su13137160

Luan, H., Geczy, P., Lai, H., Gobert, J., Yang, S. J., Ogata, H., Baltes, J., Guerra, R., Li, P., & Tsai, C. C. (2020). Challenges and future directions of big data and artificial intelligence in education. *Frontiers in Psychology*, *11*, 580820. DOI: 10.3389/fpsyg.2020.580820 PMID: 33192896

Morabito, V. (2015). Big data and analytics. Strategic and organisational impacts.

Ouali, I., Ben Halima, M., Masmoudi, N., Ayadi, M., Almuqren, L., & Wali, A. (2024). Text recuperated using ontology with stable marriage optimization technique and text visualization using AR. *Multimedia Tools and Applications*, 1–28.

Ouali, I., Fourati, R., Halima, M. B., & Wali, A. (2023, July). A novel method for arabic text detection with interactive visualization. In *2023 IEEE Symposium on Computers and Communications (ISCC)* (pp. 1046-1050). IEEE.

Ouali, I., Hadj Sassi, M. S., Ben Halima, M., & Wali, A. (2021, April). Architecture for real-time visualizing arabic words with diacritics using augmented reality for visually impaired people. In *International conference on advanced information networking and applications* (pp. 285-296). Cham: Springer International Publishing. DOI: 10.1007/978-3-030-75100-5_25

Ouali, I., Halima, M. B., & Ali, W. A. L. I. (2022b, May). Real-time application for recognition and visualization of arabic words with vowels based dl and ar. In 2022 International Wireless Communications and Mobile Computing (IWCMC) (pp. 678-683). IEEE.

Ouali, I., Halima, M. B., & Wali, A. (2022, March). Text detection and recognition using augmented reality and deep learning. In *International conference on advanced information networking and applications* (pp. 13-23). Cham: Springer International Publishing.

Ouali, I., Halima, M. B., & Wali, A. (2023a). An augmented reality for an arabic text reading and visualization assistant for the visually impaired. *Multimedia Tools and Applications*, *82*(28), 43569–43597. DOI: 10.1007/s11042-023-14880-6

Ouali, I., Halima, M. B. E. N., & Wali, A. (2022c). Augmented reality for scene text recognition, visualization and reading to assist visually impaired people. *Procedia Computer Science*, *207*, 158–167. DOI: 10.1016/j.procs.2022.09.048

Rehman, A., Naz, S., & Razzak, I. (2022). Leveraging big data analytics in healthcare enhancement: Trends, challenges and opportunities. *Multimedia Systems*, *28*(4), 1339–1371.

Russom, P. (2011). Big data analytics. *TDWI best practices report, fourth quarter, 19*(4), 1-34.

Sabir, Z., Raja, M. A. Z., Arbi, A., Altamirano, G. C., & Cao, J. (2021). Neuro-swarms intelligent computing using Gudermannian kernel for solving a class of second order Lane-Emden singular nonlinear model. *AIMS Mathematics*, *6*(3), 2468–2485.

Sabir, Z., Saoud, S., Raja, M. A. Z., Wahab, H. A., & Arbi, A. (2020). Heuristic computing technique for numerical solutions of nonlinear fourth order Emden–Fowler equation. *Mathematics and Computers in Simulation*, *178*, 534–548. DOI: 10.1016/j.matcom.2020.06.021

Sassi, M. S. H., Beltaief, I., Zekri, M., & Yahia, S. B. (2019, November). Multi-oriented real-time arabic scene text detection with deep fully convolutional networks. In 2019 IEEE/ACS 16th International Conference on Computer Systems and Applications (AICCSA) (pp. 1-6). IEEE.

Sassi, M. S. H., & Fourati, L. C. (2020, June). Investigation on deep learning methods for privacy and security challenges of cognitive IoV. In 2020 International Wireless Communications and Mobile Computing (IWCMC) (pp. 714-720). IEEE.

Sassi, M. S. H., Fourati, L. C., & Jedidi, F. G. (2019, June). Business information architecture for big data and Internet of Things. In 2019 15th International Wireless Communications & Mobile Computing Conference (IWCMC) (pp. 1749-1756). IEEE.

Sassi, M. S. H., Jedidi, F. G., & Fourati, L. C. (2019, June). Computer-aided software engineering (CASE) tool for big data and IoT architecture. In 2019 15th International wireless communications & mobile computing conference (IWCMC) (pp. 1403-1410). IEEE.

Sedkaoui, S., & Khelfaoui, M. (2019). Understand, develop and enhance the learning process with big data. *Information Discovery and Delivery*, *47*(1), 2–16. DOI: 10.1108/IDD-09-2018-0043

Chapter 3
Integrating IoT and AI Solutions for Addressing Urbanism Challenges

Oussama Wali
https://orcid.org/0009-0002-3197-0360
University of Tübingen, Germany

Mohamed Saifeddine Hadj Sassi
IT for Innovative Services Department, Luxembourg Institute of Science and Technology, Luxembourg

ABSTRACT

Urban areas face numerous challenges related to population growth, resource management, environmental sustainability, and infrastructure efficiency. The integration of Internet of Things (IoT) and Artificial Intelligence (AI) technologies offers innovative solutions to tackle these urbanism problems. This article explores the application of IoT and AI in addressing various urban challenges, including traffic congestion, energy consumption, waste management, public safety, and urban planning. By leveraging real-time data collection, predictive analytics, and autonomous systems, IoT and AI solutions empower cities to optimize resource utilization, enhance service delivery, and improve overall quality of life

DOI: 10.4018/979-8-3693-8141-0.ch003

for residents.

1. INTRODUCTION

Urbanization is a global phenomenon characterized by the rapid growth of cities and metropolitan areas. With more than half of the world's population residing in urban areas, cities face a myriad of complex challenges, ranging from traffic congestion and pollution to inadequate infrastructure and limited resources. These challenges are exacerbated by the increasing demand for energy, water, and other essential services, as well as the need for improved public safety and environmental sustainability. In response to these challenges, there is a growing interest in leveraging advanced technologies such as the Internet of Things (IoT) and Artificial Intelligence (AI) to transform urban environments into smarter, more efficient, and sustainable spaces.

IoT technology enables the integration of various devices and systems, allowing for the collection and exchange of vast amounts of data in real time. Sensors, connected devices, and smart infrastructure can monitor and manage urban systems more effectively, providing valuable insights into city operations and enabling data-driven decision-making. AI, on the other hand, offers powerful tools for analyzing and interpreting this data, automating processes, and optimizing the performance of urban systems. The combination of IoT and AI has the potential to revolutionize urban management by enhancing resource allocation, improving service delivery, and fostering innovation.

The application of IoT and AI in urban settings is already showing promising results across various domains. For instance, smart traffic management systems use real-time data to optimize traffic flow and reduce congestion, while environmental monitoring networks help track pollution levels and support efforts to improve air quality. Additionally, smart grids and energy management systems enhance the efficiency of energy distribution and consumption, contributing to the sustainability of urban areas. Public safety is also being enhanced through AI-driven surveillance and emergency response systems, which can detect and respond to incidents more quickly and effectively.

This article provides an overview of how IoT and AI solutions can be applied to address urbanism problems and create smarter cities. It explores the potential benefits of these technologies, such as improved efficiency, reduced costs, and enhanced quality of life for urban residents. Furthermore, it discusses the challenges and considerations associated with implementing IoT and AI in urban environments, including issues related to data privacy, security, and interoperability. By examining current examples and case studies, the article highlights best practices and strategies for successfully integrating IoT and AI into urban planning and management.

In summary, the integration of IoT and AI technologies offers a promising pathway to addressing the complex challenges of urbanization. By harnessing the power of these advanced technologies, cities can become more resilient, sustainable, and livable, ultimately improving the well-being of their inhabitants.

2. IoT APPLICATIONS IN URBANISM

2.1 Smart Transportation

Smart transportation systems leverage IoT and AI technologies to revolutionize how people and goods move within urban areas. By integrating real-time data collection, predictive analytics, and autonomous vehicles, smart transportation solutions aim to enhance mobility, reduce congestion, and improve overall transportation efficiency in cities.

2.1.1 Real-Time Traffic Monitoring

IoT sensors and connected devices deployed across road networks collect data on traffic flow, vehicle speeds, and congestion levels in real-time. This data is transmitted to centralized control centers where AI algorithms analyze and process it to provide actionable insights to traffic management authorities. By monitoring traffic conditions dynamically, authorities can identify congestion hotspots, optimize traffic signal timings, and reroute vehicles to alleviate traffic congestion and reduce travel times (ALAHI *et al.*, 2023).

2.1.2 Predictive Traffic Management

AI algorithms analyze historical traffic data, weather patterns, and special events to forecast traffic conditions and anticipate congestion in advance. By predicting future traffic volumes and congestion levels, transportation authorities can implement proactive measures such as adjusting speed limits, deploying additional public transportation services, and coordinating traffic flow to prevent bottlenecks and minimize disruptions.

2.1.3 Autonomous Vehicles and Mobility Services

IoT-enabled sensors and AI-powered algorithms enable the development and deployment of Autonomous Vehicles (AVs) and ride-sharing services that provide on-demand transportation solutions. AVs equipped with sensors, cameras, and lidar systems navigate urban environments autonomously, reducing the need for human intervention and improving safety and efficiency on roads. Ride-sharing platforms leverage AI algorithms to match riders with nearby vehicles, optimize route planning, and reduce vehicle emissions by promoting carpooling and shared mobility options (ALAHI *et al.,* 2023).

2.1.4 Integrated Multimodal Transport Systems

Smart transportation systems integrate various modes of transportation, including public transit, cycling, walking, and micro-mobility solutions, to provide seamless and efficient mobility options for residents. IoT-connected transit systems enable real-time tracking of buses, trains, and other public transportation services, allowing commuters to plan their journeys more effectively and reduce wait times. AI algorithms optimize route planning and scheduling to enhance service reliability and accessibility, encouraging more people to use sustainable modes of transportation and reduce reliance on private vehicles (ALAHI *et al.,* 2023).

2.1.5 Smart Infrastructure and Traffic Management

IoT sensors embedded in roads, traffic lights, and infrastructure assets provide real-time data on road conditions, infrastructure usage, and environmental factors. AI-powered traffic management systems analyze this data to optimize traffic signal timings, manage traffic flow, and prioritize emergency vehicles, improving overall road safety and reducing congestion-related accidents. Smart infrastructure solutions, such as dynamic tolling and congestion pricing, incentivize behavior change and promote more sustainable and efficient transportation choices among commuters (ALAHI *et al.,* 2023).

In summary, smart transportation systems leverage IoT and AI technologies to create more efficient, reliable, and sustainable mobility solutions for urban residents. By optimizing traffic management, promoting shared mobility options, and integrating various modes of transportation, smart transportation initiatives aim to transform urban mobility and improve quality of life in cities around the world.

2.2 Energy Management

Energy management in urban areas involves the efficient utilization of resources, reduction of waste, and adoption of renewable energy sources to address sustainability challenges. Leveraging IoT and AI technologies, energy management systems optimize energy consumption, monitor energy usage patterns, and enhance the integration of renewable energy sources into the urban grid.

2.2.1 Smart Grid Infrastructure

IoT-enabled smart grid technologies facilitate the bidirectional flow of electricity between power producers and consumers, enabling more efficient energy distribution and consumption (see Figure 1). Smart meters, sensors, and advanced communication networks collect real-time data on energy consumption, grid performance, and demand patterns, allowing utilities to better manage electricity supply and demand, reduce transmission losses, and optimize grid operations (KAGINALKAR *et al.*, 2021).

Figure 1. Conceptual Framework of Smart Grids.

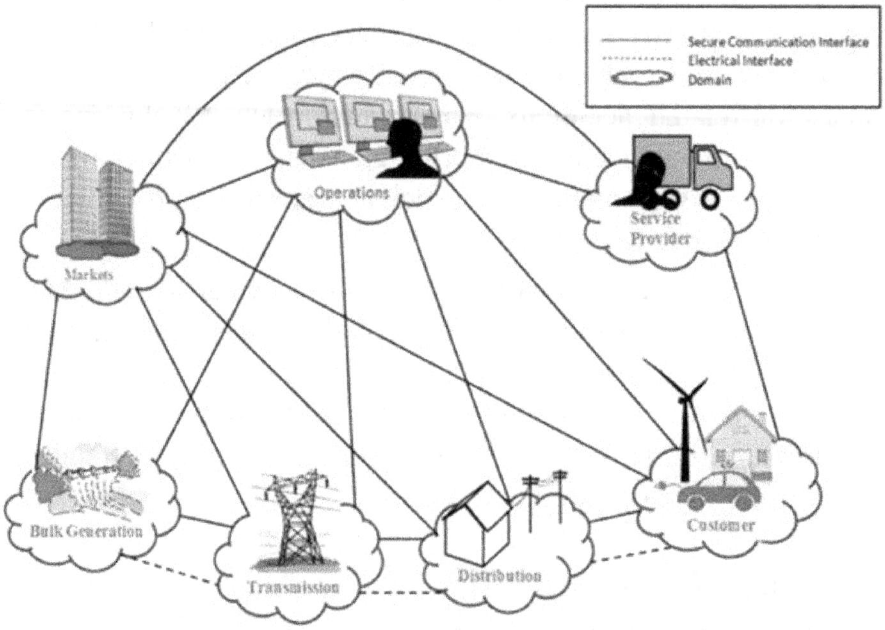

2.2.2 Demand Response and Load Management

AI algorithms analyze historical energy consumption data, weather forecasts, and market prices to predict energy demand patterns and optimize load distribution in real-time. Demand response programs incentivize consumers to adjust their energy usage during peak hours through dynamic pricing schemes, smart appliances, and automated energy management systems. By shifting energy-intensive tasks to off-peak hours and reducing peak demand, utilities can alleviate strain on the grid, prevent blackouts, and lower overall energy costs.

2.2.3 Energy Efficiency and Conservation

IoT sensors and smart devices monitor energy usage patterns within buildings, homes, and industrial facilities, identifying opportunities for energy efficiency improvements and waste reduction. AI-powered energy management systems analyze this data to optimize HVAC systems, lighting fixtures, and equipment operation, minimizing energy wastage and reducing carbon emissions. Energy-efficient building designs, green construction practices, and sustainable materials further enhance energy conservation efforts and promote eco-friendly urban development (KAGINALKAR *et al.,* 2021).

2.2.4 Renewable Energy Integration

IoT-enabled renewable energy systems, such as solar panels, wind turbines, and geothermal heat pumps, generate clean and sustainable energy to power urban infrastructure and meet growing energy demands. AI algorithms optimize the integration of renewable energy sources into the urban grid, balancing supply and demand, managing energy storage systems, and maximizing renewable energy generation. Energy storage technologies, such as batteries and pumped hydro storage, store excess renewable energy for later use, ensuring grid stability and reliability during periods of high demand or intermittent renewable energy generation.

2.2.5 Microgrid and Distributed Energy Systems

Microgrid solutions leverage IoT and AI technologies to create decentralized energy networks that integrate renewable energy sources, energy storage systems, and distributed energy resources. Microgrids provide localized energy generation, distribution, and consumption capabilities, enhancing energy resilience, reliability, and security in urban areas. AI algorithms optimize microgrid operations, manage energy flows, and coordinate grid-connected and off-grid energy assets to maximize efficiency and minimize environmental impact (ARBI, 2018).

In summary, energy management initiatives leveraging IoT and AI technologies play a crucial role in promoting sustainability, resilience, and efficiency in urban environments. By optimizing energy usage, integrating renewable energy sources, and implementing smart grid solutions, cities can reduce their carbon footprint, enhance energy security, and create more sustainable and livable communities for residents.

2.3 Waste Management

Efficient waste management is essential for maintaining cleanliness, hygiene, and environmental sustainability in urban areas. Leveraging IoT and AI technologies, waste management systems optimize waste collection, recycling processes, and landfill management, leading to reduced environmental pollution and improved resource utilization (see Figure 2).

Figure 2. IoT Integration in Smart Waste Management Systems.

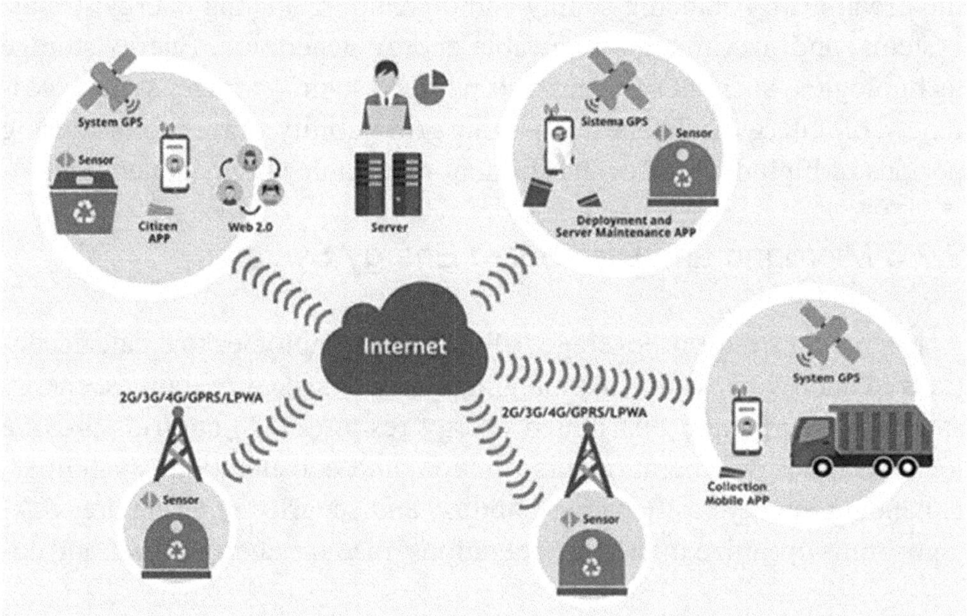

2.3.1 Smart Waste Collection

IoT-enabled smart waste bins equipped with sensors and actuators monitor waste levels in real-time and automatically trigger waste collection processes when bins reach capacity. These smart bins communicate with waste management authorities, routing collection trucks to the most efficient routes based on demand and optimizing collection schedules to minimize fuel consumption and reduce carbon emissions. AI algorithms analyze historical data on waste generation patterns, population density, and traffic conditions to predict future waste generation trends and optimize collection routes accordingly (BIBRI *et al.,* 2024).

2.3.2 Waste Sorting and Recycling

AI-powered image recognition technologies identify and classify different types of waste materials at recycling facilities, enabling automated sorting processes and enhancing recycling efficiency. IoT sensors track the movement of recyclable materials throughout the recycling supply chain, from collection to processing and manufacturing, ensuring transparency and traceability. Smart recycling bins equipped with RFID tags incentivize residents to separate recyclable materials from general waste, promoting recycling behavior and reducing contamination in recycling streams (BIBRI *et al.,* 2024).

2.3.3 Landfill Management and Monitoring

IoT sensors and satellite imaging technologies monitor landfill sites in real-time, detecting methane emissions, leachate leakage, and environmental pollution risks. AI algorithms analyze sensor data and satellite imagery to identify potential environmental hazards, optimize landfill operations, and mitigate negative impacts on surrounding ecosystems. Predictive analytics models forecast landfill capacity, waste decomposition rates, and long-term environmental risks, guiding waste management authorities in planning future landfill expansions, closures, and remediation efforts (BIBRI *et al.,* 2024).

2.3.4 Composting and Organic Waste Management

IoT-enabled composting systems monitor temperature, moisture levels, and nutrient content in compost piles, optimizing composting processes and accelerating the decomposition of organic waste materials. AI algorithms analyze environmental data and composting parameters to optimize composting conditions, minimize odor emissions, and produce high-quality compost for soil enrichment and agricultural applications. Smart composting solutions integrate with urban farming initiatives, community gardens, and green spaces, promoting circular economy principles and reducing reliance on chemical fertilizers and synthetic pesticides.

2.3.5 Waste-to-Energy Conversion

Advanced waste-to-energy technologies, such as anaerobic digestion, pyrolysis, and gasification, convert organic waste materials into biogas, biofuels, and renewable energy sources. IoT sensors monitor energy production processes, optimize reactor temperatures, and regulate feedstock inputs to maximize energy output and minimize emissions. AI algorithms analyze operational data, predict equipment failures, and optimize maintenance schedules to ensure continuous and reliable operation of waste-to-energy facilities. Integrated energy recovery systems harness waste heat and biogas emissions for district heating, industrial processes, and electricity generation, enhancing energy efficiency and resource utilization in urban environments.

In summary, IoT and AI technologies play a vital role in revolutionizing waste management practices in urban areas, promoting circular economy principles, and mitigating environmental pollution. By optimizing waste collection, recycling processes, landfill management, and energy recovery systems, cities can achieve significant reductions in waste generation, improve resource efficiency, and create more sustainable and resilient urban ecosystems for future generations.

2.4 Public Safety

Ensuring public safety is paramount for sustainable urban development, and the integration of IoT and AI technologies offers innovative solutions to address various challenges in this domain. From crime prevention to emergency response, smart urban systems powered by IoT and AI enhance situational awareness, enable proactive risk management, and improve the overall safety and security of urban environments.

2.4.1 Smart Surveillance and Monitoring

IoT-enabled surveillance cameras, acoustic sensors, and environmental monitoring devices enhance situational awareness by capturing real-time data on various urban parameters, including pedestrian traffic, vehicle movements, environmental conditions, and public gatherings. AI algorithms process and analyze this data to detect anomalies, identify potential security threats, and alert law enforcement agencies or emergency responders in real-time. Smart video analytics techniques, such as object recognition and behavior analysis, enable automated threat detection, suspicious activity monitoring, and crowd behavior prediction, enhancing the effectiveness of urban surveillance systems and reducing response times to security incidents.

2.4.2 Predictive Policing and Crime Prevention

AI-powered predictive analytics models leverage historical crime data, demographic profiles, and socio-economic indicators to forecast crime hotspots, trends, and patterns in urban areas. IoT sensors deployed in high-risk locations, such as street corners, public parks, and transportation hubs, monitor environmental factors, human behavior, and social interactions, providing real-time data inputs for predictive policing algorithms. Law enforcement agencies use predictive insights to allocate resources more effectively, deploy patrol units proactively, and implement targeted intervention strategies to deter criminal activities, prevent incidents, and enhance community safety (SIMIĆ *et al.,* 2020).

2.4.3 Emergency Response and Disaster Management

IoT-enabled emergency response systems integrate sensors, communication networks, and AI-driven decision support tools to streamline disaster preparedness, response, and recovery efforts in urban environments. Smart sensors installed in critical infrastructure, such as buildings, bridges, and transportation networks, monitor structural integrity, seismic activity, and environmental conditions, providing early warnings and alerts during natural disasters, such as earthquakes, floods, and hurricanes. AI algorithms analyze sensor data, prioritize emergency calls, and optimize dispatch routes for first responders, ensuring rapid and coordinated response to emergencies, minimizing casualties, and reducing property damage (SIMIĆ *et al.,* 2020).

2.4.4 Public Health Monitoring and Disease Surveillance

IoT devices, wearable sensors, and mobile applications enable real-time monitoring of public health indicators, such as air quality, temperature, humidity, and disease outbreaks, in urban communities. AI-powered epidemiological models analyze health data from diverse sources, including electronic health records, social media feeds, and environmental sensors, to track the spread of infectious diseases, identify at-risk populations, and predict future outbreaks. Smart health surveillance systems facilitate early detection, containment, and mitigation of public health threats, enabling authorities to implement targeted interventions, allocate healthcare resources efficiently, and safeguard community well-being (ARBI *et al.,* 2018).

2.4.5 Traffic Management and Pedestrian Safety

IoT-connected traffic signals, smart streetlights, and pedestrian crossing systems improve traffic flow, reduce congestion, and enhance pedestrian safety in urban areas. AI algorithms process real-time traffic data, predict traffic patterns, and optimize signal timings to minimize delays, prioritize emergency vehicles, and improve overall transportation efficiency. Smart crosswalks equipped with sensors and warning signals detect pedestrian movements, monitor traffic speeds, and provide visual cues to drivers, cyclists, and pedestrians, reducing the risk of accidents and promoting safer mobility options in urban environments.

In summary, the integration of IoT and AI technologies enhances public safety and security in urban areas by enabling proactive risk management, real-time threat detection, and rapid emergency response. By leveraging smart surveillance, predictive analytics, emergency response systems, and public health monitoring solutions, cities can create safer, more resilient communities, improve quality of life, and foster sustainable urban development for residents and visitors alike (OUALI *et al.,* 2022b).

2.5 Urban Planning

Urban planning is undergoing a transformative shift with the integration of IoT and AI technologies, enabling data-driven decision-making, sustainable development, and enhanced quality of life in urban areas. By harnessing real-time data insights, predictive analytics, and smart infrastructure solutions, cities can optimize land use, transportation networks, environmental sustainability, and community engagement, shaping resilient, inclusive, and livable urban environments for future generations.

2.5.1 Smart Land Use and Zoning

IoT-enabled sensors, geospatial mapping technologies, and AI-driven analytics empower urban planners to optimize land use, development density, and zoning regulations based on real-time data insights and predictive modeling. Smart city platforms integrate diverse datasets, including population demographics, economic indicators, environmental factors, and urban amenities, to assess land suitability, identify growth opportunities, and design mixed-use neighborhoods that promote walkability, accessibility, and social equity. AI algorithms analyze spatial data patterns, simulate urban scenarios, and recommend policy interventions to support sustainable land management practices, preserve natural resources, and enhance urban resilience to climate change and population growth (YANG *et al.,* 2020).

2.5.2 Integrated Transportation Systems

IoT-connected vehicles, smart traffic signals, and multimodal transportation networks revolutionize urban mobility and accessibility, enabling seamless, efficient, and sustainable transportation solutions for residents and commuters. AI-powered traffic management systems optimize traffic flow, reduce congestion, and minimize travel times by dynamically adjusting signal timings, rerouting vehicles, and coordinating public transit services based on real-time demand and traffic conditions. Smart parking solutions leverage sensor data, predictive analytics, and mobile applications to guide drivers to available parking spaces, alleviate parking congestion, and promote alternative transportation modes, such as cycling, walking, and ridesharing, reducing emissions and improving air quality in urban areas (OUALI et al., 2022a).

2.5.3 Sustainable Infrastructure Development

IoT-enabled infrastructure monitoring, predictive maintenance, and asset management systems enhance the resilience, efficiency, and sustainability of urban infrastructure networks, including water supply, energy distribution, and waste management systems. AI algorithms analyze sensor data, detect anomalies, and predict equipment failures, enabling proactive maintenance interventions, optimizing resource allocation, and minimizing downtime for critical infrastructure assets. Smart grid technologies integrate renewable energy sources, energy storage systems, and demand-response mechanisms to optimize energy consumption, reduce carbon emissions, and promote renewable energy integration in urban communities, advancing climate change mitigation and environmental sustainability goals (YANG *et al.,* 2020).

2.5.4 Community Engagement and Participatory Planning

IoT-enabled citizen engagement platforms, digital feedback mechanisms, and virtual reality tools empower residents, businesses, and community stakeholders to actively participate in urban planning processes, voice their concerns, and contribute to decision-making outcomes. AI-driven sentiment analysis, social media mining, and crowd-sourced data collection methods provide valuable insights into public preferences, perceptions, and priorities, enabling planners to design more responsive, inclusive, and equitable urban policies and initiatives. Smart city initiatives foster collaboration, transparency, and co-creation opportunities between government agencies, private sector partners, and civil society organizations, fostering social cohesion, trust, and resilience in urban communities (YANG *et al.,* 2020).

2.5.5 Resilient Urban Design and Climate Adaptation

IoT sensors, remote sensing technologies, and AI-based climate modeling tools support evidence-based decision-making and adaptive urban design strategies to mitigate climate risks, enhance disaster resilience, and protect vulnerable communities from environmental hazards. Smart building design principles, green infrastructure solutions, and nature-based urban interventions promote energy efficiency, water conservation, and natural habitat preservation, creating climate-resilient urban landscapes that are adaptable to changing environmental conditions and extreme weather events. AI-driven predictive modeling techniques enable planners to anticipate future climate impacts, assess risk exposure, and prioritize adaptation measures, ensuring long-term sustainability and livability in urban areas (YANG *et al.,* 2020).

In summary, the convergence of IoT and AI technologies is revolutionizing urban planning practices, enabling data-driven insights, evidence-based decision-making, and stakeholder engagement in the design and management of sustainable, resilient, and inclusive urban environments. By leveraging smart land use strategies, integrated transportation systems, sustainable infrastructure solutions, community engagement tools, and climate adaptation measures, cities can address complex urban challenges, promote social equity, and create thriving, resilient communities for current and future generations (SASSI *et al.,* 2019b).

3. AI TECHNOLOGIES FOR URBANISM

3.1 Machine Learning

Machine Learning (ML) plays a pivotal role in leveraging IoT data for urbanism solutions, enabling automated data analysis, pattern recognition, and predictive modeling to extract actionable insights and optimize decision-making processes in urban environments. ML algorithms process vast amounts of heterogeneous data streams generated by IoT sensors, devices, and urban infrastructure systems, transforming raw data into meaningful information, knowledge, and intelligence for urban planners, policymakers, and stakeholders.

3.1.1 Supervised Learning for Predictive Analytics

Supervised learning algorithms, such as regression, classification, and ensemble methods, enable predictive analytics applications in urban planning, transportation management, and infrastructure optimization. By training ML models on historical IoT data, sensor readings, and environmental parameters, cities can forecast future trends, anticipate demand patterns, and optimize resource allocation for various urban services, including energy consumption, water distribution, and waste management. Supervised learning techniques empower decision-makers to identify potential risks, assess the impact of policy interventions, and prioritize investments in critical infrastructure projects to enhance urban resilience and sustainability (YIGITCANLAR *et al.*, 2021).

3.1.2 Unsupervised Learning for Anomaly Detection

Unsupervised learning algorithms, including clustering, anomaly detection, and dimensionality reduction techniques, facilitate anomaly detection and pattern recognition tasks in IoT data streams, enabling early warning systems, fault detection, and proactive maintenance strategies for urban infrastructure assets. By analyzing real-time sensor data, ML models can detect abnormal behavior, identify performance deviations, and trigger automated responses to mitigate risks and prevent service disruptions in transportation networks, energy grids, and public utilities. Unsupervised learning approaches enable cities to optimize operational efficiency, minimize downtime, and improve service reliability for urban residents and businesses.

3.1.3 Reinforcement Learning for Adaptive Control

Reinforcement learning algorithms enable adaptive control and decision-making processes in dynamic urban environments, where systems must continuously learn and adapt to changing conditions, uncertainties, and user preferences. By modeling urban systems as Markov Decision Processes (MDPs), RL agents can interact with the environment, learn optimal policies, and optimize resource allocation strategies to achieve predefined objectives, such as minimizing traffic congestion, maximizing energy efficiency, or optimizing waste collection routes. Reinforcement learning techniques enable autonomous agents, such as self-driving vehicles, smart grid controllers, and robotic systems, to navigate complex urban landscapes, make real-time decisions, and coordinate actions in response to evolving environmental stimuli and user demands (ALAHI *et al.*, 2023).

3.1.4 Deep Learning for Image and Sensor Data Analysis

Deep learning algorithms, such as Convolutional Neural Networks (CNNs) and Recurrent Neural Networks (RNNs), excel at processing high-dimensional, multimodal data sources, including images, videos, and time-series sensor readings, enabling advanced analytics and computer vision applications in urban environments. By leveraging deep learning techniques, cities can analyze urban imagery, satellite data, and aerial footage to monitor land use changes, detect urban sprawl, and assess environmental impacts on natural ecosystems. Deep learning models can also interpret sensor data from IoT devices, smart meters, and wearable sensors to monitor air quality, noise pollution, and environmental health indicators, enabling real-time decision support systems for urban planners and policymakers.

In summary, machine learning techniques play a critical role in harnessing IoT data for urbanism applications, enabling predictive analytics, anomaly detection, adaptive control, and image analysis tasks to optimize urban infrastructure, enhance public services, and improve quality of life in cities. By leveraging supervised, unsupervised, reinforcement, and deep learning algorithms, cities can unlock the full potential of IoT data streams, transform urban governance, and create smarter, more sustainable urban environments for residents, businesses, and future generations.

3.2 Deep Learning

Deep learning, a subset of machine learning, has emerged as a powerful approach for processing complex and high-dimensional data in various urbanism domains. Leveraging artificial neural networks with multiple layers of abstraction, deep learning models excel at capturing intricate patterns, extracting meaningful features, and performing advanced analytics tasks on diverse data modalities, including images, texts, and sequential data. In the context of IoT and AI for urbanism, deep learning techniques offer unprecedented capabilities for understanding, analyzing, and optimizing urban systems and infrastructure (SASSI et al., 2019a).

3.2.1 Image Recognition and Semantic Segmentation

Deep learning models, particularly Convolutional Neural Networks (CNNs), have revolutionized image recognition and semantic segmentation tasks in urban environments. By training CNNs on large-scale datasets of urban imagery, satellite images, and street-level photos, cities can automate the analysis of land use patterns, urban morphology, and infrastructure assets. Deep learning algorithms can detect and classify objects, such as buildings, roads, parks, and vehicles, enabling fine-grained spatial analysis, urban planning, and environmental monitoring. Semantic segmentation techniques further enable pixel-level labeling of urban scenes, facilitating the identification of specific features and anomalies for infrastructure maintenance, public safety, and disaster response applications (ATITALLAH *et al.,* 2020).

3.2.2 Natural Language Processing for Urban Data Analysis

Deep learning methods, including Recurrent Neural Networks (RNNs) and transformer architectures, are widely used for Natural Language Processing (NLP) tasks in urban data analysis. By processing textual data sources, such as social media feeds, news articles, and citizen reports, deep learning models can extract valuable insights, sentiment analysis, and public opinion trends related to urban issues, events, and policies. NLP techniques enable cities to monitor public sentiment, identify emerging concerns, and engage with residents to address community needs, enhance civic participation, and foster inclusive urban governance.

3.2.3 Time-Series Forecasting and Predictive Analytics

Deep learning architectures, such as Long Short-Term Memory networks (LSTMs) and Gated Recurrent Units (GRUs), are well-suited for time-series forecasting and predictive analytics tasks in urban contexts. By analyzing historical IoT data, sensor readings, and environmental parameters, deep learning models can capture temporal dependencies, detect patterns, and forecast future trends in various urban phenomena, including traffic congestion, air quality, energy consumption, and water demand. Time-series forecasting enables cities to anticipate changes, optimize resource allocation, and implement proactive interventions to mitigate risks, improve service delivery, and enhance urban resilience (ATITALLAH *et al.,* 2020).

3.2.4 Graph Neural Networks for Spatial Data Analysis

Deep learning techniques, such as Graph Neural Networks (GNNs), are increasingly applied to spatial data analysis and graph-based representations of urban networks, such as transportation networks, social networks, and utility networks. By modeling urban systems as graphs, GNNs can capture complex relationships, spatial dependencies, and network dynamics, enabling tasks such as route optimization, community detection, and infrastructure planning. Graph-based deep learning enables cities to optimize urban mobility, enhance connectivity, and design resilient infrastructure networks that meet the evolving needs of urban residents and businesses (ATITALLAH *et al.,* 2020).

In summary, deep learning techniques offer a diverse set of tools and methodologies for unlocking insights from IoT data and AI-driven applications in urban environments. By harnessing the power of deep neural networks for image analysis, natural language processing, time-series forecasting, and spatial data analysis, cities can address complex urban challenges, optimize resource management, and create more livable, sustainable, and resilient urban spaces for future generations.

3.3 Natural Language Processing (NLP)

Natural Language Processing (NLP) plays a crucial role in harnessing the potential of IoT and AI for addressing urbanism problems by enabling the analysis and understanding of unstructured textual data generated from various sources such as social media, news articles, citizen reports, and administrative documents. NLP techniques empower cities to extract valuable insights, sentiments, and trends from textual data, facilitating informed decision-making, proactive intervention, and community engagement in urban governance and planning processes.

3.3.1 Sentiment Analysis and Opinion Mining

Sentiment analysis, a core NLP task, involves determining the sentiment expressed in textual content, such as positive, negative, or neutral sentiments. By applying sentiment analysis techniques to social media feeds, citizen reports, and online forums, cities can gauge public sentiment towards urban policies, infrastructure projects, and community initiatives. Opinion mining extends sentiment analysis by identifying specific opinions, concerns, or viewpoints expressed by residents regarding urban issues, enabling city authorities to understand public perceptions, address grievances, and foster constructive dialogue with stakeholders.

3.3.2 Topic Modeling and Trend Detection

Topic modeling algorithms, such as Latent Dirichlet Allocation (LDA) and Non-negative Matrix Factorization (NMF), enable cities to uncover latent topics and themes from large volumes of textual data. By clustering related documents into coherent topics, cities can identify emerging trends, prioritize policy agendas, and allocate resources effectively. Topic modeling techniques also facilitate trend detection and tracking, allowing cities to monitor evolving urban issues, anticipate public concerns, and adapt policy responses in real-time to address emerging challenges (TUBALLA *et al.,* 2016).

3.3.3 Named Entity Recognition (NER) and Information Extraction

Named Entity Recognition (NER) is a fundamental NLP task that involves identifying and classifying named entities, such as locations, organizations, and people, mentioned in textual data. By employing NER techniques, cities can extract valuable information from unstructured text, such as identifying key stakeholders, geographical references, and relevant entities related to urban infrastructure and services. Information extraction extends NER by extracting structured data from unstructured text, enabling cities to populate knowledge graphs, build databases, and automate data integration processes for urban analytics and decision support systems (TUBALLA *et al.,* 2016).

3.3.4 Language Translation and Multilingual Analysis

Language translation technologies, powered by machine translation algorithms such as Neural Machine Translation (NMT), facilitate communication and collaboration across linguistic barriers in diverse urban contexts. By supporting multilingual analysis, cities can engage with linguistically diverse communities, translate public communications, and provide access to information and services in multiple languages. Multilingual NLP enables cities to ensure inclusivity, accessibility, and cultural sensitivity in urban planning, public service delivery, and community engagement initiatives (TUBALLA *et al.,* 2016).

3.3.5 Text Summarization and Information Retrieval

Text summarization techniques, including extractive and abstractive summarization, enable cities to distill key information and insights from large volumes of textual data. By generating concise summaries of documents, reports, and articles, cities can facilitate information retrieval, decision-making, and knowledge dissemination among policymakers, urban planners, and stakeholders. Text summarization algorithms also support information retrieval tasks by indexing and organizing textual data, enabling efficient search, retrieval, and access to relevant information for urban analysis and decision support (TUBALLA *et al.,* 2016).

In summary, Natural Language Processing (NLP) techniques offer powerful tools and methodologies for extracting insights, sentiments, and knowledge from textual data in urban contexts. By leveraging NLP capabilities for sentiment analysis, topic modeling, named entity recognition, language translation, and text summarization, cities can enhance their understanding of urban issues, engage with residents, and make data-driven decisions to address complex urban challenges and foster inclusive, sustainable, and resilient urban development.

3.4 Reinforcement Learning

Reinforcement Learning (RL) presents a promising approach to address urbanism problems by enabling intelligent decision-making in dynamic and uncertain environments. In the context of IoT and AI for urbanism, RL algorithms empower autonomous agents, such as smart infrastructure systems and urban management platforms, to learn optimal actions through interaction with the urban environment, receive feedback based on the consequences of their actions, and adapt their behavior to achieve long-term objectives and goals. RL techniques offer several applications in urban domains, ranging from traffic management and energy optimization to environmental monitoring and public safety (ARBI *et al.,* 2024).

3.4.1 Traffic Management and Control

Reinforcement Learning algorithms can optimize traffic flow and reduce congestion by learning adaptive control policies for traffic signals, dynamic lane management, and route guidance systems. RL agents deployed in smart transportation networks can learn to make real-time decisions, such as adjusting signal timings, rerouting vehicles, and coordinating traffic flow based on traffic conditions, road congestion, and user preferences. By leveraging RL-based traffic management systems, cities can enhance mobility, reduce travel times, and improve the overall efficiency of urban transportation networks (BRATTON *et al* 2021).

3.4.2 Energy Optimization and Demand Response

RL techniques enable intelligent energy management systems to optimize energy consumption, generation, and distribution in urban environments. RL agents deployed in smart grid infrastructure can learn to schedule energy generation, storage, and distribution resources efficiently, adapt to fluctuating energy demand, and respond to dynamic pricing signals and environmental conditions. By applying RL-based demand response strategies, cities can incentivize consumers to adjust their energy usage patterns, minimize peak demand, and promote energy conservation and renewable energy integration, leading to enhanced energy efficiency and sustainability (BRATTON *et al* 2021).

3.4.3 Environmental Monitoring and Pollution Control

Reinforcement Learning algorithms can support proactive environmental monitoring and pollution control initiatives in urban areas by optimizing resource allocation, sensor deployment, and pollution mitigation strategies. RL agents deployed in IoT-enabled environmental monitoring networks can learn to identify pollution sources, predict pollutant concentrations, and recommend mitigation measures based on real-time sensor data, weather conditions, and geographical factors. By leveraging RL-based pollution control systems, cities can mitigate environmental risks, improve air and water quality, and protect public health and ecological integrity (SABIR *et al.,* 2021).

3.4.4 Public Safety and Emergency Management

RL techniques offer innovative solutions for enhancing public safety and emergency management capabilities in urban environments. RL agents deployed in IoT-enabled public safety systems can learn adaptive patrol routes, emergency response plans, and evacuation strategies to optimize resource allocation and response times during emergencies, natural disasters, and crisis situations. By applying RL-based decision support systems, cities can improve incident detection, coordination, and mitigation efforts, ensuring effective response and recovery operations and enhancing urban resilience and community safety.

In summary, Reinforcement Learning (RL) presents a powerful paradigm for addressing complex urbanism problems by enabling autonomous decision-making, adaptive control, and learning-based optimization in diverse urban domains. By leveraging RL capabilities for traffic management, energy optimization, environmental monitoring, and public safety, cities can enhance their resilience, sustainability, and livability, paving the way for smarter, safer, and more sustainable urban futures (BRATTON *et al* 2021).

4. CASE STUDIES AND BEST PRACTICES

4.1 Singapore's Smart Nation Initiative

Singapore's Smart Nation Initiative serves as a pioneering example of how IoT and AI technologies are being harnessed to address urban challenges and enhance quality of life. As one of the world's leading smart cities, Singapore has embarked on a comprehensive strategy to leverage advanced technologies for urban development, economic growth, and social progress. At the heart of Singapore's Smart Nation vision lies a concerted effort to harness the power of data, connectivity, and intelligence to create a more efficient, sustainable, and inclusive urban environment.

4.1.1 Integrated Urban Solutions

Singapore's Smart Nation Initiative encompasses a wide array of integrated urban solutions that leverage IoT and AI technologies to optimize various aspects of urban life. From smart transportation and energy management to healthcare, education, and governance, Singapore's smart city initiatives aim to enhance the efficiency, resilience, and livability of the urban landscape. By deploying sensor networks, data analytics platforms, and AI-driven applications, Singapore has implemented innovative solutions for traffic congestion management, energy conservation, waste reduction, and public safety, transforming the city into a testbed for urban innovation and experimentation (HO *et al.,* 2017).

4.1.2 Digital Infrastructure and Connectivity

Central to Singapore's Smart Nation agenda is the development of robust digital infrastructure and connectivity capabilities to support the seamless integration and interoperability of IoT devices, sensors, and systems. Singapore has invested heavily in building a nationwide network of sensors, communication networks, and data centers to enable real-time data collection, processing, and sharing across various urban domains. By establishing ubiquitous connectivity and high-speed broadband access, Singapore has laid the foundation for the proliferation of smart applications and services that drive economic growth, social development, and environmental sustainability (ARBI *et al.,* 2021).

4.1.3 Open Data Ecosystem and Collaboration

Singapore's Smart Nation strategy emphasizes the importance of fostering an open data ecosystem and promoting collaboration between government agencies, industry partners, academia, and the community to co-create innovative solutions and services. Singapore has launched several initiatives to facilitate data sharing, transparency, and collaboration, including the Data.gov.sg portal, which provides access to a wide range of government datasets for research, analysis, and application development. By engaging citizens, businesses, and stakeholders in the co-creation process, Singapore aims to harness collective intelligence and creativity to address complex urban challenges and enhance civic engagement and participation (OUALI *et al.,* 2024).

4.1.4 Citizen-Centric Services and Governance

Singapore's Smart Nation initiatives are driven by a strong emphasis on delivering citizen-centric services and governance models that prioritize user needs, preferences, and feedback. Through the use of AI-powered chatbots, mobile applications, and online platforms, Singapore has transformed the delivery of public services, such as healthcare, education, transportation, and utilities, to make them more accessible, efficient, and personalized. By leveraging data analytics and machine learning algorithms, Singapore has also enhanced decision-making processes, policy formulation, and urban planning efforts to better meet the evolving needs and aspirations of its citizens (HO *et al.,* 2017).

4.1.5 Global Leadership and Innovation Hub

Singapore's Smart Nation vision has positioned the city-state as a global leader and innovation hub in the field of urban technology and sustainability. Through strategic partnerships, international collaborations, and knowledge exchange initiatives, Singapore has emerged as a testbed for cutting-edge technologies, best practices, and innovative solutions that address common urban challenges faced by cities around the world. By showcasing successful smart city projects and initiatives, Singapore aims to inspire and catalyze urban transformation efforts globally, fostering a culture of innovation, collaboration, and continuous improvement in the pursuit of sustainable urban development (OUALI *et al.,* 2021).

In summary, Singapore's Smart Nation Initiative exemplifies the transformative potential of IoT and AI technologies in addressing complex urban challenges and creating more sustainable, resilient, and livable cities. By embracing innovation, collaboration, and citizen engagement, Singapore has established itself as a global leader in urban technology and set a compelling example for cities seeking to harness the power of data-driven insights and intelligent systems to build smarter, more inclusive, and sustainable urban futures.

4.2 Barcelona's Urban Innovation

Barcelona has emerged as a prominent global leader in urban innovation, leveraging IoT and AI technologies to address pressing urban challenges and enhance the quality of life for its residents. The city's commitment to sustainable urban development, coupled with its innovative approach to technology adoption, has positioned Barcelona as a model smart city and a beacon of urban innovation. Numerous scholarly articles explore the realm of Smart City Technologies, as depicted in Figures 3, which analyze publications from 2010 to present.

Figure 3. Evolution of Academic Interest in Smart City Technologies: Analyzing Publications from 2010 to Present.

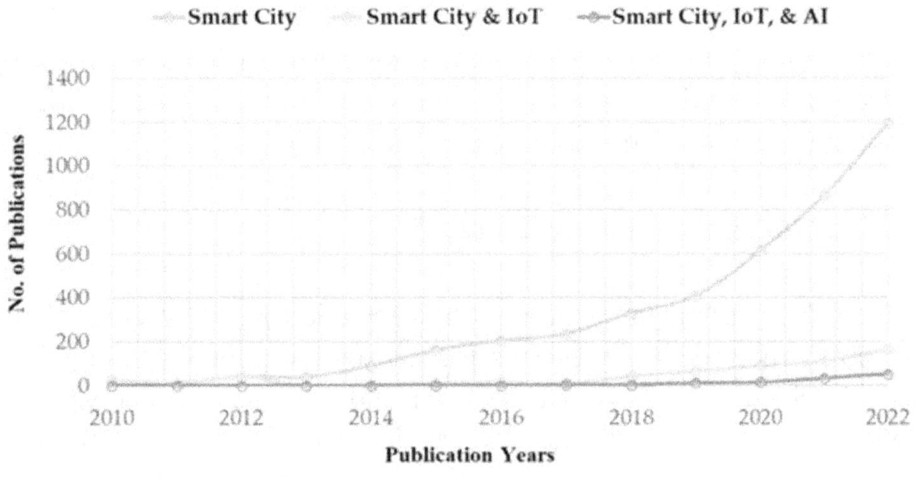

Figure 4. Methodological Overview for Integrating IoT and AI Applications in Smart Cities.

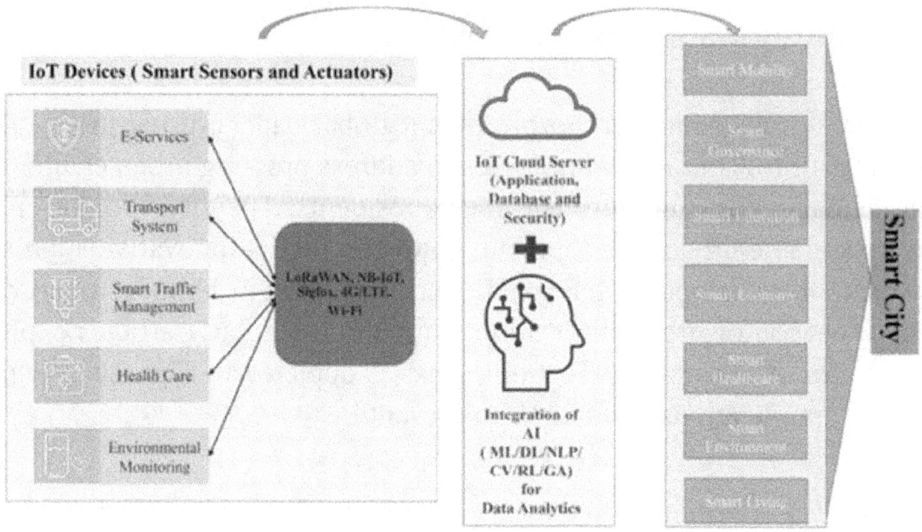

This figure provides a comprehensive outline of the methodology employed to introduce applications within a smart city framework, emphasizing the integration of IoT and AI technologies.

4.2.1 Smart City Infrastructure

Barcelona's urban innovation efforts are underpinned by a robust smart city infrastructure that integrates IoT sensors, data analytics platforms, and AI-driven applications to monitor and manage various aspects of urban life (see Figure 5). The city has deployed sensor networks across its urban landscape to collect real-time data on traffic flow, air quality, energy consumption, waste management, and public services, enabling data-driven decision-making and proactive interventions to improve efficiency, sustainability, and resilience.

Figure 5. Assessment of Communication Technologies Across Smart City Applications.

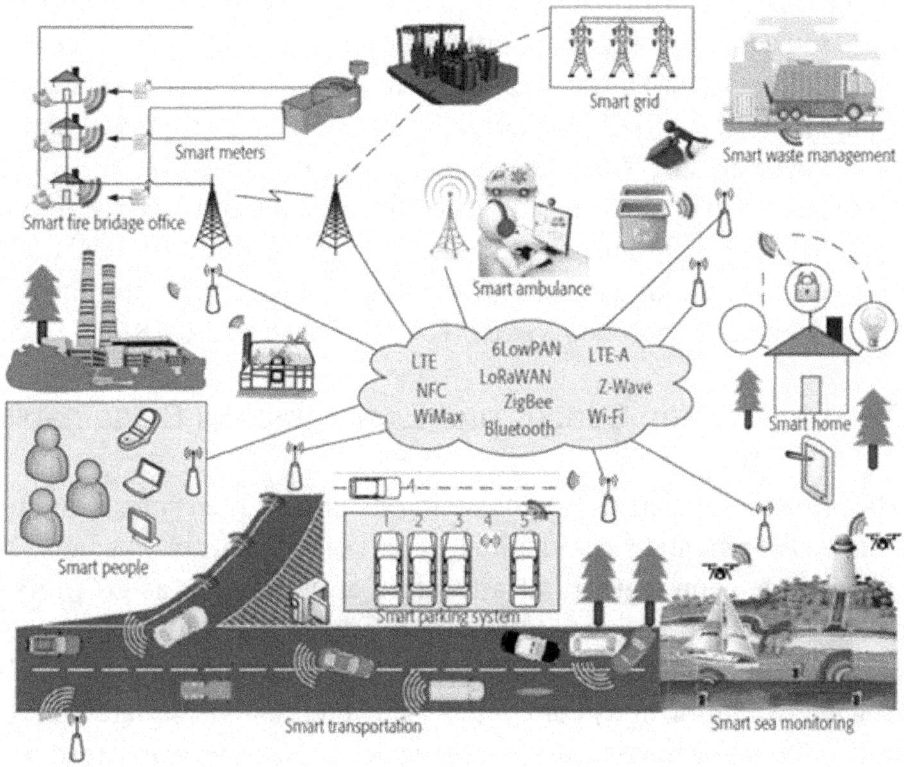

4.2.2 Citizen Engagement and Participation

Central to Barcelona's smart city initiatives is a strong emphasis on citizen engagement and participation, empowering residents to actively contribute to the co-creation of urban solutions and services. Through digital platforms, such as the Decidim Barcelona participatory democracy platform, residents can voice their opinions, ideas, and concerns on urban issues and collaboratively shape the city's development agenda. By fostering a culture of open governance and transparency, Barcelona aims to build trust, accountability, and social cohesion among its diverse communities (ORTEGA-FERNÁNDEZ *et al.,* 2020).

4.2.3 Innovative Mobility Solutions

Barcelona has prioritized the development of innovative mobility solutions to address congestion, pollution, and accessibility challenges in urban transportation. The city has implemented a comprehensive network of smart mobility initiatives, including bike-sharing programs, electric vehicle charging infrastructure, and intelligent transportation systems that optimize traffic flow and reduce carbon emissions. By promoting sustainable modes of transportation and encouraging multi-modal mobility, Barcelona is creating a more efficient, equitable, and environmentally friendly urban transport ecosystem (CALZADA *et al.,* 2018).

4.2.4 Urban Green Spaces and Environmental Sustainability

Barcelona is committed to enhancing its urban green spaces and promoting environmental sustainability as part of its smart city agenda. The city has implemented green infrastructure projects, such as green roofs, urban gardens, and park revitalization initiatives, to mitigate the urban heat island effect, improve air quality, and enhance biodiversity. Through IoT-enabled monitoring systems and AI-powered analytics, Barcelona can optimize the management of its green spaces, conserve water resources, and create healthier and more resilient urban environments for its residents (SABIR, *et al.* 2020).

4.2.5 Digital Innovation Ecosystem

Barcelona has fostered a vibrant digital innovation ecosystem that brings together startups, research institutions, corporations, and government agencies to collaborate on cutting-edge projects and initiatives. The city's innovation hubs, such as the Barcelona Urban Lab and the 22@Barcelona innovation district, serve as catalysts for entrepreneurship, research, and technology transfer in areas such as smart cities, digital health, and sustainable urban development. By nurturing talent, fostering collaboration, and supporting entrepreneurship, Barcelona is driving innovation and economic growth while addressing urban challenges.

4.2.6 International Collaboration and Knowledge Sharing

Barcelona actively engages in international collaboration and knowledge sharing initiatives to exchange best practices, lessons learned, and innovative solutions with cities around the world. Through partnerships with organizations like the C40 Cities Climate Leadership Group and the European Innovation Partnership on Smart Cities and Communities, Barcelona collaborates on global urban sustainability initiatives, shares expertise, and contributes to the advancement of smart city standards and frameworks. By leveraging the collective intelligence and resources of global networks, Barcelona seeks to accelerate urban innovation and build more resilient and sustainable cities for future generations (CALZADA *et al.,* 2018).

In conclusion, Barcelona's urban innovation journey demonstrates the transformative potential of IoT and AI technologies in addressing complex urban challenges and building more sustainable, resilient, and inclusive cities. By embracing innovation, citizen engagement, and collaboration, Barcelona has established itself as a global leader in smart city development and set a compelling example for cities worldwide seeking to leverage technology for urban sustainability and prosperity (SASSI *et al.,* 2020b).

5. CHALLENGES AND OPPORTUNITIES

Barcelona's pioneering efforts in integrating IoT and AI technologies into urban development are accompanied by a set of unique challenges and opportunities that shape the trajectory of its smart city journey.

5.1 Challenges

5.1.1 Data Privacy and Security: As Barcelona collects and analyzes vast amounts of data from IoT sensors and AI-driven applications, ensuring the privacy and security of citizens' personal information becomes paramount. The city must implement robust data protection measures, including encryption, anonymization, and access controls, to safeguard sensitive data against cyber threats and unauthorized access (NIŽETIĆ *et al.,* 2020).

5.1.2 Digital Inclusion and Equity: While digital technologies have the potential to enhance urban services and improve quality of life, there is a risk of exacerbating existing socio-economic disparities. Barcelona must address digital literacy gaps, bridge the digital divide, and ensure equitable access to digital infrastructure and services for all residents, particularly marginalized communities, to prevent further social exclusion (SASSI *et al.,* 2019c).

5.1.3 Interoperability and Standardization: The proliferation of IoT devices and AI systems from various vendors poses challenges related to interoperability and standardization. Barcelona needs to develop common technical standards, protocols, and interfaces to enable seamless integration and interoperability between heterogeneous systems, ensuring data compatibility, consistency, and interoperability across different platforms and domains (OUALI *et al.,* 2023b).

5.1.4 Ethical and Regulatory Frameworks: As AI technologies become increasingly pervasive in urban environments, Barcelona must grapple with ethical and regulatory considerations related to algorithmic bias, transparency, accountability, and liability. The city needs to establish clear guidelines, regulations, and ethical frameworks governing the responsible use of AI in decision-making processes, ensuring fairness, accountability, and transparency in the deployment of smart city technologies (SYED *et al.,* 2021).

5.2 Opportunities

5.2.1 Innovation Ecosystem: Barcelona's vibrant innovation ecosystem provides fertile ground for collaboration, experimentation, and co-creation of novel solutions to urban challenges. By fostering partnerships between academia, industry, government, and civil society, the city can harness collective intelligence, foster entrepreneurship, and accelerate the development and adoption of innovative technologies and business models that address urban challenges and create new economic opportunities.

5.2.2 Sustainability and Resilience: Barcelona's commitment to sustainability and resilience positions it as a global leader in urban sustainability innovation. The city has an opportunity to leverage IoT and AI technologies to advance its sustainability goals, reduce carbon emissions, enhance resource efficiency, and build climate-resilient infrastructure. By investing in renewable energy, green mobility, and circular economy initiatives, Barcelona can create a more sustainable and resilient urban environment for future generations.

5.2.3 Citizen Engagement and Co-Creation: Barcelona's emphasis on citizen engagement and participatory governance empowers residents to actively contribute to the co-creation of smart city solutions. By leveraging digital platforms, such as participatory budgeting tools, crowdsourcing platforms, and civic engagement apps, the city can harness collective intelligence, gather feedback, and involve citizens in decision-making processes, fostering a sense of ownership, accountability, and social cohesion (HADJ SASSI *et al.,* 2024).

5.2.4 Knowledge Sharing and Collaboration: Barcelona's active participation in international networks and knowledge-sharing platforms provides an opportunity to exchange best practices, lessons learned, and innovative solutions with cities worldwide. By collaborating with global partners, sharing data, and participating in peer-to-peer learning networks, Barcelona can leverage external expertise, accelerate innovation, and amplify the impact of its smart city initiatives on a global scale.

In conclusion, Barcelona faces a set of complex challenges and opportunities in its quest to harness IoT and AI technologies for urban innovation. By addressing key challenges, seizing emerging opportunities, and leveraging its strengths as a global innovation hub, Barcelona can continue to lead the way in smart city development, drive sustainable urban transformation, and improve quality of life for its residents (OUALI *et al.,* 2023a).

6. FUTURE DIRECTIONS AND OUTLOOK

As Barcelona continues to embrace IoT and AI technologies to address urban challenges and enhance quality of life, several key trends and future directions emerge, shaping the trajectory of its smart city journey.

6. 1. AI-Powered Decision-Making: Barcelona is poised to leverage advanced AI algorithms and machine learning models to enhance decision-making processes across various domains, including transportation, energy management, and public safety. By harnessing the predictive capabilities of AI, the city can optimize resource allocation, improve service delivery, and respond more effectively to emerging urban trends and challenges (GUO *et al.,* 2022).

6. 2. Edge Computing and IoT Integration: The proliferation of IoT devices and sensors in urban environments generates vast amounts of data that need to be processed, analyzed, and acted upon in real-time. Barcelona is exploring edge computing solutions that bring computation and analytics closer to the data sou rce, reducing latency, bandwidth requirements, and operational costs. By integrating edge computing capabilities with IoT infrastructure, the city can unlock new possibilities for real-time monitoring, analysis, and decision-making at the network edge (ALAHI *et al.,* 2023).

6. 3. Smart Infrastructure and Autonomous Systems: Barcelona is increasingly investing in smart infrastructure and autonomous systems that leverage IoT sensors, AI algorithms, and robotics to optimize urban operations and improve service delivery. From smart buildings and intelligent transportation systems to autonomous drones and robots, the city is embracing automation and autonomy to enhance efficiency, safety, and sustainability across its infrastructure networks (Rahimi *et al.,* 2020).

6. 4. Data Sharing and Collaboration: Barcelona recognizes the importance of data sharing and collaboration in driving innovation and fostering ecosystem growth. The city is exploring new models of data governance, interoperability, and collaboration that enable public and private stakeholders to share data, insights, and resources in a secure and transparent manner. By fostering open data initiatives, public-private partnerships, and collaborative platforms, Barcelona can accelerate innovation, stimulate entrepreneurship, and create new economic opportunities in the digital economy.

6. 5. Resilience and Adaptation: In the face of growing urban challenges, including climate change, natural disasters, and pandemics, Barcelona is prioritizing resilience and adaptation in its smart city strategy. The city is investing in resilient infrastructure, emergency response systems, and adaptive planning processes to enhance its capacity to withstand and recover from shocks and stresses. By integrating resilience principles into urban design, policy-making, and governance frameworks, Barcelona can build a more resilient and adaptive city that is better prepared to confront future uncertainties.

6. 6. Ethics and Responsible AI: Barcelona is committed to ensuring the ethical and responsible use of AI technologies in its smart city initiatives. The city is developing ethical guidelines, regulatory frameworks, and governance mechanisms that promote transparency, fairness, and accountability in AI-driven decision-making processes. By embedding ethical considerations into the design, deployment, and evaluation of AI systems, Barcelona can build trust, mitigate risks, and safeguard the rights and interests of its residents.

In conclusion, Barcelona's journey towards a smarter, more sustainable, and resilient city is driven by a shared vision of harnessing the transformative power of IoT and AI technologies. By embracing emerging trends, fostering collaboration, and upholding ethical principles, Barcelona can navigate the complexities of urbanization, address pressing challenges, and create a more inclusive, equitable, and livable city for all its residents.

7. CONCLUSION

In conclusion, the integration of IoT and AI technologies offers unprecedented opportunities to address the multifaceted challenges of urbanization and create smarter, more sustainable cities. These technologies provide real-time data insights, predictive analytics, and autonomous systems that can significantly optimize resource allocation, enhance service delivery, and improve the overall quality of life for urban residents. For instance,

IoT-enabled infrastructure can monitor and manage traffic flow, reducing congestion and emissions, while AI-driven analytics can predict maintenance needs for utilities, preventing outages and conserving resources.

However, realizing the full potential of IoT and AI in urban contexts is not without its challenges. It requires strategic planning, collaborative partnerships between public and private sectors, and active citizen engagement to ensure that urban development is inclusive, equitable, and ethical. Privacy and security concerns must be addressed to gain public trust and ensure that data is used responsibly. Interoperability of systems and standardization of technologies are also critical to achieving seamless integration and widespread adoption.

Moreover, the successful deployment of IoT and AI solutions necessitates a robust digital infrastructure and a skilled workforce capable of managing and maintaining these advanced systems. Investment in education and training is essential to prepare the next generation of urban planners, engineers, and data scientists who will drive this transformation (OUALI *et al.,* 2022c).

As cities continue to evolve and embrace digital transformation, the integration of IoT and AI solutions will play a pivotal role in shaping the future of urbanism. These technologies will enable cities to become more resilient to environmental changes, more responsive to the needs of their inhabitants, and more efficient in their operations. By fostering innovation and leveraging data-driven insights, cities can build a sustainable framework for urban growth that promotes economic vitality, social equity, and environmental stewardship.

In summary, IoT and AI represent transformative forces that have the potential to revolutionize urban living. As we move forward, it is imperative to adopt a holistic approach that combines technological advancements with thoughtful policy-making and community involvement. This will ensure that the benefits of smart cities are realized by all, paving the way for resilient, livable, and thriving urban environments for generations to come.

REFERENCES

Alahi, M. E. E., Sukkuea, A., Tina, F. W., Nag, A., Kurdthongmee, W., Suwannarat, K., & Mukhopadhyay, S. C. (2023). Integration of IoT-enabled technologies and artificial intelligence (AI) for smart city scenario: Recent advancements and future trends. *Sensors (Basel), 23*(11), 5206. DOI: 10.3390/s23115206 PMID: 37299934

Alahi, M. E. E., Sukkuea, A., Tina, F. W., Nag, A., Kurdthongmee, W., Suwannarat, K., & Mukhopadhyay, S. C. (2023). Integration of IoT-enabled technologies and artificial intelligence (AI) for smart city scenario: Recent advancements and future trends. *Sensors (Basel), 23*(11), 5206. DOI: 10.3390/s23115206 PMID: 37299934

Arbi, A. (2018). Dynamics of BAM neural networks with mixed delays and leakage time-varying delays in the weighted pseudo–almost periodic on time-space scales. *Mathematical Methods in the Applied Sciences, 41*(3), 1230–1255. DOI: 10.1002/mma.4661

Arbi, A., Cao, J., & Alsaedi, A. (2018). Improved synchronization analysis of competitive neural networks with time-varying delays. *Nonlinear Analysis (Vilnius), 23*(1), 82–107. DOI: 10.15388/NA.2018.1.7

Arbi, A., Guo, Y., & Cao, J. (2021). Convergence analysis on time scales for HOBAM neural networks in the Stepanov-like weighted pseudo almost automorphic space. *Neural Computing & Applications, 33*(8), 3567–3581. DOI: 10.1007/s00521-020-05183-0

Arbi, A., & Tahri, N. (2024). Synchronization analysis of novel delayed dynamical Clifford-valued neural networks on timescales. *Journal of Algorithms & Computational Technology, 18*, 17483026241241492. DOI: 10.1177/17483026241241492

Atitallah, S. B., Driss, M., Boulila, W., & Ghézala, H. B. (2020). Leveraging Deep Learning and IoT big data analytics to support the smart cities development: Review and future directions. *Computer Science Review, 38*, 100303. DOI: 10.1016/j.cosrev.2020.100303

Bibri, S. E., Krogstie, J., Kaboli, A., & Alahi, A. (2024). Smarter eco-cities and their leading-edge artificial intelligence of things solutions for environmental sustainability: A comprehensive systematic review. *Environmental Science and Ecotechnology*, *19*, 100330. DOI: 10.1016/j.ese.2023.100330 PMID: 38021367

Bratton, B. (2021). AI urbanism: A design framework for governance, program, and platform cognition. *AI & Society*, *36*(4), 1307–1312. DOI: 10.1007/s00146-020-01121-9

Calzada, I. (2018). (Smart) citizens from data providers to decision-makers? The case study of Barcelona. *Sustainability (Basel)*, *10*(9), 3252. DOI: 10.3390/su10093252

Guo, Y., Ge, S. S., & Arbi, A. (2022). Stability of traveling waves solutions for nonlinear cellular neural networks with distributed delays. *Journal of Systems Science and Complexity*, *35*(1), 18–31. DOI: 10.1007/s11424-021-0180-7

Hadj Sassi, M. S., & Chaari Fourati, L. (2024). Design cognitive IoT architecture framework for immersive visual technologies of air quality monitoring systems. *Multimedia Tools and Applications*, *83*(17), 51615–51646. DOI: 10.1007/s11042-023-17249-x

Ho, E. (2017). Smart subjects for a Smart Nation? Governing (smart) mentalities in Singapore. *Urban Studies (Edinburgh, Scotland)*, *54*(13), 3101–3118. DOI: 10.1177/0042098016664305

Kaginalkar, A., Kumar, S., Gargava, P., & Niyogi, D. (2021). Review of urban computing in air quality management as smart city service: An integrated IoT, AI, and cloud technology perspective. *Urban Climate*, *39*, 100972. DOI: 10.1016/j.uclim.2021.100972

Nižetić, S., Šolić, P., Gonzalez-De, D. L. D. I., & Patrono, L. (2020). Internet of Things (IoT): Opportunities, issues and challenges towards a smart and sustainable future. *Journal of Cleaner Production*, *274*, 122877. DOI: 10.1016/j.jclepro.2020.122877 PMID: 32834567

Ortega-Fernández, A., Martín-Rojas, R., & García-Morales, V. J. (2020). Artificial intelligence in the urban environment: Smart cities as models for developing innovation and sustainability. *Sustainability (Basel)*, *12*(19), 7860. DOI: 10.3390/su12197860

Ouali, I., Ben Halima, M., Masmoudi, N., Ayadi, M., Almuqren, L., & Wali, A. (2024). Text recuperated using ontology with stable marriage optimization technique and text visualization using AR. *Multimedia Tools and Applications*, *83*(41), 1–28. DOI: 10.1007/s11042-024-18795-8

Ouali, I., Fourati, R., Halima, M. B., & Wali, A. (2023b, July). A novel method for arabic text detection with interactive visualization. In *2023 IEEE Symposium on Computers and Communications (ISCC)* (pp. 1046-1050). IEEE. DOI: 10.1109/ISCC58397.2023.10218141

Ouali, I., Hadj Sassi, M. S., Ben Halima, M., & Wali, A. (2021, April). Architecture for real-time visualizing arabic words with diacritics using augmented reality for visually impaired people. In *International conference on advanced information networking and applications* (pp. 285-296). Cham: Springer International Publishing. DOI: 10.1007/978-3-030-75100-5_25

Ouali, I., Halima, M. B., & Ali, W. A. L. I. (2022b, May). Real-time application for recognition and visualization of arabic words with vowels based dl and ar. In *2022 International Wireless Communications and Mobile Computing (IWCMC)* (pp. 678-683). IEEE. DOI: 10.1109/IWCMC55113.2022.9825089

Ouali, I., Halima, M. B., & Ali, W. A. L. I. (2022c). Augmented reality for scene text recognition, visualization and reading to assist visually impaired people. *Procedia Computer Science*, *207*, 158–167. DOI: 10.1016/j.procs.2022.09.048

Ouali, I., Halima, M. B., & Wali, A. (2022a, March). Text detection and recognition using augmented reality and deep learning. In *International conference on advanced information networking and applications* (pp. 13-23). Cham: Springer International Publishing. DOI: 10.1007/978-3-030-99584-3_2

Ouali, I., Halima, M. B., & Wali, A. (2023). An augmented reality for an arabic text reading and visualization assistant for the visually impaired. *Multimedia Tools and Applications*, *82*(28), 43569–43597. DOI: 10.1007/s11042-023-14880-6

Rahimi, M., Songhorabadi, M., & Kashani, M. H. (2020). Fog-based smart homes: A systematic review. *Journal of Network and Computer Applications*, *153*, 102531. DOI: 10.1016/j.jnca.2020.102531

Sabir, Z., Raja, M. A. Z., Arbi, A., Altamirano, G. C., & Cao, J. (2021). Neuro-swarms intelligent computing using Gudermannian kernel for solving a class of second order Lane-Emden singular nonlinear model. *AIMS Mathematics*, *6*(3), 2468–2485. DOI: 10.3934/math.2021150

Sabir, Z., Saoud, S., Raja, M. A. Z., Wahab, H. A., & Arbi, A. (2020). Heuristic computing technique for numerical solutions of nonlinear fourth order Emden–Fowler equation. *Mathematics and Computers in Simulation*, *178*, 534–548. DOI: 10.1016/j.matcom.2020.06.021

Sassi, M. S. H., Beltaief, I., Zekri, M., & Yahia, S. B. (2019c, November). Multi-oriented real-time arabic scene text detection with deep fully convolutional networks. In *2019 IEEE/ACS 16th International Conference on Computer Systems and Applications (AICCSA)* (pp. 1-6). IEEE. DOI: 10.1109/AICCSA47632.2019.9035340

Sassi, M. S. H., & Fourati, L. C. (2020, June). Investigation on deep learning methods for privacy and security challenges of cognitive IoV. In *2020 International Wireless Communications and Mobile Computing (IWCMC)* (pp. 714-720). IEEE. DOI: 10.1109/IWCMC48107.2020.9148417

Sassi, M. S. H., Fourati, L. C., & Jedidi, F. G. (2019b, June). Business information architecture for big data and Internet of Things. In *2019 15th International Wireless Communications & Mobile Computing Conference (IWCMC)* (pp. 1749-1756). IEEE.

Sassi, M. S. H., Jedidi, F. G., & Fourati, L. C. (2019a, June). Computer-aided software engineering (CASE) tool for big data and IoT architecture. In *2019 15th International wireless communications & mobile computing conference (IWCMC)* (pp. 1403-1410). IEEE.

Simić, M., Perić, M., Popadić, I., Perić, D., Pavlović, M., Vučetić, M., & Stanković, M. S. (2020). Big Data and development of Smart City: System architecture and practical public safety example. *Serbian Journal of Electrical Engineering*, *17*(3), 337–355. DOI: 10.2298/SJEE2003337S

Syed, A. S., Sierra-Sosa, D., Kumar, A., & Elmaghraby, A. (2021). IoT in smart cities: A survey of technologies, practices and challenges. *Smart Cities*, *4*(2), 429–475. DOI: 10.3390/smartcities4020024

Tuballa, M. L., & Abundo, M. L. (2016). A review of the development of Smart Grid technologies. *Renewable & Sustainable Energy Reviews*, *59*, 710–725. DOI: 10.1016/j.rser.2016.01.011

Yang, P. P., & Yamagata, Y. (2020). Urban systems design: Shaping smart cities by integrating urban design and systems science. In *Urban Systems Design* (pp. 1–22). Elsevier. DOI: 10.1016/B978-0-12-816055-8.00001-4

Yigitcanlar, T., Mehmood, R., & Corchado, J. M. (2021). Green artificial intelligence: Towards an efficient, sustainable and equitable technology for smart cities and futures. *Sustainability (Basel)*, *13*(16), 8952. DOI: 10.3390/su13168952

Chapter 4
The Role of Artificial Intelligence in Revolutionizing Healthcare Domains

Achraf Wali
https://orcid.org/0009-0001-2071-0136
FSEGS, Tunisia

Imene Ouali
https://orcid.org/0000-0001-5176-5482
ENIS, Tunisia

Adnène Arbi
https://orcid.org/0000-0002-2834-0248
Tunisia Polytechnic School, Tunisia

ABSTRACT

Artificial Intelligence (AI) has emerged as a transformative force in healthcare, revolutionizing the industry through its ability to analyze complex data, optimize processes, and enhance decision-making. This article provides an overview of the applications of AI in healthcare, including disease diagnosis, treatment personalization, predictive analytics, and

DOI: 10.4018/979-8-3693-8141-0.ch004

administrative tasks. Additionally, challenges and opportunities associated with AI implementation in healthcare are discussed, highlighting the potential for AI to improve patient outcomes, reduce costs, and transform the delivery of healthcare services.

1. INTRODUCTION

Artificial Intelligence (AI) technologies, including machine learning, natural language processing, and robotics, have rapidly advanced in recent years, offering unprecedented opportunities to transform healthcare delivery. AI has the potential to revolutionize various aspects of healthcare, from diagnosis and treatment to administrative tasks and patient engagement. This article explores the role of AI in healthcare and its implications for patients, healthcare providers, and the broader healthcare ecosystem.

The integration of AI in healthcare is driven by the increasing availability of big data, advancements in computing power, and the development of sophisticated algorithms capable of analyzing complex medical data. AI systems can process vast amounts of information at speeds unattainable by human professionals, identifying patterns and insights that can lead to more accurate diagnoses, personalized treatment plans, and early detection of diseases. These capabilities are particularly significant in the context of chronic diseases, where early intervention can drastically improve patient outcomes.

Moreover, AI's potential extends beyond clinical applications. In administrative functions, AI can streamline operations, reduce costs, and minimize human errors, thereby improving the efficiency of healthcare delivery. AI-powered chatbots and virtual assistants are enhancing patient engagement by providing round-the-clock support and personalized health information, thus empowering patients to take an active role in their health management.

The adoption of AI in healthcare also poses several ethical and practical challenges. Concerns about data privacy, the need for transparency in AI decision-making processes, and the potential for algorithmic biases are critical issues that must be addressed to ensure the safe and equitable use of AI technologies. Additionally, the integration of AI into existing healthcare systems requires significant investment in infrastructure, training, and regulatory frameworks.

Despite these challenges, the potential benefits of AI in healthcare are immense. As AI technologies continue to evolve, they are likely to become increasingly integrated into all facets of healthcare, leading to improved patient outcomes, enhanced efficiency, and reduced costs. This article delves into the current applications of AI in healthcare, the benefits and challenges associated with its use, and the future directions of AI-driven healthcare innovation.

2. APPLICATIONS OF AI IN HEALTHCARE

2.1 Disease Diagnosis

Artificial Intelligence (AI) has made significant strides in revolutionizing disease diagnosis by leveraging advanced algorithms to interpret medical images and data with unprecedented accuracy and efficiency. AI-powered diagnostic systems have demonstrated remarkable capabilities in detecting abnormalities and assisting healthcare professionals in diagnosing a wide range of diseases, including cancer, cardiovascular disorders, and neurological conditions(See Figure 1).

One of the primary applications of AI in disease diagnosis is medical imaging analysis. AI algorithms trained on vast datasets of medical images, such as X-rays, MRIs, and CT scans, can identify subtle abnormalities that may be overlooked by human observers. For instance, in the field of radiology, AI-powered image analysis systems can detect early signs of cancer, such as tumors or lesions, with high sensitivity and specificity. Moreover, AI can aid in the interpretation of pathology slides, identifying cellular patterns indicative of various diseases, including cancer subtypes(Iqbal,*et al.,*2021).

AI-driven diagnostic tools not only enhance the accuracy of disease detection but also expedite the diagnostic process, leading to faster treatment initiation and improved patient outcomes. By automating the analysis of medical images and data, AI reduces the burden on healthcare professionals, allowing them to focus on clinical decision-making and patient care. Furthermore, AI algorithms can continuously learn and improve over time, adapting to new data and refining their diagnostic capabilities (Esmaeilzadeh *et al.,*2020).

In addition to medical imaging, AI is increasingly being applied to other diagnostic modalities, such as genomic analysis and Electronic Health Records (EHR) data mining(See Table 1). AI algorithms can analyze genetic information to identify genetic markers associated with disease susceptibility and treatment response, enabling personalized medicine approaches. Furthermore, AI-powered analytics of EHR data can identify patterns and correlations indicative of disease risk factors, facilitating early intervention and preventive care strategies(Lin *et al.,*2020).

Applying Artificial Intelligence (AI) to Electronic Health Record (EHR) data has yielded significant advancements across various domains. For instance, studies in cardiology have extensively utilized AI techniques with EHR data for the early detection of heart failure and risk assessment of Diabetic Retinopathy (DR). In the comprehensive process of literature review, one author (WL) meticulously curated articles for inclusion based on manual title, abstract, and content review. Subsequently, two authors (WL and JSC) meticulously extracted pertinent data for each study, including the aim, disease, algorithm, specific techniques, performance assessment, and conclusions of the articles meeting the inclusion criteria, as summarized in the Table 1.

These studies have predominantly employed three major techniques: supervised machine learning, deep learning, and Natural Language Processing (NLP) to derive actionable insights from EHR data. Supervised machine learning techniques, encompassing random forest, logistic regression, decision trees, and Support Vector Machines (SVMs), have been adeptly utilized to develop predictive models or classifiers. Deep learning, a subset of machine learning techniques reliant on Artificial Neural Networks (ANNs), has been instrumental in distinguishing various ocular diseases from normal images, predicting treatment responses, and improving clinical calculations. Additionally, NLP has been pivotal in extracting structured data from unstructured clinical notes.

Studies investigating glaucoma diagnosis and progression have demonstrated promising results using supervised machine learning techniques. For instance, Chaganti et al. achieved a remarkable AUC of 88% for glaucoma diagnosis by incorporating EMR phenotypes into the classification process, whereas Baxter et al. reported moderate performance in predicting progression to surgical intervention. Similarly, studies focusing on cataract diagnosis have leveraged NLP to extract pertinent information from clinical notes. Peissig et al. demonstrated robust performance with a predictive positive value exceeding 95%.

Moreover, AI techniques have shown efficacy in diagnosing age-related macular degeneration (AMD) and predicting diabetic retinopathy (DR) risk. Lee et al. achieved high accuracy (AUC 97%) in distinguishing AMD from normal images using deep learning techniques, while Saleh et al. and Yoo and Park demonstrated substantial accuracy in predicting DR risk. Additionally, hybrid decision support systems have exhibited excellent performance in estimating DR risk among diabetic patients.

In essence, the integration of AI techniques with EHR data holds immense potential in enhancing disease diagnosis, predicting treatment outcomes, and optimizing clinical decision-making processes. These findings underscore the transformative impact of AI-driven approaches in revolutionizing ocular disease management and fostering personalized patient care.

Table 1. Exploring Ocular Disease Research: Artificial Intelligence Applications with Electronic Health Record Data(EHR).

Ref	Disease	Goal	Algorithm	Techniques	Performance	Objective
Gaskin *et al.*, (2016),	Cataract	Identify and predict risks of cataract surgery complications	Supervised machine learning, Text- mining	RandomforestNLP, Bootstrapped LASSO	Based on the LASSO model, younger age (<60 years old), prior anterior vitrectomy or refractive surgery, history of AMD, and complex cataract surgery were risk factors associated with postoperative complications The random forest model shows high NPV > 95% and moderate sensitivity (67%) and AUC (65%)	Bootstrapped LASSO analysis serves as a valuable tool in identifying risk factors associated with postoperative complications following cataract surgery. Additionally, Random Forest analysis demonstrates strong reliability in predicting complications associated with cataract surgery.
Chaganti *et al.*, (2017),	Glaucoma, intrinsic optic nerve ailments, optic nerve edema, orbital inflammation, and thyroid eye disease	Identifying pertinent risk factors and enhancing diagnostic precision.	Supervised machine learning	Randomforest	AUC of classifiers:glaucoma (88%), intrinsicopticneuritis (76%), optic nerve edema (78%), orbital inflammation (77%), thyroideyedisease (85%)	Utilizing EMR phenotype data obtained from pyPheWAS enhances the predictive capabilities of a random forest classifier when combined with imaging biomarkers.
Fraccaro *et al.*, (2015),	AMD	Improve diagnostic accuracy	Supervised machine learning	Logistic regression, decision trees, SVM, random forests, and AdaBoost	AUC of random forest, logistic regression, and AdaBoost (92%); SVM, decision trees (90%)	Machine learning algorithms leveraging clinical EHR data offer a means to enhance the diagnostic accuracy of AMD.
Saleh *et al.*, (2018),	DR	Risk assessment	Supervised machine learning	DRSA, FRF	Performance of DRSA:Accuracy (77.32%), sensitivity (76.89%), specificity (77.43%) of DRSA. Performance of FRF:Accuracy (80.29%), sensitivity (80.67%), specificity (80.18%)	Ensemble classifiers such as RFR and DRSA offer valuable applications in assessing the risk of diabetic retinopathy. A recommended approach involves employing a two-step aggregation procedure.

continued on following page

Table 1. Continued

Ref	Disease	Goal	Algorithm	Techniques	Performance	Objective
Lin *et al.*, (2018),	Myopia	Diseasedetection	Supervised machine learning	Randomforest	95% confidence intervals were calculated for predicting the onset of high myopia over different time frames: 3 years (AUC: 94%–98.5%), 5 years (85.6%–90.1%), and 8 years (80.1%–83.7%).	Machine learning utilizing EHR data demonstrates a high degree of accuracy in predicting the onset of myopia.
Lee *et al.*, (2017),	AMD	Improve diagnostic accuracy	Deep learning	CNN	For each patient, the AUC is 97.45%, with corresponding accuracy, sensitivity, and specificity rates of 93.54%, 92.64%, and 93.69%, respectively.	The integration of OCT images with EMR data demonstrates enhanced accuracy in deep learning models for distinguishing AMD from normal OCT images.
Baxter *et al.*, (2019),	Open-angle glaucoma	Risk assessment	Supervised machine learning Deep learning	Random forests, Logistic regression, ANNs	Random forest (65%), AUC of logistic model (67%), ANNs (65%)	Utilizing pre-existing systemic data within the EHR facilitates the identification of POAG patients who are susceptible to progressing towards surgical intervention.
Apostolova *et al.*, (2017),	Open globe injury	Patient identification	Text-mining, Supervised machine learning	SVMNLP–Word embeddings	Text classification: precision (92.50%), recall (89.83%)	Machine learning methods applied to free-form text can effectively identify cases of open globe injury.
Rohm *et al.*, (2018),	AMD	Predict progression	Supervised machine learning	AdaBoost, Gradient Boosting, Random Forests, Extremely Randomized trees, LASSO	Accuracy of logMAR VA prediction after VEGF injections. 3 months: MAE (0.14), RMSE (0.18) 12 months: MAE (0.16), RMSE (0.2)	Machine learning models applied to EHR data from patients with neovascular AMD can effectively predict visual acuity.
Oh *et al.*, (2013),	DR	Risk assessment	Supervised machine learning	Ridge, elastic net, and LASSO	In external validation, LASSO predicted DR: AUC (82%), accuracy (75.2%), sensitivity (72.1%), and specificity (76.0%)	LASSO with EHR data can be used to predict DR risk among diabetic patients

continued on following page

Table 1. Continued

Ref	Disease	Goal	Algorithm	Techniques	Performance	Objective
Sramka *et al.*, (2019),	Cataracts	Improve surgical outcome	Supervised machine learning, Deep learning	SVM-RM MLNN-EM	Both SVM-RM and MLNN-EM achieved significantly better results than the Barrett Universal II formula in the ±0.50 D PE category	SVM-RM and MLNN-EM, when applied to EHR data, demonstrate the potential to enhance clinical IOLcalculations and optimize refractive outcomes in cataract surgery.
Peissig *et al.*, (2012),	Cataracts	Patient identification	Text-mining	NLP	The multimodal model shows results including sensitivity (84.6%), specificity (98.7%), PPV (95.6%), and NPV (95.1%)	A multimodal approach integrating optical character recognition and natural language processing can effectively augment the identification of cataract cases, thereby enhancing diagnostic capabilities.
Skevofilakas *et al.*, (2010),	DR	Risk assessment	Deep learning Supervised machine learning	FNN and iHWNN CART	AUC of hybrid DSS (98%), iHWNN (97%), FNN (88%), and CART (86%).	A Hybrid DSS trained on imaging data and correlated EHR information proves effective in estimating the risk of diabetic retinopathy development in patients with type 1 diabetes.

Overall, AI is revolutionizing disease diagnosis by augmenting the capabilities of healthcare professionals, improving diagnostic accuracy, and accelerating the diagnostic process. As AI technologies continue to evolve and mature, they hold the potential to transform healthcare delivery, making diagnosis more precise, efficient, and accessible to patients worldwide.

Figure 1. Utilization of AI, ML, and DL in Digital Healthcare and Oncology: Addressing Healthcare Challenges and Predicting Optimal Treatment Outcomes.

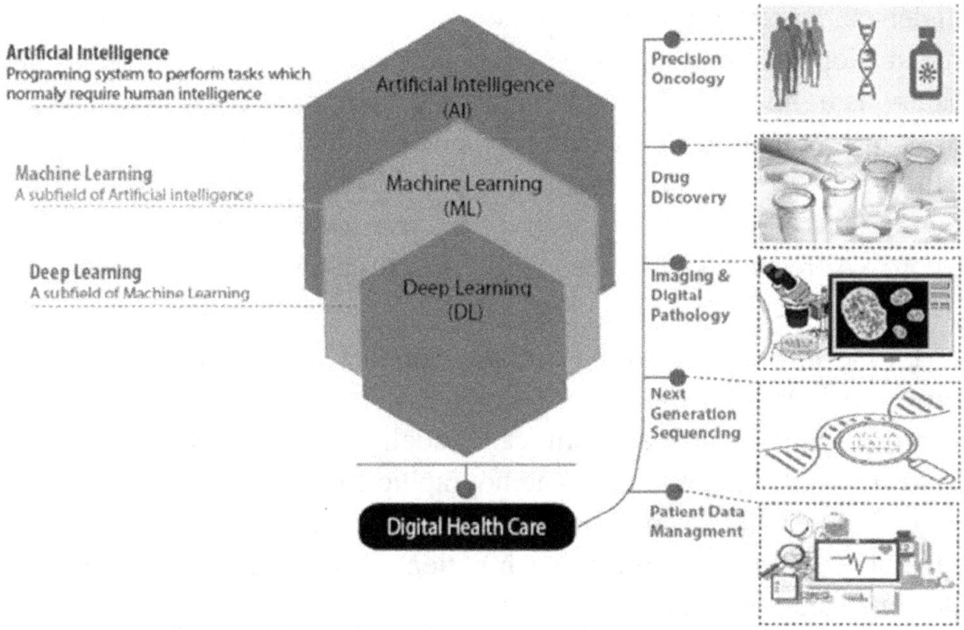

2.2 Treatment Personalization

Artificial Intelligence (AI) is revolutionizing the field of healthcare by enabling personalized treatment approaches tailored to the individual characteristics and needs of patients. Through advanced data analytics and machine learning algorithms, AI empowers healthcare providers to develop and implement treatment plans that optimize therapeutic outcomes and minimize adverse effects(Sabir, *et al.*2020).

One of the key applications of AI in treatment personalization is precision medicine. By analyzing vast datasets of patient information, including genetic data, medical history, lifestyle factors, and treatment responses, AI algorithms can identify patterns and correlations that inform personalized treatment recommendations. For example, in oncology, AI-driven genomic analysis can identify specific genetic mutations in tumors and predict the efficacy of targeted therapies, allowing for tailored treatment strategies that maximize therapeutic benefit while minimizing side effects(Alowais *et al.,*2023).

AI also plays a critical role in pharmacogenomics, which focuses on understanding how genetic variations influence individual responses to medications. By integrating genetic information with drug efficacy and safety data, AI algorithms can identify genetic markers associated with drug metabolism, drug interactions, and treatment response variability. This information enables healthcare providers to prescribe medications that are most likely to be effective and safe for each patient, leading to improved treatment outcomes and reduced adverse drug reactions(Abdelhalim *et al.,*2022).

Furthermore, AI-powered decision support systems assist healthcare providers in making evidence-based treatment decisions by synthesizing complex patient data and clinical guidelines. These systems analyze patient-specific factors, such as demographic information, medical history, comorbidities, and treatment preferences, to generate personalized treatment recommendations tailored to each patient's unique circumstances. This personalized approach to treatment enhances clinical decision-making, promotes patient engagement, and improves adherence to treatment regimens(Johnson, *et al.,*2021).

Moreover, AI facilitates continuous monitoring and adaptation of treatment plans based on real-time patient data and feedback. Wearable devices and remote monitoring technologies equipped with AI algorithms can track patient health metrics, such as vital signs, activity levels, and medication adherence, and provide timely insights to healthcare providers. This enables proactive interventions and adjustments to treatment plans to optimize patient outcomes and prevent disease progression(Guo *et al.,*2022).

Overall, AI-driven treatment personalization holds tremendous promise for improving patient care by tailoring treatments to individual patients' characteristics, preferences, and responses. As AI technologies continue to evolve and integrate into clinical practice, personalized medicine approaches will become increasingly prevalent, leading to more effective, efficient, and patient-centered healthcare delivery(Ouali et al., 2022a).

2.3 Predictive Analytics

Predictive analytics powered by Artificial Intelligence (AI) is transforming healthcare by enabling proactive and preventive approaches to patient care. By analyzing large volumes of patient data and identifying patterns and trends, predictive analytics algorithms can forecast future health outcomes, anticipate disease risks, and guide early intervention strategies(Sassi *et al.,*2020b).

In healthcare, predictive analytics encompasses a wide range of applications, including disease risk prediction, hospital readmission forecasting, and treatment response prediction. One of the primary uses of predictive analytics is in identifying individuals at high risk of developing specific diseases or health complications. By analyzing diverse data sources, such as Electronic Health Records (EHR), medical imaging, genetic information, and lifestyle factors, predictive models can assess an individual's likelihood of developing conditions such as diabetes, cardiovascular disease, or sepsis. These risk prediction models empower healthcare providers to implement targeted preventive measures, such as lifestyle modifications, screening programs, or early medical interventions, to mitigate the risk of disease onset or progression.

Predictive analytics also plays a crucial role in predicting hospital readmissions, which are associated with increased healthcare costs and adverse patient outcomes. By analyzing patient data, including clinical history, medication adherence, socioeconomic factors, and prior healthcare utilization patterns, predictive models can identify patients at high risk of readmission following discharge. Healthcare providers can then implement personalized care plans and interventions, such as post-discharge monitoring, care coordination, and patient education, to reduce the likelihood of readmission and improve patient outcomes(Rana *et al.,*2024).

Furthermore, predictive analytics can forecast individual patient responses to specific treatments, medications, or interventions, facilitating personalized treatment planning and optimization. By leveraging patient data, including genetic information, biomarkers, treatment history, and demographic factors, predictive models can predict treatment efficacy, adverse drug reactions, and treatment response variability. This enables healthcare providers to tailor treatment regimens to each patient's unique characteristics and maximize therapeutic outcomes while minimizing risks.

Moreover, predictive analytics enables healthcare organizations to optimize resource allocation, streamline operations, and enhance healthcare delivery efficiency. By analyzing patient flow, demand patterns, resource utilization, and staffing levels, predictive models can forecast future healthcare needs, optimize scheduling, and allocate resources effectively to meet patient demand and improve operational efficiency. This proactive approach to resource management helps healthcare organizations enhance patient satisfaction, reduce waiting times, and optimize resource utilization(Richardson *et al.,*2021).

Overall, predictive analytics powered by AI holds immense potential for transforming healthcare by enabling proactive, personalized, and efficient approaches to patient care. As predictive models continue to evolve and integrate into clinical practice, they will play an increasingly pivotal role in improving patient outcomes, reducing healthcare costs, and advancing population health management initiatives(See Figure 2).

Figure 2. Harnessing Patient Data Potential through AI-Enabled Predictive Analytics.

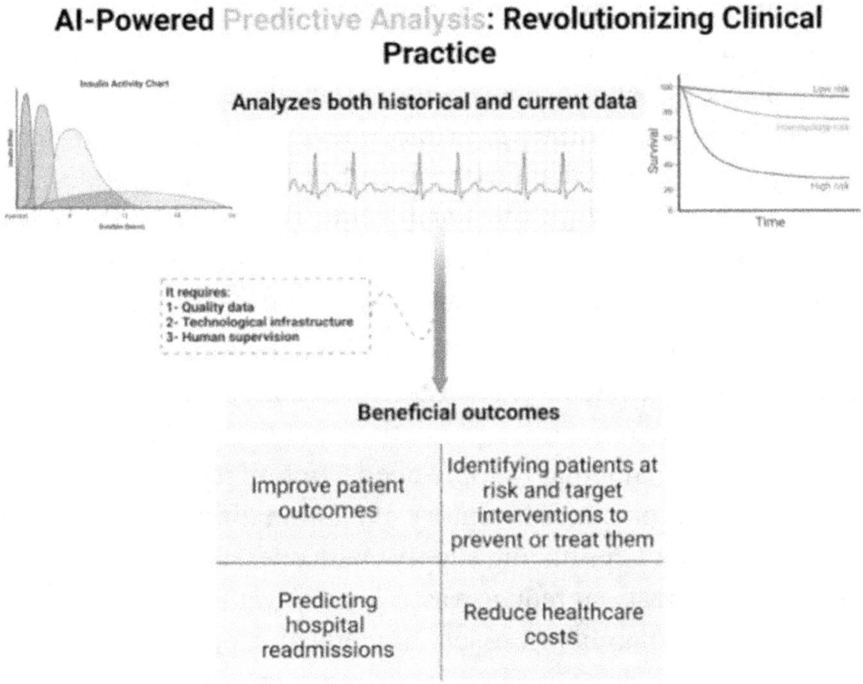

2.4 Administrative Tasks

Artificial Intelligence (AI) is increasingly being leveraged to automate and streamline administrative tasks within healthcare organizations, freeing up valuable time for healthcare professionals to focus on patient care and clinical decision-making(Ouali *et al.*,2022b). From patient scheduling and billing to inventory management and regulatory compliance, AI-driven solutions are revolutionizing administrative workflows and enhancing operational efficiency across the healthcare ecosystem.

One of the primary applications of AI in administrative tasks is in patient scheduling and appointment management. AI-powered scheduling systems utilize machine learning algorithms to optimize appointment scheduling, taking into account factors such as patient preferences, physician availability, clinic capacity, and appointment urgency. By automating appointment scheduling and reminders, AI systems help reduce no-show rates, minimize appointment wait times, and improve overall patient access to care.

Furthermore, AI-enabled billing and revenue cycle management solutions streamline the complex process of medical billing and claims processing. These systems leverage Natural Language Processing (NLP) and machine learning algorithms to extract relevant information from medical documentation, such as diagnoses, procedures, and billing codes, and generate accurate billing statements and claims submissions. By automating billing workflows, AI solutions accelerate reimbursement cycles, reduce billing errors, and optimize revenue capture for healthcare providers.

Inventory management is another area where AI is driving significant improvements in efficiency and cost-effectiveness. AI-powered inventory optimization platforms utilize predictive analytics and demand forecasting algorithms to anticipate supply needs, optimize inventory levels, and prevent stockouts or excess inventory. By automating inventory replenishment processes and optimizing supply chain operations, AI solutions help healthcare organizations reduce waste, lower inventory carrying costs, and ensure timely availability of essential medical supplies and equipment.

Moreover, AI-driven solutions are transforming regulatory compliance and quality assurance processes within healthcare organizations. These solutions leverage Natural Language Processing (NLP) and machine learning algorithms to analyze and interpret regulatory requirements, identify compliance gaps, and generate actionable insights for process improvement. By automating compliance monitoring and reporting tasks, AI solutions help healthcare organizations ensure adherence to regulatory standards, mitigate compliance risks, and maintain high-quality care delivery standards(Shaheen *et al.*,2021).

Additionally, AI-powered virtual assistants and chatbots are revolutionizing patient engagement and communication, enabling patients to access information, schedule appointments, request prescription refills, and receive personalized health recommendations through conversational interfaces. These virtual assistants leverage Natural Language Understanding (NLU) and sentiment analysis algorithms to interact with patients in a conversational manner, providing timely assistance and support while reducing the burden on frontline staff.

In summary, AI-driven solutions are playing a transformative role in automating and optimizing administrative tasks within healthcare organizations. By streamlining workflows, improving efficiency, and enhancing patient engagement, AI technologies are helping healthcare providers deliver high-quality care, reduce operational costs, and improve overall organizational performance. As AI continues to advance, its impact on administrative tasks in healthcare is expected to grow, driving further innovation and efficiency gains across the industry.

3. CHALLENGES AND OPPORTUNITIES

The integration of Artificial Intelligence (AI) into healthcare presents both challenges and opportunities that must be addressed to realize the full potential of AI-driven innovations in improving patient outcomes, enhancing operational efficiency, and advancing population health management. Understanding these challenges and opportunities is essential for healthcare organizations, policymakers, and technology developers to navigate the evolving landscape of AI in healthcare effectively.

One of the key challenges in the adoption of AI in healthcare is the ethical and regulatory considerations surrounding data privacy, security, and patient consent. Healthcare data, including electronic health records (EHR), medical imaging, and genomic information, are sensitive and subject to strict privacy regulations such as the Health Insurance Portability and Accountability Act (HIPAA). Ensuring compliance with regulatory requirements while harnessing the full potential of AI for data-driven decision-making poses complex ethical dilemmas. Balancing patient privacy rights with the need for data access and sharing for research and innovation is a critical challenge that healthcare organizations and policymakers must address.

Another challenge is the interoperability and standardization of healthcare data across disparate systems and platforms. The fragmentation of healthcare data silos and the lack of standardized data formats and interoperability protocols hinder the seamless exchange and integration of data needed for AI-driven analytics and decision support. Overcoming interoperability barriers requires collaborative efforts among healthcare stakeholders to develop common data standards, interoperability frameworks, and data governance policies to facilitate data sharing and integration while safeguarding data integrity and security.

Furthermore, the quality and reliability of AI algorithms in healthcare pose significant challenges, particularly in the context of clinical decision support and patient care. AI algorithms are only as good as the data they are trained on, and biases, inaccuracies, and errors in training data can propagate through AI models, leading to erroneous predictions and decisions. Ensuring the transparency, fairness, and accountability of AI algorithms, as well as robust validation and testing frameworks, are essential for building trust and confidence in AI-driven healthcare solutions among clinicians, patients, and regulators (Arbi *et al.,*2024).

Additionally, the implementation and adoption of AI in healthcare require overcoming organizational and cultural barriers, including resistance to change, workforce readiness, and stakeholder engagement. Healthcare professionals must be equipped with the necessary skills and training to effectively leverage AI technologies and integrate them into clinical workflows. Moreover, fostering a culture of innovation, collaboration, and continuous learning is essential for driving successful AI adoption and transformation within healthcare organizations.

Despite these challenges, AI presents immense opportunities for transforming healthcare delivery and improving patient outcomes. AI-driven innovations have the potential to enhance diagnostic accuracy, personalize treatment plans, optimize resource allocation, and empower patients to actively participate in their care. By leveraging AI technologies such as machine learning, natural language processing, and predictive analytics, healthcare organizations can unlock actionable insights from vast amounts of data, accelerate medical discoveries, and revolutionize care delivery models (Arbi *et al.,*2018, Hamdi et al.,2024).

Furthermore, AI holds promise for addressing pressing healthcare challenges, such as population health management, chronic disease management, and healthcare disparities. AI-powered predictive analytics and population health models can identify high-risk patient populations, prioritize interventions, and allocate resources effectively to prevent disease onset and progression. Moreover, AI-enabled telemedicine and remote monitoring solutions expand access to healthcare services, particularly in underserved and rural communities, bridging geographical barriers and improving health equity(Ouali *et al.,*2023b).

In conclusion, while the integration of AI into healthcare presents challenges and complexities, it also offers unprecedented opportunities for innovation, transformation, and improvement in patient care. By addressing ethical, regulatory, technical, and organizational challenges, healthcare stakeholders can harness the full potential of AI to create a more efficient, effective, and equitable healthcare system that delivers personalized, patient-centered care at scale. Embracing a collaborative, multidisciplinary approach and investing in education, infrastructure, and research are essential for realizing the promise of AI in healthcare and shaping the future of medicine.

4. FUTURE TRENDS AND IMPLICATIONS

4.1. AI-Powered Robotics in Surgery

AI-powered robotics in surgery epitomize the convergence of cutting-edge technologies to revolutionize the field of medicine. These sophisticated systems, equipped with artificial intelligence capabilities, are poised to redefine surgical procedures by augmenting human expertise with advanced automation and data-driven decision-making(Sabir *et al.,*2021).

One of the primary applications of AI-powered robotics in surgery lies in the realm of minimally invasive procedures. By integrating high-resolution imaging, real-time feedback sensors, and AI-driven algorithms, these robotic systems enable surgeons to perform intricate maneuvers with enhanced precision and accuracy through small incisions. This minimally invasive approach offers numerous advantages over traditional open surgery, including reduced trauma to surrounding tissues, faster recovery times, and minimized postoperative pain for patients(Arbi,2018).

Moreover, AI-powered surgical robots are capable of performing a wide range of procedures across various medical specialties, from cardiac and neurosurgery to orthopedics and urology. Their versatility and adaptability make them invaluable tools for addressing complex surgical challenges, such as tumor resections, organ transplants, and reconstructive surgeries(Racine *et al.,*2019).

In addition to their role in enhancing surgical precision, AI-powered robotics offer significant potential for improving patient safety. These systems can autonomously monitor vital parameters, detect anomalies in real-time, and alert surgeons to potential complications during procedures. By providing this continuous feedback loop, AI-powered robots help mitigate the risk of adverse events and ensure optimal patient outcomes.

Furthermore, AI algorithms integrated into surgical robots have the capacity to learn from vast datasets of surgical procedures, patient outcomes, and clinician interventions. This machine learning capability enables the refinement of surgical techniques, the optimization of treatment pathways, and the development of personalized approaches tailored to individual patient needs(Arbi *et al.,*2021).

As AI-powered robotics continue to evolve, they hold promise for addressing some of the longstanding challenges in surgery, such as disparities in access to specialized care, variability in surgical outcomes, and the shortage of skilled surgeons in certain regions. By democratizing access to advanced surgical techniques, empowering healthcare providers with AI-driven decision support tools, and improving patient outcomes, these transformative technologies are poised to shape the future of surgery and pave the way for a new era of precision medicine(Ouali *et al.,*2024).

4.2. Predictive Analytics for Disease Prevention

Predictive analytics in disease prevention harness the power of data-driven insights to anticipate and mitigate health risks before they manifest into clinical conditions (OUALI *et al.,*2021). By leveraging advanced statistical models, machine learning algorithms, and large-scale health data repositories, predictive analytics enable healthcare providers to identify individuals at heightened risk of developing specific diseases and intervene proactively to prevent their onset(Alanazi *et al.,*2022).

One of the key components of predictive analytics for disease prevention is the integration of diverse datasets encompassing demographic information, genetic profiles, lifestyle factors, environmental exposures, and clinical biomarkers(OUALI *et al.,*2022c). By aggregating and analyzing this multifaceted data, predictive models can discern patterns, trends, and risk factors associated with various diseases, ranging from chronic conditions like diabetes and cardiovascular disease to infectious outbreaks and cancer(Ramírez *et al.,*2024).

These predictive models employ a variety of techniques, including logistic regression, decision trees, neural networks, and ensemble methods, to forecast individualized risk scores and probabilities of disease occurrence. By stratifying populations into different risk categories based on these predictive scores, healthcare providers can tailor preventive interventions and allocate resources more efficiently to those who stand to benefit most.

Moreover, predictive analytics for disease prevention extend beyond individual risk assessment to encompass population health management and public health surveillance(HADJ SASSI *et al.,*2024). By analyzing trends in health indicators, disease incidence rates, and social determinants of health at a population level, public health agencies can anticipate emerging health threats, allocate resources for preventive interventions, and implement targeted interventions to mitigate the spread of infectious diseases and reduce the burden of chronic conditions(Kalis Brian, *et al.,*2018).

In addition to their role in early detection and risk stratification, predictive analytics empower individuals to take proactive steps towards maintaining their health and well-being. By leveraging personalized risk assessments and actionable insights generated by predictive models, individuals can make informed lifestyle choices, adhere to preventive screenings, and engage in health-promoting behaviors to reduce their risk of developing chronic diseases(Rana *et al.,*2024).

Looking ahead, the integration of predictive analytics into routine clinical practice holds promise for transforming healthcare delivery from a reactive, episodic model to a proactive, preventive paradigm(OUALI *et* *al.,*2023a). By harnessing the power of data-driven insights to anticipate and preempt disease onset, predictive analytics have the potential to usher in a new era of precision prevention, where healthcare interventions are tailored to individual risk profiles, resources are allocated more effectively, and the burden of preventable diseases is significantly reduced(Sassi *et al.,*2019b).

4.3. AI-Enabled Remote Healthcare Services

AI-enabled remote healthcare services represent a paradigm shift in healthcare delivery, leveraging artificial intelligence technologies to overcome geographical barriers, improve access to care, and enhance patient outcomes(SASSI et al., 2019a). These innovative solutions harness the power of AI algorithms, telecommunication platforms, and digital health tools to deliver timely, personalized, and cost-effective healthcare services to individuals regardless of their location(Kasula *et al.,* 2023).

One of the primary applications of AI-enabled remote healthcare services is telemedicine, which enables healthcare providers to deliver virtual consultations, diagnosis, and treatment to patients remotely. AI-driven telemedicine platforms leverage advanced algorithms to analyze patient data, interpret medical images, and assist clinicians in making informed decisions about patient care. This includes the use of Natural Language Processing (NLP) to transcribe and analyze patient-provider interactions, computer vision algorithms to interpret diagnostic images, and predictive analytics to identify patients at risk of adverse health outcomes.

Moreover, AI-enabled remote monitoring devices and wearable sensors empower patients to track their health parameters, monitor chronic conditions, and transmit real-time data to healthcare providers for remote monitoring and management. These devices leverage AI algorithms to analyze physiological data, detect anomalies, and alert clinicians to potential health issues, enabling early intervention and preventive care.

Furthermore, AI-enabled chatbots and virtual health assistants provide patients with round-the-clock access to medical information, symptom triage, and self-care guidance. These conversational AI platforms leverage Natural Language Understanding (NLU) and machine learning algorithms to understand patient queries, provide personalized responses, and escalate complex cases to human providers when necessary. By offering instant access to healthcare information and support, AI-powered chatbots enhance patient engagement, improve health literacy, and reduce unnecessary healthcare utilization(Kasula *et al.,*2023).

In addition to improving access to primary and specialty care, AI-enabled remote healthcare services play a crucial role in extending healthcare reach to underserved populations, rural areas, and regions with limited access to healthcare infrastructure. By leveraging telecommunication technologies and mobile health solutions, these services bridge geographical gaps, connect patients with specialized providers, and facilitate continuity of care across diverse settings(Sassi *et al.,*2019c).

Looking ahead, the integration of AI-enabled remote healthcare services into mainstream healthcare delivery holds promise for transforming the healthcare landscape, making healthcare more accessible, affordable, and patient-centered. By leveraging the power of artificial intelligence to deliver high-quality care remotely, these innovative solutions have the potential to enhance healthcare equity, improve health outcomes, and empower individuals to take control of their health, regardless of their location or socioeconomic status.

5. CONCLUSION

In conclusion, Artificial Intelligence holds immense promise for revolutionizing healthcare by enhancing diagnostic accuracy, personalizing treatment plans, predicting health outcomes, and streamlining administrative tasks. The integration of AI technologies in healthcare can lead to more precise and timely diagnoses, reducing the incidence of misdiagnoses and enabling earlier interventions. Personalized treatment plans can be developed through AI-driven analysis of patient data, improving treatment efficacy and patient satisfaction.

Moreover, AI's predictive capabilities can transform preventive care, allowing healthcare providers to anticipate and mitigate potential health issues before they become critical. Administrative efficiencies gained through AI can significantly reduce the burden on healthcare professionals, allowing them to focus more on patient care.

However, the implementation of AI in healthcare is not without challenges. Ethical considerations, data privacy concerns, and the need for robust regulatory frameworks must be addressed to ensure the safe and effective use of AI technologies. Additionally, there is a need for continuous collaboration between technologists, healthcare providers, and policymakers to navigate these challenges and maximize the benefits of AI in healthcare.

Despite these challenges, the potential benefits of AI in healthcare are substantial, paving the way for a future where healthcare is more efficient, effective, and patient-centered. Continued research, investment, and innovation in AI technologies will be crucial in realizing this future, ultimately improving health outcomes and the overall quality of care for patients worldwide.

REFERENCES

Abdelhalim, H., Berber, A., Lodi, M., Jain, R., Nair, A., Pappu, A., Patel, K., Venkat, V., Venkatesan, C., Wable, R. and Dinatale, M., , (2022). Artificial intelligence, healthcare, clinical genomics, and pharmacogenomics approaches in precision medicine. *Frontiers in Genetics*, *13*, 929736. DOI: 10.3389/fgene.2022.929736 PMID: 35873469

Alanazi, A.,, (2022). Using machine learning for healthcare challenges and opportunities. *Informatics in Medicine Unlocked*, *30*, 100924. DOI: 10.1016/j.imu.2022.100924

Alowais, S.A., Alghamdi, S.S., Alsuhebany, N., Alqahtani, T., Alshaya, A.I., Almohareb, S.N., Aldairem, A., Alrashed, M., Bin Saleh, K., Badreldin, H.A. and Al Yami, M.S.,, (2023). Revolutionizing healthcare: The role of artificial intelligence in clinical practice. *BMC Medical Education*, *23*(1), 689. DOI: 10.1186/s12909-023-04698-z PMID: 37740191

Apostolova, E., White, H.A., Morris, P.A., Eliason, D.A. and Velez, T.,, (2017). Open globe injury patient identification in warfare clinical notes. *AMIA Annual Symposium Proceedings*, 403.

Arbi, A. (2018). Dynamics of BAM neural networks with mixed delays and leakage time-varying delays in the weighted pseudo–almost periodic on time-space scales. *Mathematical Methods in the Applied Sciences*, *41*(3), 1230–1255. DOI: 10.1002/mma.4661

Arbi, A., & Tahri, N., (2024). Synchronization analysis of novel delayed dynamical Clifford-valued neural networks on timescales. *Journal of Algorithms & Computational Technology*, *18*, 17483026241241492. DOI: 10.1177/17483026241241492

Arbi, A., & Cao, J. & Alsaedi, A.,, (2018). Improved synchronization analysis of competitive neural networks with time-varying delays. *Nonlinear Analysis (Vilnius)*, *23*(1), 82–107. DOI: 10.15388/NA.2018.1.7

Baxter, S.L., Marks, C., Kuo, T.T., Ohno-Machado, L. and Weinreb, R.N.,, (2019). Machine learning-based predictive modeling of surgical intervention in glaucoma using systemic data from electronic health records. *American Journal of Ophthalmology*, *208*, 30–40. DOI: 10.1016/j.ajo.2019.07.005 PMID: 31323204

Chaganti, S., Nabar, K.P., Nelson, K.M., Mawn, L.A. & Landman, B.A. (2017). Phenotype analysis of early risk factors from electronic medical records improves image-derived diagnostic classifiers for optic nerve pathology. In *Medical Imaging 2017: Imaging Informatics for Healthcare, Research, and Applications* (pp. 99-105). SPIE. https://doi.org/DOI: 10.1117/12.2255739

Esmaeilzadeh, P., (2020). Use of AI-based tools for healthcare purposes: A survey study from consumers' perspectives. *BMC Medical Informatics and Decision Making*, *20*(1), 1–19. DOI: 10.1186/s12911-020-01191-1 PMID: 32698869

Fraccaro, P., Nicolo, M., Bonetto, M., Giacomini, M., Weller, P., Traverso, C.E., Prosperi, M. & OSullivan, D., (2015). Combining macula clinical signs and patient characteristics for age-related macular degeneration diagnosis: A machine learning approach. *BMC Ophthalmology*, *15*(1), 1–9. DOI: 10.1186/1471-2415-15-10 PMID: 25623470

Gaskin, J. C., Pershing, S., & Shah, N. (2016). Predictive modeling of risk factors and complications of cataract surgery. *European Journal of Ophthalmology*, *26*(4), 328–337. DOI: 10.5301/ejo.5000706 PMID: 26692059

Iqbal, M.J., Javed, Z., Sadia, H., Qureshi, I.A., Irshad, A., Ahmed, R., Malik, K., Raza, S., Abbas, A., Pezzani, R. & Sharifi-Rad, J., (2021). Clinical applications of artificial intelligence and machine learning in cancer diagnosis: Looking into the future. *Cancer Cell International*, *21*(1), 270. DOI: 10.1186/s12935-021-01981-1 PMID: 34020642

Johnson, K.B., Wei, W.Q., Weeraratne, D., Frisse, M.E., Misulis, K., Rhee, K., Zhao, J. & Snowdon, J.L., (2021). Precision medicine, AI, and the future of personalized health care. *Clinical and Translational Science*, *14*(1), 86–93. DOI: 10.1111/cts.12884 PMID: 32961010

Kalis, B., Collier, M., & Fu, R. (2018). 10 promising AI applications in health care. *Harvard Business Review*, •••, 2–5.

Kasula, A., Singh, D., & Verma, P. (2023). AI-driven machine learning solutions for sustainable development in healthcare—Pioneering efficient, equitable, and innovative health service. *International Journal of Sustainable Development Through AI. ML and IoT*, *2*(2), 1–7.

Lee, C. S., Baughman, D. M., & Lee, A. Y. (2017). Deep learning is effective for classifying normal versus age-related macular degeneration OCT images. *Ophthalmology Retina*, *1*(4), 322–327. DOI: 10.1016/j.oret.2016.12.009 PMID: 30693348

Lin, W.C., Chen, J.S., Chiang, M.F. & Hribar, M.R., (2020). Applications of artificial intelligence to electronic health record data in ophthalmology. *Translational Vision Science & Technology*, *9*(2), 13-23. DOI: 10.1167/tvst.9.2.13 PMID: 32704419

Lin, H., Long, E., Ding, X., Diao, H., Chen, Z., Liu, R., Huang, J., Cai, J., Xu, S., Zhang, X. & Wang, D., (2018). Prediction of myopia development among Chinese school-aged children using refraction data from electronic medical records: A retrospective, multicentre machine learning study. *PLoS Medicine*, *15*(11), e1002674. DOI: 10.1371/journal.pmed.1002674 PMID: 30399150

Ouali, I., & Halima, M.B (2022b). Real-time application for recognition and visualization of Arabic words with vowels based DL and AR. In *2022 International Wireless Communications and Mobile Computing (IWCMC)* (pp. 678-683). IEEE. https://doi.org/DOI: 10.1109/IWCMC55113.2022.9825089

Peissig, P. L., White, T., & McCarty, C. A. (2012). Importance of multimodal approaches to effectively identify cataract cases from electronic health records. *Journal of the American Medical Informatics Association : JAMIA*, *19*(2), 225–234. DOI: 10.1136/amiajnl-2011-000456 PMID: 22319176

Ramírez, J., (2024). AI in healthcare: Revolutionizing patient care with predictive analytics and decision support systems. [JAIGS]. *Journal of Artificial Intelligence General Science*, *1*(1), 31–37.

Rana, S., Gupta, R., & Kumar, N. (2024). AI in healthcare: Transforming patient care through predictive analytics and decision support systems. [JAIGS]. *Journal of Artificial Intelligence General Science*, *1*(1). Advance online publication. DOI: 10.60087/jaigs.v1i1.30

Richardson, S., Brown, K., & Carter, M. (2021). Patient apprehensions about the use of artificial intelligence in healthcare. *NPJ Digital Medicine*, *4*(1), 140. DOI: 10.1038/s41746-021-00509-1 PMID: 34548621

Shaheen, H., Ali, B., & Khan, N. (2021). Applications of artificial intelligence (AI) in healthcare: A review. *ScienceOpenPreprints*.

Skevofilakas, M., Konstantia Z., Basil G. K., and Konstantina S. N., (2010). A hybrid decision support system for the risk assessment of retinopathy development as a long-term complication of Type 1 Diabetes Mellitus. In *2010 Annual International Conference of the IEEE Engineering in Medicine and Biology* (pp. 6713-6716). IEEE. https://doi.org/DOI: 10.1109/IEMBS.2010.5626245

Sramka, M., Patel, P., & Varadarajan, A. (2019). Improving clinical refractive results of cataract surgery by machine learning. *PeerJ*, *7*, e7202. https://doi.org/10.xxxx. DOI: 10.7717/peerj.7202 PMID: 31304064

Chapter 5
Artificial Intelligence in Autonomous Vehicles Advancing Sustainable Transportation Goals

Fatima Ezzahra Khalloufi
https://orcid.org/0009-0004-0450-9688
Ibn Tofail University, Morocco

Najat Rafalia
Ibn Tofail University, Marocco

Jaafar Abouchabaka
Ibn Tofail University, Marocco

ABSTRACT

This paper provides a concise review of the role of artificial intelligence in the development of autonomous vehicles for sustainable development goals. It highlights the significance of artificial intelligence in enabling autonomous vehicles to achieve sustainable transportation goals such as reduced emissions, improved traffic efficiency, and enhanced safety. The paper discusses the fundamental components of autonomous vehicles and the key artificial intelligence techniques used in perception, decision making, and control system. It also explores the challenges and perspectives

DOI: 10.4018/979-8-3693-8141-0.ch005

associated the use of autonomous vehicles for achieving the sustainable development goals. This review serves as a valuable resource for researchers, and professionals interested in leveraging artificial intelligence for sustainable autonomous vehicles development.

1. INTRODUCTION

The Sustainable Development Goals (SDGs) consist of 17 global objectives introduced by the United Nations in 2015 as part of the 2030 Agenda for Sustainable Development (*United Nations System Staff College, Sustainable Development and the SDGs*.). These goals aim to tackle pressing global issues, including poverty, inequality, environmental degradation, and peace, striving to foster a better and more sustainable future for all. Sustainability is divided into several categories, with the first being environmental sustainability. This focuses on preserving healthy ecosystems and reducing the negative impact of human activities on the environment. Its main objectives include promoting the use of renewable energy sources and reducing pollutants, such as carbon emission (Ziaul & Shuwei, n.d.). The second category is economic sustainability. It involves building a thriving economy that can support both present and future generations (Spangenberg, 2005). Another category of sustainability is the social one, which focuses on promoting justice, equity, and fostering a sense of belonging within society (De Fine Licht & Folland, 2019). The transportation sector can significantly advance the global effort toward achieving the SDGs.It has significant impact on the environments, energy consumption, and public safety. Conventional vehicles that run on fossil fuels release greenhouse gases, intensifying climate change. Traffic congestion leads to wasted time and fuel, diminishing productivity and increasing pollution levels. Road accidents, often caused by human error, result in traffic loss of life and economic burdens. In light of these challenges, there is a pressing need to transform the transportation sector into a sustainable and efficient system. The development of autonomous vehicles (Avs) holds great promise for revolutionizing the transportation industry and contributing to sustainable development goals. Consequently, the advancement of Avs relies on various technological innovations, including artificial intelligence

(AI), fifth-generation cellular networks (5G), and more. AI algorithms play a crucial role in enabling these vehicles to navigate, perceive, and adapt to changing environments, enhancing both safety and efficiency. The evolution of autonomous systems has been significantly shaped by AI integration. This paper seeks to provide a comprehensive analysis of AI's role in developing autonomous cars for sustainable transportation. It will explore the fundamentals components of Avs, including perception system, decision making system, and control systems, highlighting the AI techniques utilized in each component. The review will discuss the applications of autonomous cars in achieving sustainable development goals. However, the path towards widespread adoption of AI-driven autonomous cars not without challenges. This paper will address these challenges and provide insights into ongoing research efforts and the future directions in the field of AI-driven autonomous cars development.

2. THE DEVELOPMENT OF Avs USING AI

The future of Avs depends on various factors, including technological advancements, regulations, government support, and social acceptance. This section highlights the key technologies driving Avs. Self-driving cars rely on a combination of cameras, radar, and radio antennas to navigate safely. In modern autonomous systems, these technologies work together, with each contributing a layer of autonomy that enhances overall reliability and robustness. Key innovations such as AI, fifth-generation cellular networks (5G), and other advanced technologies play a crucial role in their development. The progression of AI has profoundly influenced the development and implementation of Avs within the transportation industry. Leveraging vast amounts of data from various sensors and advanced computing power, AI has become a crucial component of autonomous vehicles. Its role encompasses perceiving the surrounding environment and making informed decisions while in motion. Understanding the working of AI within AV systems is vital to achieving the ultimate objective of full automation. Here are some key ways in which AI is applied in Avs:

2.1 Perception

The perception module is a fundamental component that enables Avs to gather essential information about surroundings. It employs an array of sensors including radar, light detection and ranging (LIDAR), and cameras, to classify, detect, and track information such as vehicles, pedestrians, and traffic signs. By processing inputs from these sensors, the perception module equipes the autonomous vehicle with a comprehensive understanding of its environments, facilitating safe and efficient navigation.

Existing algorithms for autonomous perception can be categorized into three main groups: (a) object classification and detection, (b) object tracking, and (c) object segmentation. Object detection and classification utilize AI techniques such as Convolutional Neural Networks (CNNs) and YOLO to detect and classify single or multiple objects. One of the key perception tasks mastered by AI is traffic sign detection. For instance, (Mahaur et al., 2023) analyzes how architectural modifications to the YOLOv5 framework improve the detection performance of small objects like traffic signs. Similarly, (Yildiz et al., 2023) proposes a three-stage traffic sign classification approach: a preprocessing stage to enhance dataset images, a data augmentation stage to expand the dataset, and a deep learning stage for classification. For other perception tasks, nighttime pedestrian detection has been explored in (Farooq et al., 2023), which introduces a deep reinforcement learning-based architecture using scale-invariant Faster R-CNN technology. In the case of 3D object detection, (Choe et al., 2023) examines deep learning-based 3D object recognition frameworks across various Jetson platforms.

As for object tracking that is fundamental technology that empowers AI to interact safely and effectively with their environments. Various works interests of this perception task. For example, (Shan Wu et al., 2023) this work explores the potential of improving the multi-object tracking system through the utilization of the dominant convolutional neural network, and an innovative vision transformation technique called “Locality”, ”, (Manzoor et al., 2023) proposes a single pedestrian tracking system that integrates a deep learning-based YOLO model for person detection with a metric learning-based convolutional neural network, utilizing both Siamese and MobileNet-Siamese networks for re-identification.

The third category of perception tasks, object segmentation, focuses on identifying and outlining distinct objects in images or videos by dividing them into meaningful segments. There are two primary types of object segmentation:

Semantic Segmentation: This approach assigns a class label to each pixel in an image, indicating the category to which it belongs. AI-based studies on semantic segmentation have explored various techniques. For example, (Utku Ylusoy et al., 2023) developed an autonomous vehicle system using stereo imaging and AI, incorporating a stereo camera and an NVIDIA Jetson Nano for computer vision. Depth maps were generated from image disparities, and AI-driven semantic segmentation was applied to rectified images. Similarly, (Shashaani et al., 2023) introduced an innovative layer-wise training approach for semantic segmentation and evaluated it on a lightweight, efficient neural network.

Instance Segmentation: This method extends semantic segmentation by not only assigning class labels to pixels but also distinguishing between individual instances of the same class. This means that even objects belonging to the same category are given unique labels, allowing for precise differentiation. In this context, (Zhang et al., 2023) proposed a novel instance segmentation framework called RTS R-CNN, which builds upon the Mask R-CNN algorithm and is specifically designed for detecting road traffic signs.

2.2 Decision Making

Based on the acquired data, including surroundings, velocity, and steering angle, various decision-making applications such as automatic parking, path planning, and car following have been explored. Automatic parking enables a vehicle to park itself without direct human intervention. This task utilizes a combination of sensors, cameras, radar, LiDAR, and AI algorithms to discern appropriate parking locations, guide the vehicles into these spaces, and execute precise manoeuvres even in confined areas. Various studies are heading to automatic parking such as, (Wan Chenglinand Wang, 2023) this paper introduces a deep learning called FPS-Net for quickly detecting parking slots from a bird's eye view image. FPS-Net employs MobileNetv3 to predict slot location, shape, and orientation, refines the slot's corner points, and determines occupancy status using HOG feature extraction.

Path planning for Avs is dynamic process that involves combining sensor data, environmental information, and vehicle capabilities to make safe and efficient decisions about how the vehicle should navigate its environment. Path planning methods have been widely explored. AI based approaches such as Neural Network, Ant Colony Optimization, Genetic Algorithm and Simulated Annealing, Particle Swarm Optimization and Reinforcement Learning are used in the recent works. For example, (Xing et al., 2023) this work discusses the significance of ocean exploration using underwater vehicles and the challenges of ensuring these vehicles reach their target points safely in complex underwater environments. The authors propose a method called Improved Artificial Potential Field combined with Deep Reinforcement Learning for path planning. This method aims to overcome local minimum obstacles by using traction forces and optimizes the Deep Reinforcement Learning algorithm's reward function, and (Albarella et al., 2023) this work discusses the impending reality of Avs operating on highways and the role of decision-making and motion planning algorithms in handling various unpredictable traffic situations. This work aims to develop a two-layer path planning system that integrates Deep Reinforcement Learning with model-based methods. The high-level planner, driven by Deep Reinforcement Learning, enables the vehicle to make tactical decisions based on its environment, while the low-level control layer utilizes Nonlinear Model Predictive Control to translate these decisions into precise control commands.

Car following, also known as vehicular following or vehicle following, is a concept in traffic engineering and transportation science that refers to the behavior of vehicles as they follow one another on a road or highway. It involves the study and modelling of how vehicles maintain certain distances and speeds while driving in a line or a platoon. Various AI techniques, including Reinforcement Learning (RL), have been applied to car-following models. For instance, (Wang et al., 2023) introduces a self-learning algorithm based on RL to optimize a model predictive controller, comparing its performance to a conventional model predictive controller in an autonomous vehicle car-following scenario. Similarly, (Li & Okhrin, 2023) explores a two-stage Deep Reinforcement Learning approach in the context of autonomous vehicles. The method aims to enhance the performance of car following agents by incorporating real world human driving experience which is often limited by simulations. The training take place within the CARLA framework with Robot Operating System.

3. THE IMPACT OF Avs IN ADVANCING SDGs

The Sustainable Development Goals (SDGs) (*Transforming Our World : The 2030Agenda for Sustainable Development : Resolution / Adopted by the General Assembly*), also known as the Global Goals, were established by the United Nations in 2015 as a universal call to action to eradicate poverty, protect the planet, and promote peace and prosperity for all by 2030. Comprising 17 interconnected goals, the SDGs emphasize the need for a balanced approach to social, economic, and environmental sustainability. Nations have pledged to prioritize progress for the most disadvantaged communities. These goals address critical global challenges, including poverty, hunger, disease, and inequality. Additionally, the SDGs provide substantial support and capacity-building in key areas such as water, energy, climate, oceans, urbanization, transport, science, and technology. Achieving these goals requires collective efforts, leveraging creativity, expertise, technology, and financial resources from all sectors of society. Figure 1 illustrates the 17 SDGs as defined by the UN.

Figure 1. The 17 SDGs

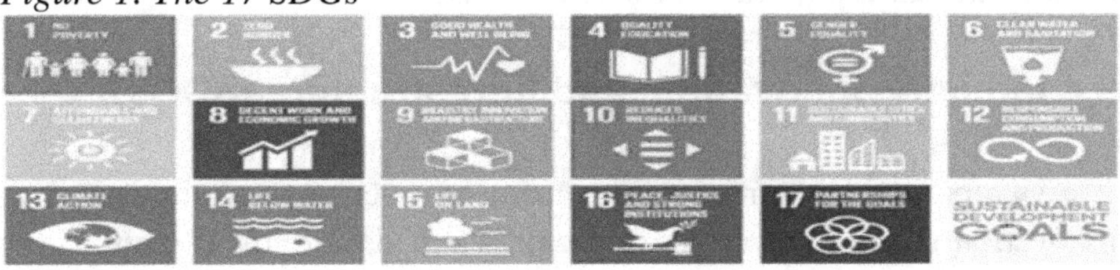

Autonomous cars have the potential to make significant contributions to various SDGs. Below are key ways in which they can contribute to sustainable development.

3.1 Climate Action (SDG13):

Avs can contribute to climate action by reducing greenhouse gas emissions. They have the potential to be more energy-efficient compared to traditional vehicles due to optimized driving patterns, reduced congestion, and smoother traffic flow. Additionally, the integration of electric and autonomous technologies can lead to a significant reduction in carbon emissions.

3.2 Sustainable Cities and Communities (SDG11):

Avs can help create more sustainable and livable cities. They can optimize traffic flow reduce congestion, and improve transportation efficiency. Shared autonomous vehicles can reduce the need for private car ownership, freeing up space for green areas and reducing the demand for parking lots. Avs can also enhance accessibility by providing transportation options to underserved communities, including the elderly and disabled.

3.3 Good Health and Well-being (SDG3):

Avs can contribute to better health outcomes. By reducing traffic accidents have the potential to save lives and reduce injuries. They can also improve air quality by promoting the adoption of electric vehicles and reducing emissions from combustion engines, leading to better respiratory health and reduced pollution related illnesses.

3.4 Industry, Innovation, and Infrastructure (SDG9):

Avs represent a significant advancement in technology and can drive innovation in the transportation sector. Their development requires the integration of various technologies such as sensors, artificial intelligence, and connectivity systems. The growth of Avs infrastructure, including charging stations for electric Avs and dedicated lanes for autonomous transport, can stimulate economic growth, create jobs, and improve transportation efficiency.

3.5 Reduced Inequalities (SDG10):

Avs can help address transportation inequalities. They can provide accessible and affordable transportation options for individuals who are unable to drive, including the elderly, disabled, and those without access to private vehicles. By offering mobility services in underserved areas and improving public transportation networks, Avs can contribute to reducing transportation disparities among different socio-economic groups.

3.6 Partnerships for the Goals (SDG17):

The development and deployment of Avs require collaboration and partnerships between various stakeholders. This includes governments, industry, players, researchers, and civil society organizations. By fostering collaboration, knowledge sharing, and coordinated efforts, Avs can contribute to the achievement of multiple SDGs through collective action.

4. Avs IN EMERGING COUNTRIES

The United States, along with countries such as France, Germany, Australia, Japan, Canada, the Netherlands, and the United Kingdom, is actively invested in intelligent transportation systems, including Avs. These nations fund numerous research projects, some of which are still in the experimental phase. Additionally, several emerging countries are making significant advancements in the autonomous vehicle industry, such as:

4.1 Avs in India

India ranks among the lowest three countries across all four pillars of the index. The government has effectively banned Avs, with road transport and highways minister Nitin Gadkari stating in July 2017 that driverless cars would not be permitted as they could threaten jobs. Consequently,

India scores zero in several policy and legislation categories, including regulation and government investment.

Despite this, India has ambitious goals. Its automotive mission plan aims to position the country among the top three globally in vehicle engineering, manufacturing, and exports. Given the socioeconomic benefits of autonomous transport and India's strong entrepreneurial ecosystem, the country could emerge as a significant Avs market in the long run. However, at present, it scores poorly in technology and innovation due to a lack of patents, low investment, and minimal adoption of driverless cars. While survey data indicates that indians are among the most open to av technology, current conditions suggest they may have limited opportunities to experience it.

4.2 Avs in Pakistan

Research on Pakistan's first autonomous vehicle was conducted in 2015 with financial support from the Office of Research. The Minister for Science and Technology emphasized the government's commitment to adopting the latest technologies in the country. In an interview with a private news outlet, he stated that driverless cars would be introduced within the government's current tenure.

The minister expressed confidence that these advanced vehicles would significantly reduce road accidents, estimating that 90% of them could be prevented through self-driving technology. He also underscored the importance of modernizing government institutions, particularly the police, highlighting how technology integration could enhance governance.

4.3 Avs in South Africa

The Department of Transport plans to introduce new regulations for self-driving cars in South Africa, anticipating that Avs will soon become a reality in the country. In its 2021/2022 strategic performance plan, the department stated that these vehicles would operate on roads with minimal or no human intervention.

It highlighted the potential benefits of Avs, including improved road safety, enhanced social inclusion, reduced emissions, and decreased traffic congestion. To capitalize on these advantages while mitigating risks and unforeseen consequences, the government is developing policies, legislation, and strategies to support the integration of autonomous vehicles.

5. CHALLENGES AND PERSPECTIVES IN DEVELOPING Avs TO ACHIEVE SDGs

5.1 Prespectives:

In this section, we offer a perspective on the future of autonomous cars (Chan, 2017) . We envision an ideal world where autonomous cars unlock their full potential, bringing significant benefits. We also briefly discuss the key challenges to scaling autonomous cars on a broader level.

Some of the targeted perspectives mentioned above in Table are well-founded and realistic, while others are harder to quantify in terms of timing or feasibility. Achieving these will depend on the growing technical viability and societal acceptance of autonomous cars. According to a report (Litman & Litman, 2013), certain benefits, such as independent mobility for affluent non-drivers, may emerge in the 2030s. However, other advantages, including reduced traffic and parking congestion, enhanced mobility for low-income individuals (potentially decreasing reliance on public transit), improved safety, energy savings, and lower pollution levels, will likely become significant only when autonomous vehicles are widely adopted and affordable, which is expected between the 2040s and 2060s.

5.2 Challenges of realizing Avs

Despite significant advancements in automated driving technology, the timeline for self-driving vehicles becoming widespread remains uncertain. Experts hold different opinions on how quickly these vehicles will enter the market and what benefits can realistically be expected. While technical challenges are one aspect, societal acceptance and driver adaptation are equally important. Additionally, existing legal frameworks and institutional barriers may slow the progress of autonomous cars deployment. This last can face many challenges that are described below:

- Although technologies have made tremendous strides across the board, significant developmental work is still needed to transform them into commercial products, which implies the initial production scale will be limited.
- The initial production costs will be relatively high, making it less accessible to a large population
- The small-scale production and deployment indicate that investments may be unsustainable, potentially leading to setbacks.
- Numerous surveys show that consumers are often unwilling to pay for automation features, with some outright rejecting the idea of owning an automated vehicle.
- The transition to handing over driving responsibilities to machines and allowing them to make decisions presents a perception challenge. Socially, it is unclear how quickly the public will accept this concept.
- Regulations and practices will need to evolve to accommodate new definitions and categories of road users, as well as the roles of drivers, owners, and vehicle operators. While these legal challenges are not insurmountable, they could pose significant obstacles in the path toward achieving widespread deployment.

Table 1. perspectives on the future of autonomous Cars

Vehicle user perspective	Transportation operation perspective	Society perspective
• Reduced traffic collisions by eliminating or minimizing human errors. • Smoother, more comfortable, and less stressful journeys. • Increased mobility freedom for individuals who are fatigued, disabled intoxicated, inattentive, children or senior. • Increased productivity and enjoyment for passengers by allowing them to focus on other activities while traveling. • A potential alternative and more efficient transportation mode. • Reduced need for individual vehicle ownership • Effective automated handling of events in cases of vehicle failure or incapacitated users.	• Lower congestion through fewer incidents and improved traffic management. • Enhanced real-time navigation, trip assignments, and dynamic routing. • Enhanced accessibility, reliability, and flexibility in shared rides for personal transportation and mobility services. • Improved infrastructure efficiency due to enhanced vehicle control and coordinated operations. • Improved financial returns and business models for private investors. • Increased resource savings in infrastructure, such as parking and roadway construction. • operate more efficiently, reducing fuel use through better driving practices, contributing to energy conservation.	• Reduced burden on those providing support services for individuals with mobility challenges. • Greater incentives to transition from personal vehicle ownership to car- and ride-sharing services. • Eased driver shortage challenges in certain countries and regions. • Lowered insurance and associated ownership costs. • Lower accident rates and reduced societal losses. • Environmentally friendly vehicles and infrastructure • Gradually achievable transportation services with enhanced safety, reliability, security, and productivity.

6. CONCLUSION

Avs technology has the potential to significantly contribute to a more sustainable and efficient transportation ecosystem when developed with careful consideration of environmental, social, and economic impacts. This paper explores the role of autonomous vehicles in achieving sustainable development goals and examines the impact of AI on the advancement of autonomous vehicle technology.

We present in this work the current researches of using AI in Avs, many AI approaches supporting Avs in perception and decision-making tasks. The future of AI in autonomous cars for sustainable development will involve a continued emphasis on reducing environmental impact, improving energy efficiency, enhancing safety, and integrating autonomous cars into broader transportation and urban. This paper presents a perspective on the future of automated driving, envisioning an ideal world of autonomous vehicles to explore their potential benefits. It also provides a brief review of the challenges involved in scaling autonomous cars on a large scale

REFERENCES

Albarella, N., Lui, D. G., Petrillo, A., & Santini, S. (2023). A Hybrid Deep Reinforcement Learning and Optimal Control Architecture for Autonomous Highway Driving. *Energies*, *16*(8), 3490. Advance online publication. DOI: 10.3390/en16083490

Chan, C. Y. (2017). Advancements, prospects, and impacts of automated driving systems. *International Journal of Transportation Science and Technology*, *6*(3), 208–216. DOI: 10.1016/j.ijtst.2017.07.008

Choe, C., Choe, M., & Jung, S. (2023). Run Your 3D Object Detector on NVIDIA Jetson Platforms:A Benchmark Analysis †. *Sensors (Basel)*, *23*(8), 4005. Advance online publication. DOI: 10.3390/s23084005 PMID: 37112347

De Fine Licht, K., & Folland, A. (2019). Defining "social sustainability": Towards a sustainable solution to the conceptual confusion. *Etikk i Praksis*, *13*(2), 21–39. DOI: 10.5324/eip.v13i2.2913

Farooq, M. S., Khalid, H., Arooj, A., Umer, T., Asghar, A. B., Rasheed, J., Shubair, R. M., & Yahyaoui, A. (2023). A Conceptual Multi-Layer Framework for the Detection of Nighttime Pedestrian in Autonomous Vehicles Using Deep Reinforcement Learning. *Entropy (Basel, Switzerland)*, *25*(1), 135. Advance online publication. DOI: 10.3390/e25010135 PMID: 36673276

Grayned, J. (n.d.). *SAE INTERNATIONAL LEVELS OF AUTONOMOUS DRIVING/ SENSOR PACKAGES*. DOI: 10.4271/J3016_201401

Li, D., & Okhrin, O. (2023). Modified DDPG car-following model with a real-world human driving experience with CARLA simulator. *Transportation Research Part C, Emerging Technologies*, *147*, 103987. Advance online publication. DOI: 10.1016/j.trc.2022.103987

Litman, T. A., & Litman, T. (2013). www.vtpi.org*Info@vtpi.org Phone 250-508-5150 Autonomous Vehicle Implementation Predictions Implications for Transport Planning*. www.vtpi.org/avip.docx

Mahaur, B., Mishra, K. K., & Kumar, A. (2023). An improved lightweight small object detection framework applied to real-time autonomous driving. *Expert Systems with Applications*, *234*, 121036. Advance online publication. DOI: 10.1016/j.eswa.2023.121036

Manzoor, S., An, Y. C., In, G. G., Zhang, Y., Kim, S., & Kuc, T. Y. (2023). SPT: Single Pedestrian Tracking Framework with Re-Identification-Based Learning Using the Siamese Model. *Sensors (Basel)*, *23*(10), 4906. Advance online publication. DOI: 10.3390/s23104906 PMID: 37430819

Shashaani, S., Teshnehlab, M., Khodadadian, A., Parvizi, M., Wick, T., & Noii, N. (2023). Using Layer-Wise Training for Road Semantic Segmentation in Autonomous Cars. *IEEE Access : Practical Innovations, Open Solutions*, *11*, 46320–46329. DOI: 10.1109/ACCESS.2023.3255988

Spangenberg, J. H. (2005). Economic sustainability of the economy: Concepts and indicators. *International Journal of Sustainable Development*, *8*(1–2), 47–64. DOI: 10.1504/IJSD.2005.007374

Wan, C., Wang, W., Yang, C., Xiang, C., & Li, Y. (2022, September). Fast Parking Slot Detection in the Bird's Eye View. In International Conference on Autonomous Unmanned Systems (pp. 1183-1193). Singapore: Springer Nature Singapore.

Wang, L., Yang, S., Yuan, K., Huang, Y., & Chen, H. (2023). A Combined Reinforcement Learning and Model Predictive Control for Car-Following Maneuver of Autonomous Vehicles. [English Edition]. *Chinese Journal of Mechanical Engineering*, *36*(1), 80. Advance online publication. DOI: 10.1186/s10033-023-00904-7

Wu, S., Hadachi, A., Lu, C., & Vivet, D. (2023). Transformer for multiple object tracking: Exploring locality to vision. *Pattern Recognition Letters*, *170*, 70–76. DOI: 10.1016/j.patrec.2023.04.016

Xing, T., Wang, X., Ding, K., Ni, K., & Zhou, Q. (2023). Improved Artificial Potential Field Algorithm Assisted by Multisource Data for AUV Path Planning. *Sensors (Basel)*, *23*(15), 6680. Advance online publication. DOI: 10.3390/s23156680 PMID: 37571463

Yildiz, G., Ulu, A., Dizdaroglu, B., & Yildiz, D. (2023). Hybrid Image Improving and CNN (HIICNN) Stacking Ensemble Method for Traffic Sign Recognition. *IEEE Access : Practical Innovations, Open Solutions, 11*, 69536–69552. DOI: 10.1109/ACCESS.2023.3292955

Ylusoy, U., Eren, O., & Demirhan, A. (2023). Development of an obstacle avoiding autonomous vehicle by using stereo depth estimation and artificial intelligence based semantic segmentation. *Engineering Applications of Artificial Intelligence*. https://doi.org/https://doi.org/10.1016/j.engappai.2023.106808

Zhang, G., Peng, Y., & Wang, H. (2023). Road Traffic Sign Detection Method Based on RTS R-CNN Instance Segmentation Network. *Sensors (Basel), 23*(14), 6543. Advance online publication. DOI: 10.3390/s23146543 PMID: 37514837

Ziaul, I.M. and Shuwei, W., 2023. Environmental sustainability: A major component of sustainable development. International Journal of Environmental, Sustainability, and Social Science, 4(3), pp.900-907, .

Chapter 6
Smart Waste Management System

S. Renuka Devi
Vellore Institute of Technology, Chennai, India

Meghna Manoj Nair
Vellore Institute of Technology, Chennai, India

Gadiparthy Harika Sai
Vellore Institute of Technology, Chennai, India

ABSTRACT

Waste management has turned out to be one of the prime issues over the last few years. Even though municipal corporations and authorities around the world have employed workers to clean and empty out garbage cans of their localities every once in few days, there are days when the garbage overflows lead to spillage of waste which attracts flies and spreads other diseases within the locality. Furthermore, in most of the cases the garbage cans are left unclean or are just washed with water which often leaves a lot of moisture content in the garbage can resulting in the growth of microbes and bacteria. In order to address this issue, we have proposed and elaborated on a smart waste management system which is automated and works using Arduino board and a set of necessary sensors. Furthermore, we have also proposed an additional feature of automated sanitation to the smart waste management system which would make use of a sprin-

DOI: 10.4018/979-8-3693-8141-0.ch006

kler mechanism to sanitize the entire garbage can using solvents which are volatile and would dissolve the dirt present in the dustbin easily and evaporate.

1. INTRODUCTION

There is a significant increase in waste generation for the past two decades and it imposes a big challenge in developing countries due to massive growth in population and urbanization. Based on research conducted worldwide, it is anticipated that by 2050, the yearly production of solid waste will amount to approximately 3.40 billion tons, resulting in an approximate expense of $635.5 billion for the management of municipal waste (Ali et al., 2020). Improper waste management may lead to huge loss. For instance, abrupt fires that break out in open waste dumping yards in crowded areas of the city have been known to cause devastating losses to the economy and human lives. It is also mentioned that any kind of waste, such as liquid, solid, or gas in a container, that can quickly catch fire can result in illnesses, injuries, financial loss, and environmental harm (Baby et al., 2017; Bhattacharya et al., 2021). Moreover, the overflowing garbage can cause unhygienic environment with unpleasant smell.

Traditional waste management will not suit the current need and it is considered inefficient. With the advancement in Internet of Things (IoT) and Artificial Intelligence (AI), the traditional waste management system can be replaced with smart system which includes sensors and Global Positioning system (GPS) to perform real-time monitoring and ensures efficient waste management. IoT makes it possible to remotely control the devices' operations via a network infrastructure, which helps in the implementation of wirelessly controlled systems into the real world. The data obtained from sensors can be transferred to cloud for storage and processing. The processed data can further be analysed to improve the overall system efficiency (Sinthiya et al (2022), Sakshi et al. (2019)).

The effectiveness of waste management systems is largely determined by the communication distance that exists between the waste collection point and the waste collection center. For long distance communication, technologies like SigFox and LoRa, which run on low power widearea networks (LPWAN) can be used and for short distance communication, technologies like Bluetooth, WiFi, and Zigbee provide better data transmission rates.

With rapid evolution in the technological industry, automation and autonomous systems have turned out to be one of the prime solutions for majority of the problems in a plethora of domains including health, finance, transportation, education, sports, etc. Smart waste management is one of the key components when it comes to smart cities and sustainable cities have been the goal for many of the developed and developing countries across the globe. With all these in mind, an appropriate model for the smart waste management has been proposed in this Chapter. Smart waste management is essential in any type of area, be it a village, town or a city in order to maintain clean and neat surroundings and as well as the public health over there. In many of the cases though the municipal authorities and the corporations are doing well with their duty, they may not get notified whenever the dustbins are full or the garbage is overflowing. This particular problem is being addressed in this chapter. There are many ways to address this problem, this chapter proposes a model in which an SMS is sent to the respective municipal authority or office whenever a garbage can is full so that they can come and empty it. Apart from this SMS notification system, an additional feature of automated sanitation is proposed which makes use of a sprinkler mechanism to sanitize the garbage, each time it is emptied. For this, a suitable solvent which is volatile and is capable of dissolving the dirt present in the dustbin is used. This helps in overcoming the foul smell or the wetness caused by the traditional way of cleaning the dustbin with water which sometimes leads to the remaining of excess water in the bin.

2. LITERATURE REVIEW

Lot of research was carried out and still on-going with respect to the waste management domains like municipal solid waste management, smart bin management, domestic waste management, medical waste management, construction and industrial waste management, and so on. Kumar et al. (2016) proposed a smart alert system which raises the alert signal to the municipal web server once the garbage filling level exceeds the threshold. It is intimation to the municipal authority to empty the garbage. Once the garbage is emptied, then the authority confirms it using RFID tag. Mohapatra and Shirapuri (2020) proposed an alarm system which is based on Arduino. Once the garbage is full, it is conveyed through blinking LED. Based on the LED output, the respective actions are taken. Jain et al. (2019) proposed a mechanism where the automatic segregation of wet waste and dry waste is achieved initially. The segregation is done with the help of moisture sensor. Based on the response from sensor, the arm is operated. The arm will lift up or down the garbage so that the waste gets loaded in the respective sections.

Apart from notifying the respective authorities regarding the overflow of garbage, the people using the dustbins should also be notified. Bhattacharya et al. (2021) designed a Smart Dustbin Utility System. It is based on the IoT where sensors are deployed in the garbage in order to get the filling level of the garbage. If the garbage is full, then the system redirects the user to the nearest garbage which has space for the wastes. In addition, it sends an alert message to the concerned authority in periodic intervals until the garbage is emptied. According to another model proposed by Hussain et al. (2019), alarm will turn ON if the dustbin is exposed to fire and the pesticides will be sprayed if there's excessive moisture content inside the bin.

Baby et al. (2017) proposed a model that relies on the concept of machine learning for garbage management. The proposed work instructs the garbage-trucks to empty the bins only when the garbage is critically filled. The information with respect to garbage filling level is gathered using the machine learning model and it is used for managing the garbage. It also makes use of the gathered information to predict the amount of waste in the future. Furthermore, the collected data is stored in the cloud in the form of graphs. Then it uses linear regression model to make decisions.

Kanade et al. (2021) proposed an IoT-based trash checking system which makes use of either Arduino board or Raspberry pi board and an open IoT to detect and clear the trash. It also includes microcontroller, ultrasonic sensor, Wi-Fi module and a heap battery. Kannan et al. (2024) proposed a framework which incorporates Industry 4.0 technologies. This framework includes four major entities that contribute to the development of Smart Waste Management 4.0 (SWM 4.0) namely, smart people, smart cities, smart enterprises, and smart factories. Moreover, the feedback from the four entities is used to identify the necessary extensions. Ali et al. (2020) proposed an IoT-based smart waste bin monitoring and municipal solid waste management system. This system is designed to serve three purposes: collecting the waste effectively, detecting fire in the bin, and forecasting the possible amount of waste generation. The bins are monitored and controlled by the IoT based devices and these devices are connected with the central hub through wireless communication. These devices periodically send the information about the bin's capacity with the existing location. By this way, the bin overflow can be detected well in advance and the bins can be emptied before it happens, thereby making a pollution free environment.

Sheng et al. (2020) proposed a smart waste management system which makes use of LoRa communication protocol and TensorFlow based deep learning model. LoRa is used for the purpose of sending the sensor data and Tensor flow is used to detect and classify the real time objects. The servo motors are used to control the segregation of waste in different compartments of bin. Ultrasonic sensor is implanted into each waste compartment to monitor the filling level of the waste. GPS module is used locate of the bin. The proposed detection model is trained with images of waste and the object detection is done through a camera which in turn is connected to the Raspberry Pi 3 Model B+. Maddileti et al. (2020) designed a model in which the lid of the dustbin automatically opens on detection of human hand and waste. Also the level of waste available in the dustbin is notified by turning on the LED and sending a message to the respective entities. They make use of Arduino, NodeMCU, Servo Motor and Ultrasonic Sensors for making it a smart dustbin.

Lincy et al. (2021) and Chand et al. (2021) proposed similar kind of smart dustbin management system which is built on top of Arduino Uno board and interfaced with GSM, GPRS and sensors. The level of waste in the dustbin is checked using the sensors. If the level exceeds the threshold, alert message is sent to the respective authority until it is emptied. In addition, a time limit is set to check whether the action is taken on the issued alert. If not, a complaint message is raised to the higher authority thereby regulating the system. Yadav et al. (2022) also proposed a similar intelligent alert system for garbage clearance but with an add-on functionality of automatic lid opening and closing using passive infrared sensor. This sensor detects a user nearby and signals the system to open the lid. Saad et al. (2023) proposed a smart dustbin prototype which includes IoT-based smart dustbin hardware and software. The height of waste is detected using Ultrasonic sensors and the weight of the waste is measured by the loadcell sensor. The location of the bin is detected by the GPS module. NodeMCU ESP8266 processes sensor data and sends it to the user. The hardware is used to operate the lid automatically to open/close. A notification is sent through WhatsApp.

3. PROPOSED SYSTEM

The proposed smart waste management system is an automated system which makes use of an Arduino board to control the sensors and process all the gathered data. The other major components of the system include ultrasonic sensor, GSM module, LM259 Buck Converter, jumper wires and USB cable. The ultrasonic sensor will be used to measure the distance of the empty area in the garbage can, if the garbage is filled above the threshold value, then the GSM module will be used to send a notification via message to the concerned authorities so that they can clean the dustbins accordingly.

3.1 Components and Requirements

The main components used for this system and their workings are mentioned below: Ultrasonic Sensor: The HC-SR04 ultrasonic sensor (as shown in figure 1) uses SONAR to determine the distance of an object just like the bats does. It offers excellent non-contact range detection with high accuracy and stable readings in an easy-to-use package from 2 cm to 400 cm or 1 inch to 13 feet.

Figure 1. Ultrasonic Sensor Arduino

Arduino Uno (as shown in figure 2) is an Atmega328 based microcontroller. Microcontrollers are typically utilized as the brains of electronic devices and are employed in embedded projects. The Arduino UNO, which has an Atmega328 microcontroller, 14 digital I/O pins, 6 analog pins, and a USB interface, is a very useful addition to the world of electronics. Using the Tx and Rx pins, serial communication is also supported. By connecting the various other sub-components in the device, it serves as the badge's brain and heart.

Figure 2. Arduino Microcontroller

Jumper Wires (Male to Male/Male to Female): Jumper wire (as shown in figure 3) is an electrical wire, or group of wires in a cable, with a connector or pin at each end. It is typically used to provide solder-less connectivity among the internal or external components of a prototype or test circuit, as well as other pieces of equipment. To link the various components of the gadget to the Arduino board, these wires are necessary.

Figure 3. Jumper Wires

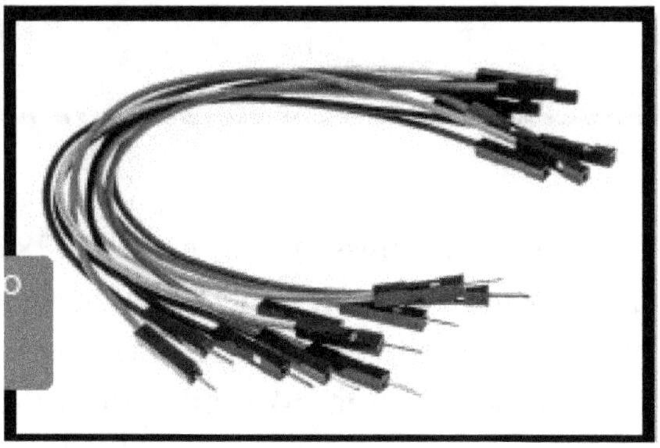

USB Cable: All instructions and programming codes which need to be embedded and executed by the Arduino board can be fed in from the computer to the microprocessor using the USB cable (as shown in figure 4) without any hassles.

Figure 4. USB Cable

GSM Module: A GSM (Global System for Mobile Communication) modem (as shown in Fig. 5) or GSM module is a piece of hardware that connects to a remote network via a data link using GSM mobile telephone technology. From the perspective of the mobile phone network, they are virtually the same as a regular mobile phone, right down to the requirement of a SIM card for network identification.

Figure 5. GSM Module

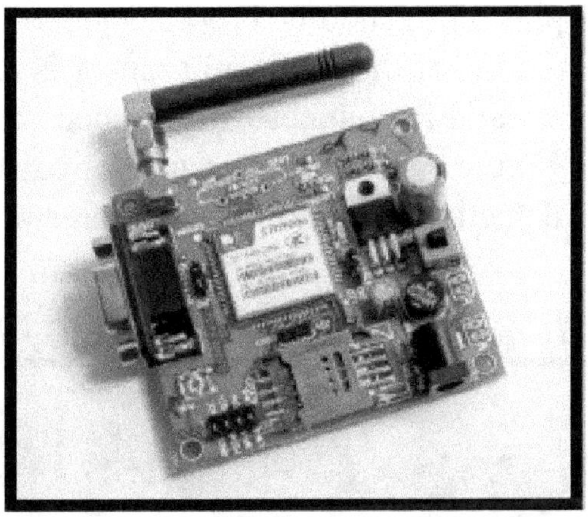

LM2596 Buck Converter: It is a step-down (buck) switching regulator (as shown in figure 6) which can operate a 3-A load with superior line and load regulation. These devices come with an adjustable output version as well as fixed output voltages of 3.3 V, 5 V, and 12 V. It facilitates lower frequency switching regulator with smaller sized filter components since LM2596 series operates at a switching frequency of 150 kHz.

Figure 6. LM2596 Buck Converter

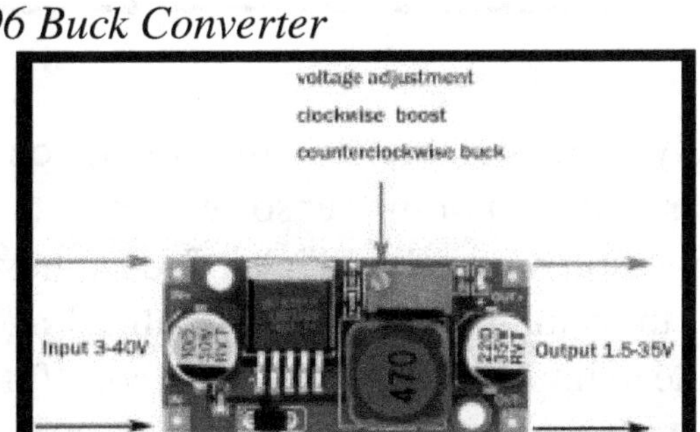

3.2 System Architecture and Circuit Design

The architecture of the basic detection mechanism of the system involves an interconnection of various sensors and required microcontrollers and power supplies. The power supply is used to power up the buck converter – LM2596D. The supplied power is regulated and reduced to a range which can be sufficiently used for the functioning of the GSM Module – SIM800L. The GSM module is thus connected to the buck converter and further the RX/TX pins of the module is connected to the Arduino board. The 'trig' and 'echo' pins of the ultrasonic sensor is used to receive and emit ultrasonic waves and is connected to the necessary digital pins of the Arduino board. Figure 7 shows the circuitry involved for curating the system involved in detecting the amount of garbage level in the dustbin.

Figure 7. TinkerCad Circuit for Detection of Level of Garbage in the Dustbin

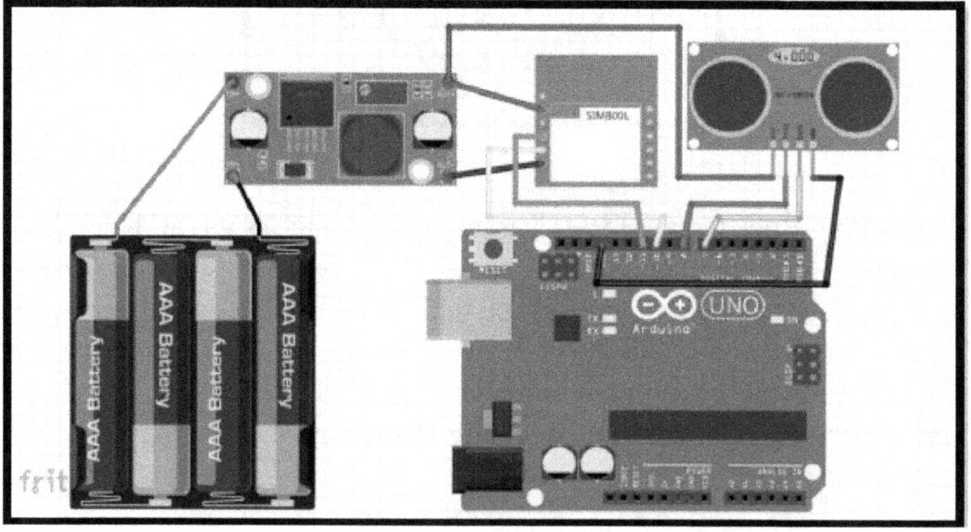

In order to analyse and comprehend the simulation of the ultrasonic sensor in depth, a simulation of the sensor with a suitable code was also implemented using a software called TinkerCad as shown in figure 8. On running the code, the simulation can be visualized and necessary code tweaks can be made to improve or optimize the code further before direct implementation. Due to the absence of other components like GSM module and buck converter, the simulations were not possible.

Figure 8. TinkerCad simulation of Ultrasonic Sensor

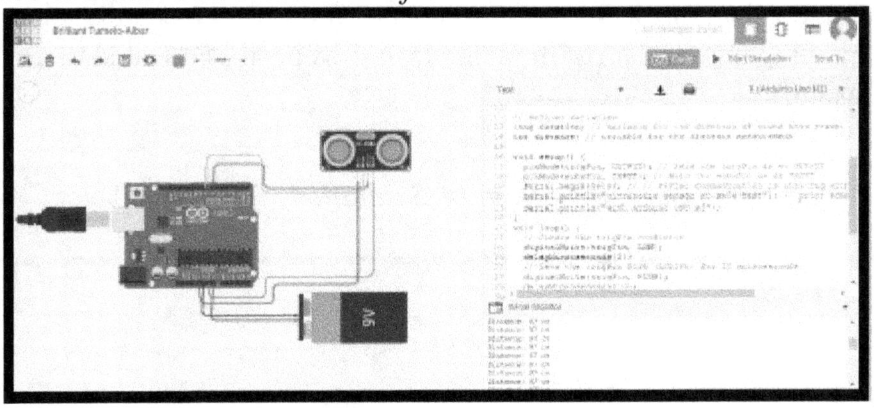

A novel feature is introduced in the proposed mechanism in order to keep the garbage hygienic immediately after the removal of waste from it. The proposed system has an additional functional module attached to it to implement this feature. This module consists of ultrasonic sensor, servo motor Arduino board and a breadboard along with jumper wires. The servo motor is used to generate torque and velocity using the voltage and current supplied to it. Servo motors come in different sizes based on which the torque generated varies. To facilitate the working of the sanitation module of our project, MG995 servo motor has been used as it provides higher torque. The main purpose of this module is to ensure that once the cleaner takes the garbage from the can, they can place their hand close to the ultrasonic sensor. When this hand movement is detected by the module, it will operate the servo motor to rotate by ninety degrees causing the strong cleansing solvent to be sprayed across the dustbin. This sanitation feature will ensure that the cleaner need not physically clean the can while exposing himself to the unhygienic environment and at the same time ensures that the garbage can is not left moist as the solvent used is a volatile and strong cleansing liquid.

In order to simulate the working of the servo motor, the circuit and the setup was created in the TinkerCad environment as shown in figure 9. On executing the Arduino code in the simulation environment, it was observed that when the distance from the ultrasonic sensor crossed the threshold value, the servo motor rotates by ninety degrees indicating that the spraying mechanism of the sanitation solvent was activated for further cleansing.

Figure 9. TinkerCad Simulation of Sanitation Feature of Smart Waste Management

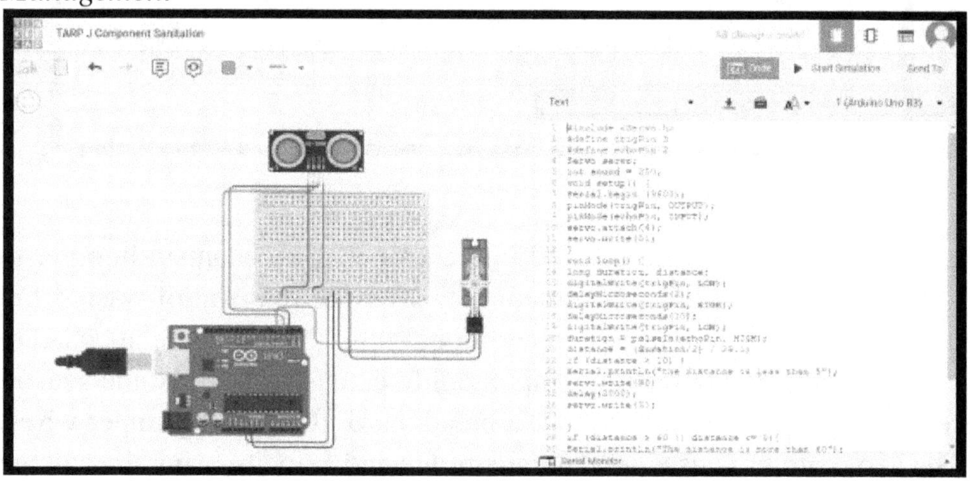

4. RESULT ANALYSIS AND PERFORMANCE EVALUATION

As observed in the circuit design of the proposed system, there will be two main modules attached to every garbage an. The first module is responsible for intimating the authorities regarding when to clean the garbage cans and is commensurate to the amount of trash in the can. While the second module is responsible for ensuring that the garbage can remains clean and free from dirt by automatic sanitation using suitable sanitation solvents. The detailed work flow of the modules one and two are shown below. As shown in figure 10, once the data is received from the ultrasonic sensor regarding the amount of distance left for the garbage to fill the can, it checks if it passes the threshold value which is set. If the condition is fulfilled, it then activates the GSM module which would then send an SMS to the concerned municipal corporation for cleaning the garbage can.

Figure 10. Flow Diagram for Garbage Level Detection

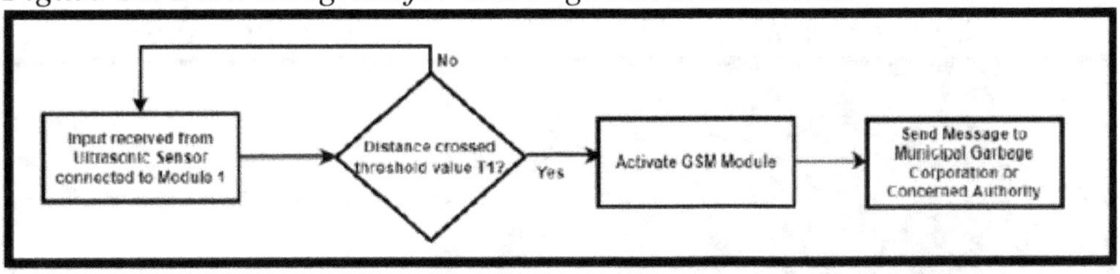

Once the garbage can is cleaned by the concerned authority, they can activate the sanitation module by keeping their hand close to the ultrasonic sensor of module 2 as shown in figure 11. Once the sensor detects the movement of hand, it then activates the servo motor which in turn activates the spraying mechanism of the cleansing solvent which would spray it and cover the garbage to its maximum reach.

Figure 11. Flow Diagram for Sanitation Feature of Smart Waste Management

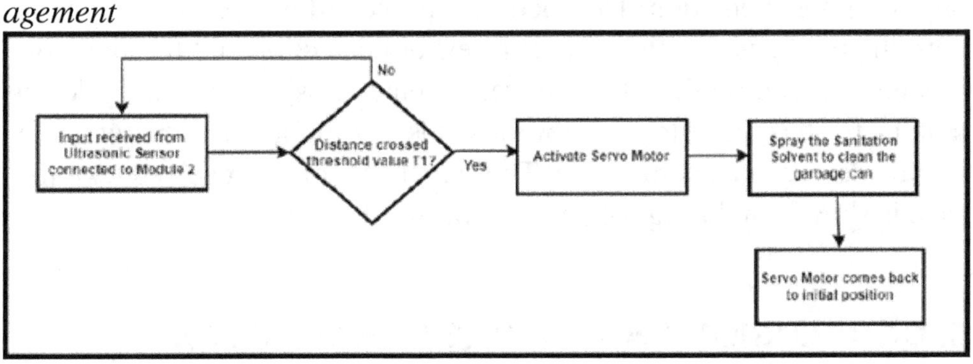

The performance and implementation of the proposed model can be contrasted with some of the existing techniques in terms of the sanitation feature available in the existing works. Most of the works explored and surveyed in the literature review have a pretty decent accuracy but most of them used IR sensors or moisture sensor to detect the garbage threshold levels and the amount of moisture content in it.

Figure 12. Implementation of Smart Waste Management System

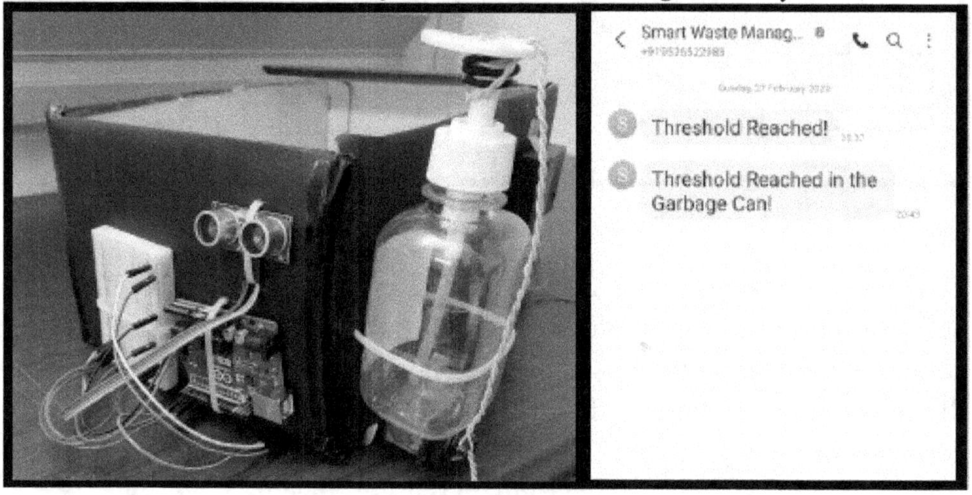

As observed in figure 12, the figure on the left-hand side shows the physical implementation of the model proposed in this paper which contains both the modules – garbage level threshold detection and the sanitation modules. As soon as the ultrasonic sensor placed inside the garbage detects that the trash is likely to overflow, it sends a notification to the registered mobile device via text message. The screenshot of the received text message is shown on the right-hand side of the above figure. 12.

5. CONCLUSION AND FUTURE ENHANCEMENTS

The proposed model of smart waste management not just provides the detection if the dustbin is filled or not but also comes with a novel part involving the sanitation of the dustbin. This kind of smart waste management can lead to a healthier life and environment as seen. This smart management can be enhanced in future in different ways. The proposed model is for one dustbin but it can be upgraded to connecting several dustbins and does the smart waste management system. This when implemented and used in villages or cities can improve the cleanliness and maintain a safer environment. Not just in the streets of cities, the proposed mechanism can also be used in our own homes to give us an alarm when the dustbin is full and as soon as we remove the waste the dustbin will be sanitized thus making the work easier for us.

REFERENCES

Ali, T., Irfan, M., Alwadie, A. S., & Glowacz, A. (2020). IoT-based smart waste bin monitoring and municipal solid waste management system for smart cities. *Arabian Journal for Science and Engineering*, *45*(12), 10185–10198. DOI: 10.1007/s13369-020-04637-w

Baby, C. J., Singh, H., Srivastava, A., & Dhawan, R.; Mahalakshmi, P. (2017). Smart bin: An intelligent waste alert and prediction system using machine learning approach. International Conference on Wireless Communications, Signal Processing and Networking (WiSPNET), pp. 771–774. DOI: 10.1109/WiSPNET.2017.8299865

Bhattacharya, K., Hazra, M., Dutta, D., Roy, K., Islam, F., & Basak, S. (2021). Smart dustbin utility system using iot. *International Journal for Research in Applied Science and Engineering Technology*, *9*(7), •••.

Chand, R. P., Sri, V. B., Lakshmi, P. M., Chakravathi, S. S., Veerendra, O. D. M., & Rao, C. V. (2021, December). Arduino based smart dustbin for waste management during Covid-19. In 2021 5th International Conference on Electronics, Communication and Aerospace Technology (ICECA) (pp. 492-496). IEEE.

Hussain, M. A., Nikhil, K., & Kalyan, K. Y. P. (2019). IOT Based Smart Dustbin Monitoring With Tracking System Using ATMega 2560 Microcontroller. *Fifteenth International Conference on Information Processing (ICINPRO)*, pp. 1–6. DOI: 10.1109/ICInPro47689.2019.9092295

Kanade, P., Alva, P., Prasad, J. P., & Kanade, S. (2021) Smart Garbage Monitoring System using Internet of Things(IoT), *5th International Conference on Computing Methodologies and Communication (ICCMC)*, pp. 330-335, DOI: 10.1109/ICCMC51019.2021.9418359

Kannan, D., Khademolqorani, S., Janatyan, N., & Alavi, S. (2024). Smart waste management 4.0: The transition from a systematic review to an integrated framework. *Waste Management (New York, N.Y.)*, *174*, 1–14. DOI: 10.1016/j.wasman.2023.08.041 PMID: 37742441

Kumar, N. S., Vuayalakshmi, B., Prarthana, R. J., & Shankar, A. (2016, November). IOT based smart garbage alert system using Arduino UNO. In 2016 IEEE region 10 conference (TENCON) (pp. 1028-1034). IEEE.

Lincy, F. A., & Sasikala, T. (2021). Smart dustbin management using IOT and Blynk application. In *5th International Conference on Trends in Electronics and Informatics (ICOEI)*, pp. 429-434. IEEE. DOI: 10.1109/ICOEI51242.2021.9452988

Maddileti, T., & Kurakula, H. (2020). IOT based smart dustbin. International Journal of Science and Technology. *Res*, *9*(2), 1297–1302.

Mohapatra, B. N., & Shirapuri, P. (2020). Arduino based smart dustbin for waste management system. *Perspectives in Communication, Embedded-systems and Signal-processing-PiCES*, *4*(3), 8–11.

Nor, M. K. M. M., Asis, I., & Saidin, M. A. (2022). Intelligent Smart Dustbin (i-SMARTBiN). *Politeknik & Kolej Komuniti Journal of Engineering and Technology*, *7*(1), 101–107.

Saad, A. M., Jul, B. O., Basalamah, A., & Sayuti, S. (2023). IoT-Based Smart Dustbin Prototype. PROtek J. *Ilm. Tek. Elektro*, *10*(2), 120.

Sakshi, J., Hardika, L., Ishika, A., & Lodha, G. M. (2019). Smart Dustbin Management System. *Journal of Advancement in Software Engineering and Testing*, *2*(2), 1–4.

Sheng, T. J., Islam, M. S., Misran, N., Baharuddin, M. H., Arshad, H., Islam, M. R., & Islam, M. T. (2020). An internet of things based smart waste management system using LoRa and tensorflow deep learning model. *IEEE Access : Practical Innovations, Open Solutions*, *8*, 148793–148811.

Sinthiya, N. J., Chowdhury, T. A., & Bahalul Haque, A. K. M. (2022). *Artificial intelligence based Smart Waste Management—a systematic review*. Computational Intelligence Techniques for Green Smart Cities. DOI: 10.1007/978-3-030-96429-0_3

Yadav, D., Pandey, A., Mishra, D., Bagchi, T., Mahapatra, A., Chandrasekhar, P., & Kumar, A. (2022). IoT enabled smart dustbin with messaging alert system. *International Journal of Information Technology: an Official Journal of Bharati Vidyapeeth's Institute of Computer Applications and Management*, *14*(7), 3601–3609. DOI: 10.1007/s41870-022-00947-4

Chapter 7
Solar Panel Tilting System Using IoT

Singaravelan Shanmugasundaram
https://orcid.org/0000-0003-4353-2261
PSR Engineering College, India

M. Sukumar
Sri Venkateswara College of Engineering, India

A. Mathan Kumar
Vel Tech Multi Tech Dr. Rengarajan Dr. Sakunthala Engineering College, India

M. Sangavi
Aalim Muhammed Salegh College of Engineering, India

V. Anusuya
Ramco Institute of Technology, India

A. Euodial
Francis Xavier Engineering College, India

A. Petchiammal
Manonmaniam Sundaranar University, India

G. Priyanga
Saveetha Engineering College, India

ABSTRACT

The optimization goal is to increase the amount of generated energy with the help of photovoltaic system considering the tracking system's consumption. Determination of the tilt angle and azimuth angle trajectories is described as a nonlinear and bounded optimization problem. For col-

DOI: 10.4018/979-8-3693-8141-0.ch007

lection of solar energy we have used sensors (LDR) for tracking of sun's path to make sure that the panel should be placed in MPPT to observe more efficiency and make sure that the panel should be placed in MPPT point. In order to maximize power output from solar panels, one needs to keep the panels aligned with the sun. In the world to avoid the dependency on non-renewable resources, solar energy is rapidly gaining the focus. Different approaches are imposed to increase the efficiency of the solar cells by tracking the sun. This system will rotate according to the position of the sun. The operation of the experimental model of the device is based on a servo motor which is intelligently controlled by an Arduino UNO board that moves a mini PV panel according to the rotation of the sun.

INTRODUCTION

In remote areas the sun is a cheap source of electricity because it uses solar cells to produce electricity. The output of solar cells depends on the intensity of sunlight to get the maximum efficiency. The solar panel remains according to the position of the sun during the whole day. But due to rotation of earth those panels can't maintain their position always in front of sun. This problem results in decrease of efficiency. In order to get a constant output, an automated system is required which should be able to rotate the solar panel according to sun's position. Automatic solar tracker is made as a prototype to solve the problem that mentioned above. Automatic solar tracker is a prototype which rotates according to the position of the sun. The unique feature of this prototype is that, it takes position of the sun as a guiding source instead of earth's rotation. The solar power is used interchangeably with solar energy but refers more specifically to the conversion of sunlight into electricity by photovoltaic cells. It has become a popular investment for companies as well as for residential users. This demand has stimulated the research for increasing the overall output power of photovoltaic

(PV) system causing people all over the globe to work hard on making the technology more efficient as well as cost effective. Solar panels are photovoltaic cells which gives voltage directly if you place them in sunlight. "Energy is non been created or not been destroyed". This is a universal law said by newton which has been proved by science. this is applicable for all things in energy sector the various forms of energy is converted into electrical energy in the process of transformation of various energy into electrical energy nonrenewable resources, after some time these resources are run out or replenished in human life we need to focused on renewable energy which are given by nature and don't make harm to the same nature so many energy have been identified from that solar energy is one of best energy from renewable energy this energy is not replenished until the sun existed.

1.1 Types of Solar Panels And Solar Tracking Techniques

Modern solar tracking methods can be classified into the following types.

1.1.1 Single Axis Solar Panel

Solar tracking systems can be classified by the mode of their motion. These tracking systems have the PV surface that can be rotated/tilted around axes to derive a proper angle that can help them get the maximum sunlight. When movement or adjustment of the PV surface happens by rotating around one axis, it is called single-axis tracking. When the movement of the PV surface happens around two axes simultaneously, it is called dual-axis tracking. Single axis solar tracker is a device that positions the panel in the direction of the sunlight to draw the maximum energy possible. As the name suggests, the tracker helps the solar panels to flex on the axis and change their angle with the Sun's direction. Simply put, the single axis solar tracking system allows the panels to move from east to west and improve energy production. It is much more efficient than fixed solar panel systems because compared to the latter, the single axis trackers generate up to 25-35% more electricity.

Figure 1. Single axis solar panel

1.1.2 Dual Axis Solar Panel

The dual axis trackers collect energy from the sun from the East, West, North, and South angles. They function on two axes – 'primary' and 'secondary'. One axis helps the solar tracker to move from East to West, and the other helps the tracker to move from North to South. Hence, they are known as 'dual-axis' solar trackers. You'll be surprised to know that the dual axis trackers can generate up to 40% more electricity than the unmovable solar panel systems that stay at a fixed position. A dual axis solar panel is a type of solar tracker. Solar trackers are used to track the sun as it moves through the sky. Solar trackers can be split into several categories based upon the type of actuation and axis of rotation. A typical dual axis solar panel can generate up to 40% more electricity than a static type, but costs perhaps 100% more and has larger maintenance costs. The amount of power required to move the solar panel must be deducted from the total amount of power gained in order to accurately record the total power gain.

Figure 2. Dual axis solar panel

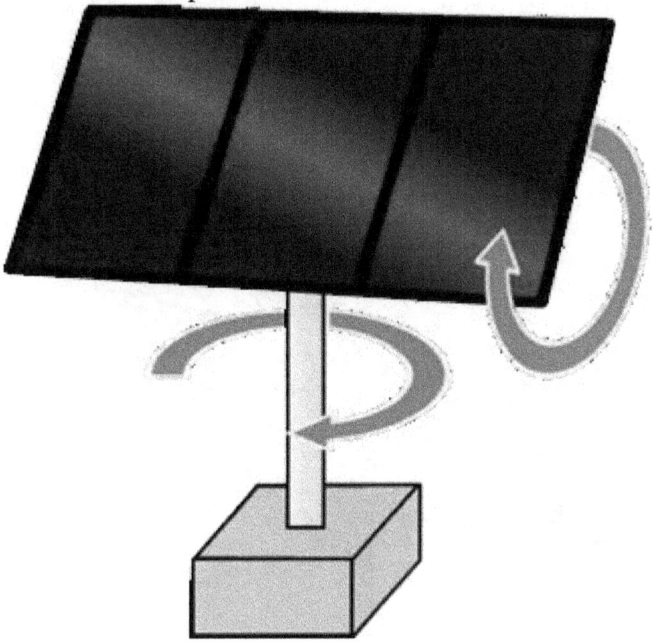

1.1.3 Active Solar Tracking

The words active and passive occur commonly in electrical engineering. Those devices which must be provided with source of energy for their full performance are classed as active. Those which do not need any external source of energy are called passive. Thus, active trackers must be provided with energy for their actuators to move. That energy may even be part of the energy harvested by the PV system they are driving. The actuator systems may consist of motors and other elaborate mechanical devices. Most tracking systems installations are active solar tracking systems. (Mamun et all, 2022). These tracking systems have an energy supply to run a motor or mechanical device. It helps to tilt the attached solar panels directly.

- An active solar tracker determines the intensity of the sunlight by utilizing light sensors.
- Then, its system evaluates where the solar modules should be oriented.

- Active solar trackers are ideally suitable for large and complicated solar arrays.

Figure 3. Active solar tracking

1.1.4 Passive Solar Tracking

Passive solar trackers will also track the sun, but they do it without requiring any external energy source, at least from us. How can they move the payload without energy. They do not! They too get their energy from the sun, but not the one we have harvested. Most often, the sun's heat is used to cause expansion of a fixed mass of material, Eg: a low boiling point gas. The expansion causes a mechanical movement of an actuator. A pair or more of actuators are positioned so that they expand differentially depending of the orientation of the payload tracker with respect to the sun. Differential expansion causes the tracker to move closer to the direction of the sun. If it derives its power from the sun how does it move at sunrise and sunset when there is virtually no solar energy to drive this dumb device. It is manually retained in a near vertical position with a self- releasing tie-down at night so that at daybreak when it gets sufficient differential energy, it can move down into position and then keep tracking. (Liu et all 2018) Passive trackers are OK for simple PV systems but unfit for concentration type PV systems which demand high aiming accuracy. Instead of gas expansion systems, actuators made of shape memory alloys (SMA), have also been used.

Figure 4. Passive solar tracking

LITERATURE SURVEY

(Amine Allouhi, et al . 2022) Photovoltaic (PV) technologies have achieved commercial acceptance, technological maturity and foresee a leading role in the current energy transition to combat the adverse environmental issues posed by fossil fuel-based power generation. The market of photovoltaic technology is rapidly evolving with a Compound Annual Growth Rate (CAGR) equal to 34% between 2010 and 2020. This review presents updated information on the solar PV development from the material, market, and engineering perspectives. Cell efficiencies, market trends, cost of PV systems, and global research efforts over the last years are provided. Real monitored performances reveal a decrease of up to 10% of PV power output due to soiling effects.

This paper discusses soiling mitigation approaches, a critical technical pathway to improve the power output of solar PV systems. A particular emphasis was put into recent and novel experimental and numerical investigations pursued by the PV research community related to heat management in PV systems. Finally, critical challenges and prospects of the solar PV technology are highlighted and discussed. the present review paper is to provide a comprehensive assessment of the solar PV technologies and its global market with updated information on relevant materials, observed efficiencies, and costs evolution.

(V.Karthikeyan, et al . 2020) Temperature reduction in a photovoltaic module can improve its efficiency. This paper presents a radiation based photovoltaic module cooled by using composite phase change material that are not in direct contact with the photovoltaic module. A thermal heat transfer network is developed which improves efficiency of the photovoltaic module by using radiation mode to eliminate the issue of phase change material re-conduction, thereby controlling excess thermal energy stagnation in the module. Pure phase change material and composite phase change material are investigated and compared by integrating them 0.6 cm behind the photovoltaic module and performing simulations to determine the optimal thickness of the phase change material matrix. It was found that by using composite phase change material, the thermal resistance between the photovoltaic and the phase change material could be reduced and the photovoltaic module temperature decreased, due to the higher thermal conductivity of the composite phase change material.

The simulated efficiency and temperature of the photovoltaic module with composite phase change material installed at the optimum thickness of 2.5 cm were 14.75% and 47.81 C, respectively. The numerical simulation of the new PV-PCM setup was validated experimentally, and simulation results were accurate within an average of 0.4 C.

(Kangmin Lee, et al . 2020) Transparent solar cells are attractive energy conversion devices because they can be used in various applications in our daily life, such as building- integrated photovoltaics (BIPV) and vehicle-integrated photovoltaics (VIPV). To date, transparent solar cells based on organic photovoltaics, dye-sensitized solar cells, and perovskite solar cells have been developed. Because most materials that are used in these solar cells could be easily made into thin films through the solution process, these thin films have light transmission properties. However, the transparent solar cells developed to date have limitations in power conversion efficiency (PCE) and stability. Furthermore, they exhibit specific colors as a result of the colors of the polymers or dyes used. To address this issue, some researchers have developed selective ultraviolet (UV)- or near-infrared (NIR)- absorbing transparent solar cells to fabricate neutral-colored transparent solar cells. However, UV- or NIR-absorbing transparent solar cells have demonstrated very low PCEs (<2%) until now. Accordingly, a different approach is required to develop transparent solar cells with neutral color, high PCE, and long-term stability.

As a method to develop neutral-colored transparent solar cells with high PCE and long-term stability, crystalline-silicon (*c*-Si)-based transparent solar cells could be considered. *c*-Si is a representative semiconductor widely used in various devices, such as transistors, integrated circuit chips, and solar cells owing to its abundance and high physical stability.

(Jiaxin Zhao, et al. 2019) In recent years, the utilization of phase change materials (PCMs) in photovoltaic (PV) module for thermal regulation has attracted wide attention in this field, as the hybrid PV-PCM technology can not only achieve higher photoelectric conversion efficiency but also make it possible to extract thermal energy stored in PCMs for cascade utilization. Although substantial research has been carried out on PV-PCM systems, the promise of practical application is still far from clear with some barriers unsolved, such as PCMs which need further improvements in both technical and economical view. In this paper, a comprehensive literature review of the state-of-the-art aspects of PV-PCM systems is presented, with the focus on technology overview and materials selection. The concept of hybrid PV-PCM system is first discussed with its general configuration and energy balance, to figure out the key factors affecting its performance. Besides, the development route of PV-PCM research is outlined through a comprehensive review of 104 research articles during 2004–2018, clarifying the representative achievements and existing problems in each stage.

Finally, the challenges and prospects of future research on PV-PCM systems are raised, advocating that more attention should be addressed on new strategies to overcome the existing problems such as insufficient reliability and economic feasibility.

(S.Mahmoudinezhad, et al, 2018) Transient response of a hybrid system composed of concentrated photovoltaic (CPV) cell and thermoelectric generator (TEG) is investigated in this study. This research is carried out by using a numerical simulation approach thermally coupled between the CPV and TEG. A transient model is established and solved by finite volume algorithm. In spite of temperatures profile in the hybrid CPV-TEG module, as results of variation of solar irradiation, power generation and efficiency of the CPV and TEG under the transient condition are presented.

The results show that efficiency of the TEG and CPV varies diversely versus changing the solar radiation and module temperature. Moreover, the thermal response of the TEG stabilizes temperature fluctuation of the hybrid module when the solar radiation rapidly changes. In this work, impact of the thermal contact resistance on the temperature profile and system efficiency is investigated. The model presented in this study provides a fundamental understanding of the thermal and electrical effect of the TEG in hybrid CPV-TEG module under transient conditions.

SYSTEM ARCHITECTURE

1.2 Flow Diagram

Figure 5. Flow diagram

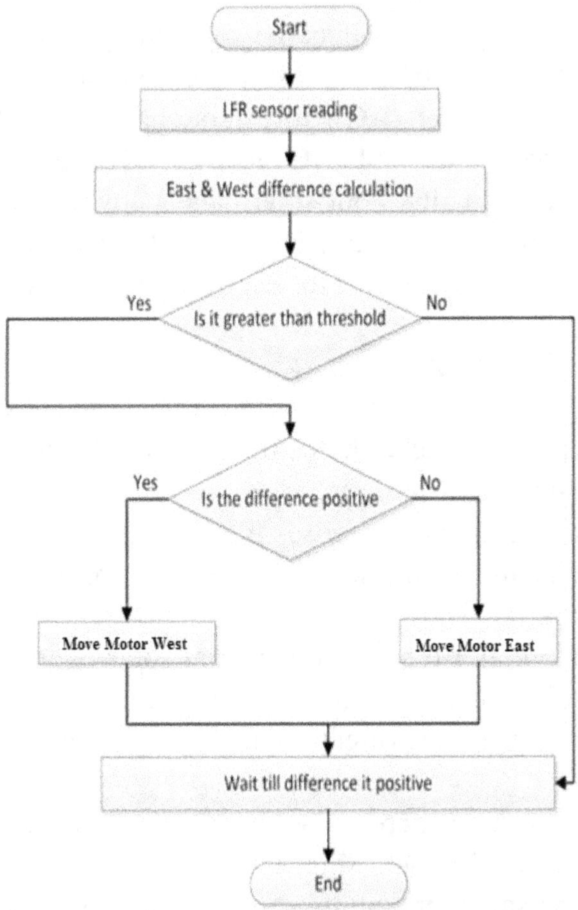

3.1 Existing System

The existing system is a fixed solar panel. These Solar panels convert the solar energy into electrical energy. There is a key component of the solar panel system.
Most commonly available panels of today are either poly-crystalline or mono- crystalline solar panels.
The cells in solar panels collect the solar energy and turn it into direct current (DC) electricity. Most homes and businesses, however, use alternating current (AC). Inverters change the DC electricity from your panels into usable AC electricity. Racking and mounting systems are used to affix your solar panels either to your roof or to the ground. (Singh et all 2021) They also allow you to position your panels at an angle that is best for capturing the sun's rays.

3.2 Proposed System

An automatic solar tracker helps by allowing the solar panel to automatically shift with sunlight.
An automatic solar tracker senses the sun's position and moves accordingly. This means the solar panel moves from east to west with respect to sun.
There are two major types of residential solar panel tracker: single axis and dual axis. The single axis solar tracker can move the angle of the tracker in one direction as the day progresses (Kim et all 2020).
These solar trackers increase solar panel's efficiency up to 25%-30% than the fixed panel. Solar trackers generate more electricity in roughly the same amount of space needed for fixed tilt systems, making them ideal optimizing land usage.

3.2.1 Advantages

Trackers generate more electricity than their stationary counterparts due to increased direct exposure to solar rays. (Awasthi et all 2022)

This increase can be as much as 10 to 25% depending on the geographic location of the tracking system.
There are many different kinds of solar trackers, such as single-axis and dual-axis trackers, all of which can be the perfect fit for a unique jobsite. Installation size, local weather, degree of latitude and electrical requirements are all important considerations that can influence the type of solar tracker best suited for a specific solar installation.
Solar trackers generate more electricity in roughly the same amount of space needed for fixed-tilt systems, making them ideal for optimizing land usage. (Abdalah et all 2017)
In certain states, some utilities offer Time of Use (TOU) rate plans for solar power, which means the utility will purchase the power generated during the peak time of the day at a higher rate. In this case, it is beneficial to generate a greater amount of electricity during these peak times of the day. Using a tracking system helps maximize the energy gains during these peak time periods.
Advancements in technology and reliability in electronics and mechanics have drastically reduced long-term maintenance concerns for tracking systems(Allouhi et all 2002).

4.1 System Requirements

4.1.1 Hardware Requirements

Arduino UNO
LDR
Solar Panel
Jumpers
Server motor
USB cable

4.1.2 Software Requiremets

Arduino IDE

4.2 Hardware Description

The Components used are,

Arduino UNO
LDR
Solar Panel
Jumpers
Server motor
USB cable

4.2.1 Arduino UNO

Arduino UNO is a low-cost, flexible, and easy-to-use programmable open- source microcontroller board that can be integrated into a variety of electronic projects. This board can be interfaced with other Arduino boards, Arduino shields, Raspberry Pi boards and can control relays, LEDs, servos, and motors as an output.

Arduino UNO features AVR microcontroller Atmega328, 6 analogue input pins, and 14 digital I/O pins out of which 6 are used as PWM output.
This board contains a USB interface i.e USB cable is used to connect the board with the computer and Arduino IDE (Integrated Development Environment) software is used to program the board.
The unit comes with 32KB flash memory that is used to store the number of instructions while the SRAM is 2KB and EEPROM is 1KB.
The operating voltage of the unit is 5V which projects the microcontroller on the board and its associated circuitry operates at 5V while the input voltage ranges between 6V to 20V and the recommended input voltage ranges from 7V to 12V.

4.2.1.1 Arduino UNO Components:

Figure 6. Components of Arduino UNO

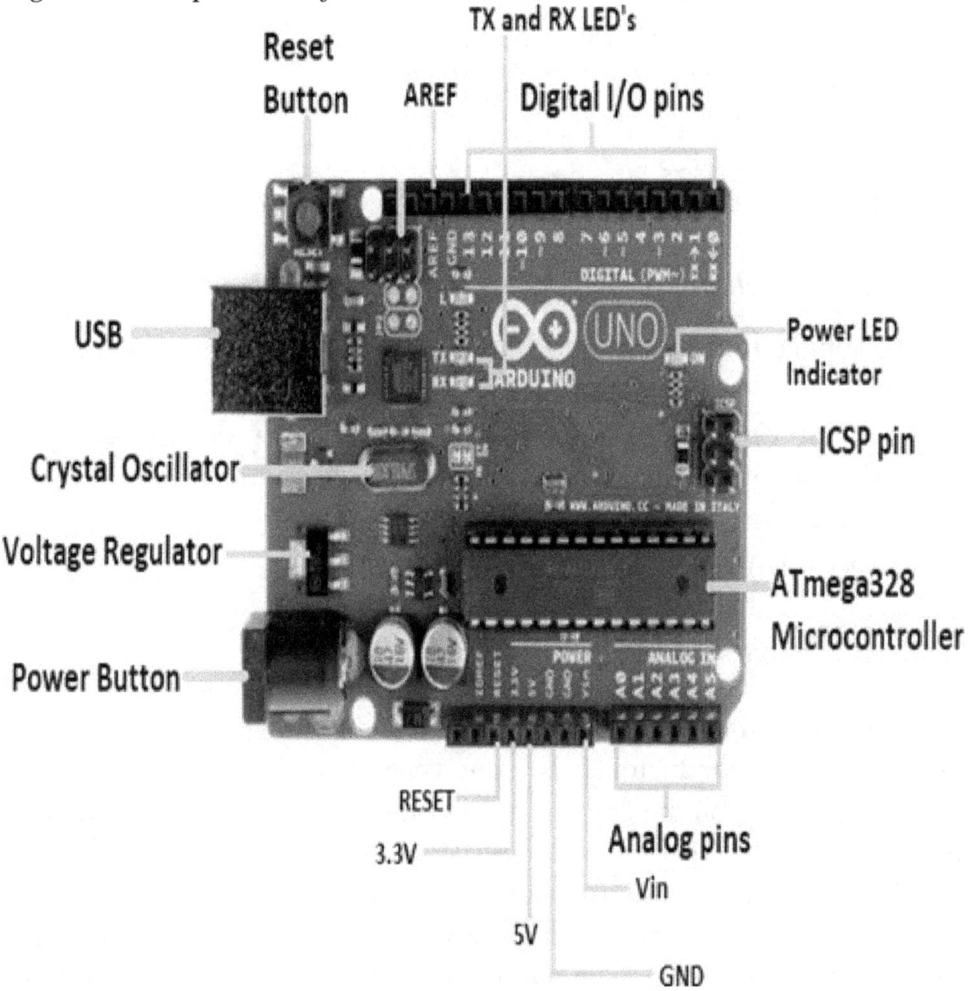

4.2.1.4. Features of Arduino Uno Board

The features of Arduino Uno ATmega328 includes the following.

The operating voltage is 5V
The recommended input voltage will range from 7v to 12V
The input voltage ranges from 6v to 20V

Digital input/output pins are 14
Analog i/p pins are 6
DC Current for each input/output pin is 40 mA
DC Current for 3.3V Pin is 50 mA
Flash Memory is 32 KB
SRAM is 2 KB
EEPROM is 1 KB
CLK Speed is 16 MH

4.2.1.5 Applications of Arduino Uno ATmega328

The applications of Arduino Uno include the following.

Arduino Uno is used in Do-it-Yourself projects prototyping.
In developing projects based on code-based control
Development of Automation System
Designing of basic circuit designs.

4.3.1 LDR (Light Dependent Resistor)

An LDR or light dependent resistor is also known as photo resistor, photocell, photoconductor. It is a one type of resistor whose resistance varies depending on the amount of light falling on its surface. When the light falls on the resistor, then the resistance changes. These resistors are often used in many circuits where it is required to sense the presence of light. These resistors have a variety of functions and resistance. For instance, when the LDR is in darkness, then it can be used to turn ON a light or to turn OFF a light when it is in the light. A typical light dependent resistor has a resistance in the darkness of 1MOhm, and in the brightness a resistance of a couple of KOhm.

This resistor works on the principle of photo conductivity. It is nothing but, when the light falls on its surface, then the material conductivity reduces and also the electrons in the valence band of the device are excited to the conduction band. These photons in the incident light must have energy greater than the band gap of the semiconductor material. This makes the electrons to jump from the valence band to conduction.

These devices depend on the light, when light falls on the LDR then the resistance decreases, and increases in the dark.When a LDR is kept in the dark place, its resistance is high and, when the LDR is kept in the light its resistance will decrease.

A photoresistor or light dependent resistor is an electronic component that is sensitive to light. When light falls upon it, then the resistance changes. Values of the resistance of the LDR may change over many orders of magnitude the value of the resistance falling as the level of light increases.

It is not uncommon for the values of resistance of an LDR or photoresistor to be several megohms in darkness and then to fall to a few hundred ohms in bright light.

With such a wide variation in resistance, LDRs are easy to use and there are many LDR circuits available. The sensitivity of light dependent resistors or photoresistors also varies with the wavelength of the incident light.

LDRs are made from semiconductor materials to enable them to have their light sensitive properties. Many materials can be used, but one popular material for these photoresistors is cadmium sulphide, CdS, although the use of these cells is now restricted in Europe because of environmental issues with the use of cadmium.Similarly other cadmium based semiconductor materials like cadmium CdSe are also restricted. Other materials that can be used include lead sulphide, PbS and indium antimonide, InSb.

Although a semiconductor material is used for these photoresistors, they are purely passive devices because they do not possess a PN junction, and this separates them from other photodetectors like photodiodes and phototransistors.

Figure 7. LDR (Light dependent resistor)

4.4.1 Solar Panel

A solar panel, or solar module, is one component of a photovoltaic system. They are constructed out of a series of photovoltaic cells arranged into a panel. They come in a variety of rectangular shapes and are installed in combination to generate electricity. Solar panels, sometimes also called photovoltaic collect energy from the Sun in the form of sunlight and convert it into electricity that can be used to power homes or businesses. These panels can be used to supplement a building's electricity or provide power at remote locations. (Chng et all 2019)

In addition to residential and commercial use, there is large-scale industrial or utility use of solar. In this case, thousands or even millions of solar panels are arranged into a vast solar array, or solar farm, which provides electricity to large urban populations.

The main component of any solar panel is a solar cell. Specifically, a number of solar cells are used to build a single solar panel. These cells are the part of the device that convert the sunlight into electricity. Most solar panels are made from crystalline silicon type solar cells.These cells are composed of layers of silicon, phosphorous, and boron (although there are several different types of photovoltaic cells). These cells, once produced, are laid out into a grid pattern.

The number of these cells used depends largely on the size of the panel being created, as many different sizing options exist.

Figure 8. Solar panel

Once the cells are laid out, the panel itself is sealed to protect the cells within and covered with a non-reflective glass. This glass protects the solar cells from damage, and is non-reflective to ensure sunlight can still reach the cells. Once sealed, this panel is placed into a rigid metallic frame. This frame is designed to prevent deformation, and includes a drainage hole to prevent water from building up on the panel as a buildup of water could reduce the efficiency of the panel.

4.4.1.1 Solar panel works

Solar panels act as a way to mount a series of solar cells so that their unique properties can be used to generate electricity. Individual cells absorb photons from the Sun, which results in the production of an electric current in the cell through a phenomenon known as the photovoltaic effect.An inverter is used to convert the direct current generated by a solar panel into alternating current. Combined, these two technologies create a photovoltaic system.When installing a solar panel, the proper orientation is chosen so that the solar panel faces in a direction that is most suitable for the specific application. This is most often to produce the maximum annual energy, but is not always the case.

4.5.1 Jumpers

Jumper wires are simply wires that have connector pins at each end, allowing them to be used to connect two points to each other without soldering. Jumper wires are typically used with breadboards and other prototyping tools in order to make it easy to change a circuit as needed. Though jumper wires come in a variety of colors, the colors don't actually mean anything. This means that a red jumper wire is technically the same as a black one. But the colors can be used to your advantage in order to differentiate between types of connections, such as ground or power.

4.5.1.1 Functions of Jumpers

When you set a jumper, you place a plug on the prongs that completes a contact. In effect, the jumper acts as a switch by closing (or opening) an electrical circuit. Jumpers can be added or removed to change the function or performance of a PC component. A group of jumpers is sometimes called a jumper block .

Jumper Connection:

A jumper is a tiny metal connector that is used to close or open part of an electrical circuit. It may be used as an alternative to a dual in-line package (DIP) switch. A jumper has two or more connecting points, which regulate an electrical circuit board.

Jumper wires in Arduino

Jumper wires are used for making connections between items on your breadboard and your Arduino's header pins. Use them to wire up all your circuits! Buy jumper wires from Amazon, SparkFun, Adafruit, or Newark.

4.6.1 Servo Motor

A servo motor is a type of motor that can rotate with great precision. Normally this type of motor consists of a control circuit that provides feedback on the current position of the motor shaft, this feedback allows the servo motors to rotate with great precision. If you want to rotate an object at some specific angles or distance, then you use a servo motor. It is just made up of a simple motor which runs through a servo mechanism. If motor is powered by a DC power supply then it is called DC servo motor, and if it is AC-powered motor then it is called AC servo motor. For this tutorial, we will be discussing only about the DC servo motor working. Apart from these major classifications, there are many other types of servo motors based on the type of gear arrangement and operating characteristics.

Figure 9. Servo motor

A servo motor usually comes with a gear arrangement that allows us to get a very high torque servo motor in small and lightweight packages. Due to these features, they are being used in many applications like toy car, RC helicopters and planes, Robotics, etc.

Servo motors are rated in kg/cm (kilogram per centimeter) most hobby servo motors are rated at 3kg/cm or 6kg/cm or 12kg/cm. This kg/cm tells you how much weight your servo motor can lift at a particular distance. For example: A 6kg/cm Servo motor should be able to lift 6kg if the load is suspended 1cm away from the motors shaft, the greater the distance the lesser the weight carrying capacity. The position of a servo motor is decided by electrical pulse and its circuitry is placed beside the motor.

4.6.1.1 Servo Motor Working Mechanism

It consists of three parts:

1. Controlled device
2. Output sensor
3. Feedback system

> It is a closed-loop system where it uses a positive feedback system to control motion and the final position of the shaft. Here the device is controlled by a feedback signal generated by comparing output signal and reference input signal.

Here reference input signal is compared to the reference output signal and the third signal is produced by the feedback system. And this third signal acts as an input signal to the control the device. This signal is present as long as the feedback signal is generated or there is a difference between the reference input signal and reference output signal. So the main task of servomechanism is to maintain the output of a system at the desired value at presence of noises.

4.6.1.2 Servo Motor Working Principle

A servo consists of a Motor (DC or AC), a potentiometer, gear assembly, and a controlling circuit. First of all, we use gear assembly to reduce RPM and to increase torque of the motor. Say at initial position of servo motor shaft, the position of the potentiometer knob is such that there is no electrical signal generated at the output port of the potentiometer. Now an electrical signal is given to another input terminal of the error detector amplifier. Now the difference between these two signals, one comes from the potentiometer and another comes from other sources, will be processed in a feedback mechanism and output will be provided in terms of error signal. This error signal acts as the input for motor and motor starts rotating. Now motor shaft is connected with the potentiometer and as the motor rotates so the potentiometer and it will generate a signal. So as the potentiometer's angular position changes, its output feedback signal changes. After sometime the position of potentiometer reaches at a position that the output of potentiometer is same as external signal provided. At this condition, there will be no output signal from the amplifier to the motor input as there is no difference between external applied signal and the signal generated at potentiometer, and in this situation motor stops rotating.

4.6.1.3 Interfacing Servo Motors with Microcontrollers:

Interfacing hobby Servo motors like s90 servo motor with MCU is very easy. Servos have three wires coming out of them. Out of which two will be used for Supply (positive and negative) and one will be used for the signal that is to be sent from the MCU. An MG995 Metal Gear Servo Motor which is most commonly used for RC cars humanoid bots etc. The picture of MG995 is shown below:

Figure 10. Servo motors with microcontrollers

The color coding of your servo motor might differ hence check for your respective datasheet.

All servo motors work directly with your +5V supply rails but we have to be careful on the amount of current the motor would consume if you are planning to use more than two servo motors a proper servo shield should be designed.

4.6.1.4 Controlling Servo Motor:

All motors have three wires coming out of them. Out of which two will be used for Supply (positive and negative) and one will be used for the signal that is to be sent from the MCU.

Servo motor is controlled by PWM (Pulse with Modulation) which is provided by the control wires. There is a minimum pulse, a maximum pulse and a repetition rate. Servo motor can turn 90 degrees from either direction form its neutral position. The servo motor expects to see a pulse every 20 milliseconds (ms) and the length of the pulse will determine how far the motor turns. For example, a 1.5ms pulse will make the motor turn to the 90° position, such as if pulse is shorter than 1.5ms shaft moves to 0° and if it is longer than 1.5ms than it will turn the servo to 180°.

Servo motor works on PWM (Pulse width modulation) principle, means its angle of rotation is controlled by the duration of applied pulse to its Control PIN. Basically servo motor is made up of DC motor which is controlled by a variable resistor (potentiometer) and some gears. High speed force of DC motor is converted into torque by Gears. We know that WORK= FORCE X DISTANCE, in DC motor Force is less and distance (speed) is high and in Servo, force is High and distance is less. The potentiometer is connected to the output shaft of the Servo, to calculate the angle and stop the DC motor on the required angle.

Figure 11. Controlling servo motor

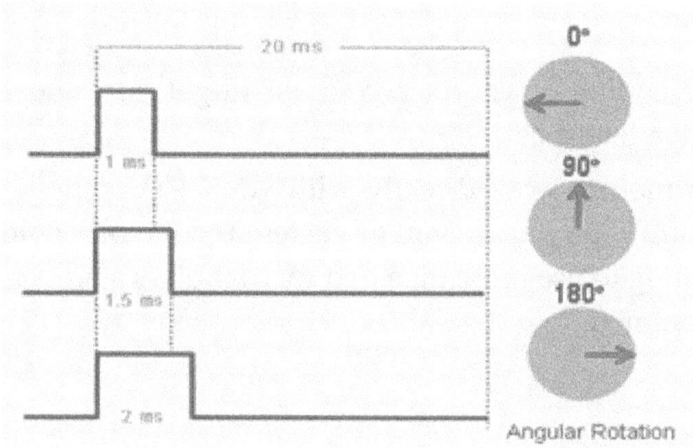

Servo motor can be rotated from 0 to 180 degrees, but it can go up to 210 degrees, depending on the manufacturing. This degree of rotation can be controlled by applying the Electrical Pulse of proper width, to its Control pin. Servo checks the pulse in every 20 milliseconds. The pulse of 1 ms (1 millisecond) width can rotate the servo to 0 degrees, 1.5ms can rotate to 90 degrees (neutral position) and 2 ms pulse can rotate it to 180 degrees.

All servo motors work directly with your +5V supply rails but we have to be careful about the amount of current the motor would consume if you are planning to use more than two servo motors a proper servo shield should be designed.

SYSTEM IMPLEMENTATION

The system does not need any power supply externally but only the sun light. All the components depend up on each other in the operation. The produced energy is supplied for the system operation and as well as to drive the load. The solar energy collected by the panel is converted into electrical energy; the collected energy is charged into a DC Battery. The motor, sensors, tracker and other components of the system is supplied by the battery to operate.

Figure 12. System functional implementation diagram

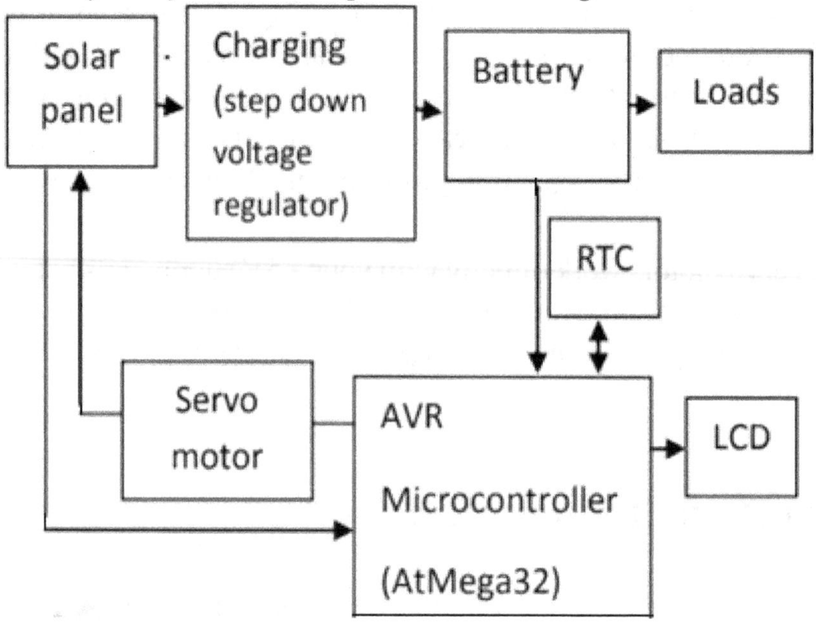

The tracking of the sun undergoes many steps. A microcontroller is used to calculate the maximum radiation of the sun. It is connected to a servo motor and LDR's to redirect the panel to the sun. The system sends the received data to the servo motor to rotate the panel towards to the sun. The position tangles are saved in registers of the microcontroller and can be displayed on the LCD. All the hardware resources like servo motor, LCD, RTC, LDR sensors are interfaced to the microcontroller. We use two light dependent resistors in the system for the detection of maximum sun light. These LDR's were placed on the solar panel, arranged each one facing east and west directions respectively. (Lee et all 2020). The tracker will measure the values of the LDR's and according to the light intensity levels gathered by the sensors; it will start rotating towards the higher intensity levels of the sun servo motor is used to rotate the panel in the system. Servo motor consists of a DC motor, gear box and a control circuitry. The servo motor works according to the pulses generated by the microcontroller.

5.1 Modules

Figure 13. Block diagram

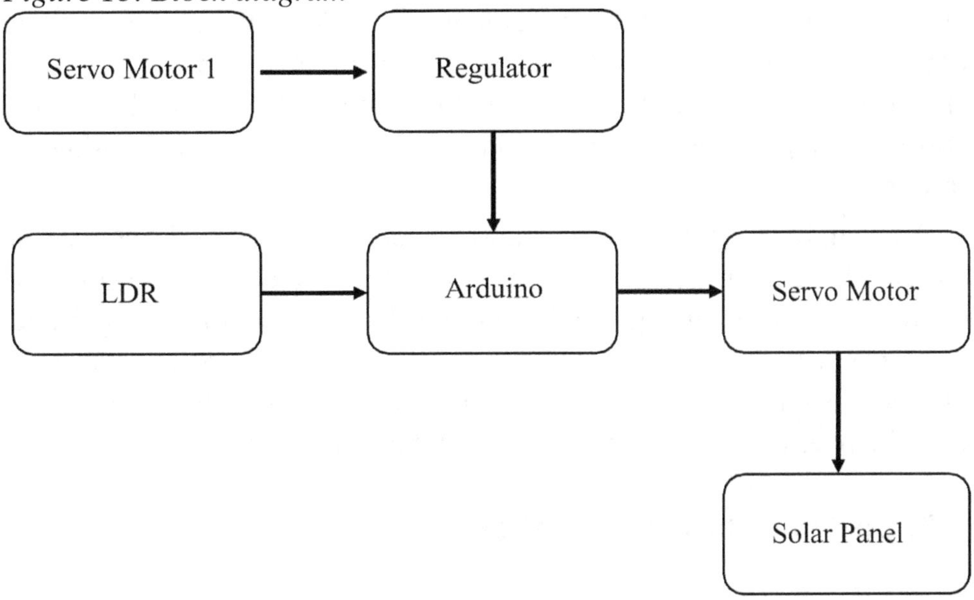

The goal of this investigation is to propose a methodology that maintains the photovoltaic (PV)value within an adequate range of Energy for Opportunity (EFO) by developing a strategy for designing a low-precision, high-efficiency PV tracking system mechanism and facilitating the instrumentation and control required for this prototype(Ma, et all 2019). This proposed methodology is based on the effect of misalignment error with respect to PV efficiency and the Norton design methodology; complementary modifications of the process, directions for the developer, as well as instrumentation and control requirements that are based on the knowledge of and devices available to the developer are made using the sequential steps.

The single axis solar tracker is the apparatus in which the sun powered board tracks the sun from east to west utilizing a solitary turn point to pivot. Under this framework there are three sorts: Horizontal single pivot following framework, Vertical single hub following framework and Tilted single hub following framework. (Karthikeyan et all 2020) In the Horizontal framework the hub of turn is flat concerning the ground, and the substance of the module is arranged corresponding to the pivot of revolution.

In the Vertical framework the hub of turn is vertical regarding the ground and the essence of the module is arranged at a point as for the hub of pivot while In the Tilted following framework the pivot is among flat and vertical and this additionally has the essence of the module situated corresponding to the hub of revolution, like the Horizontal following framework.

The single hub following framework comprises of two LDR's set on either side of the board. Contingent upon the force of the sunbeams one of the two LDR's will be shadowed and the other will be enlightened. The LDR with the most extreme force of the sun's radiation imparts more grounded sign to the controller which thus imparts sign to the engine to turn the board toward the path in which the sun's power is greatest.

5.3. Software Implementation

The Arduino Integrated Development Environment - or Arduino Software (IDE) - contains a text editor for writing code, a message area, a text console, a toolbar with buttons for common functions and a series of menus. It connects to the Arduino hardware to upload programs and communicate with them.

The code is uploaded in Arduino IDE and it upload to give the air temperature and air humidity level in the serial monitor in Arduino ID

Figure 14a. Software implementation

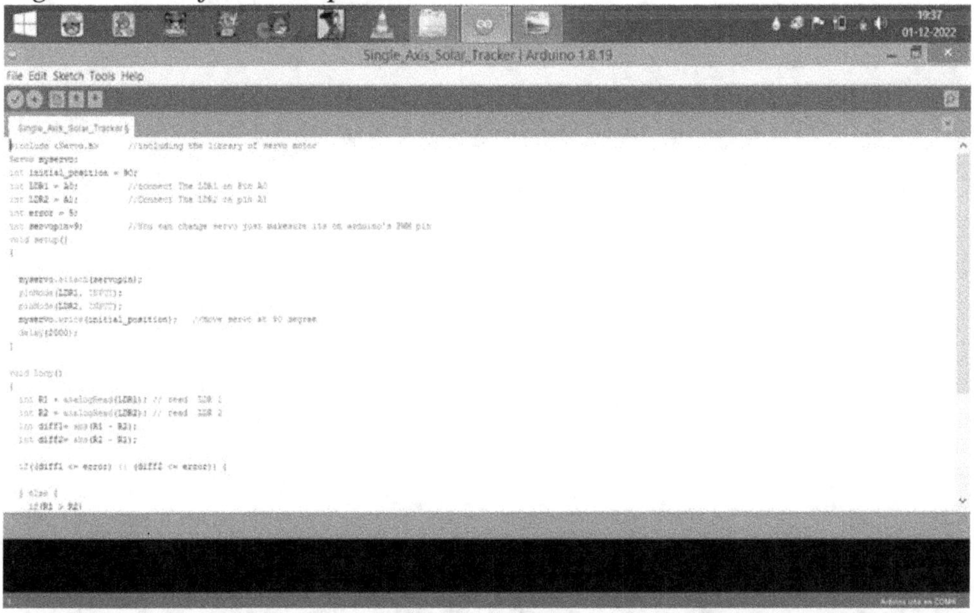

Figure 14b. Software implementation

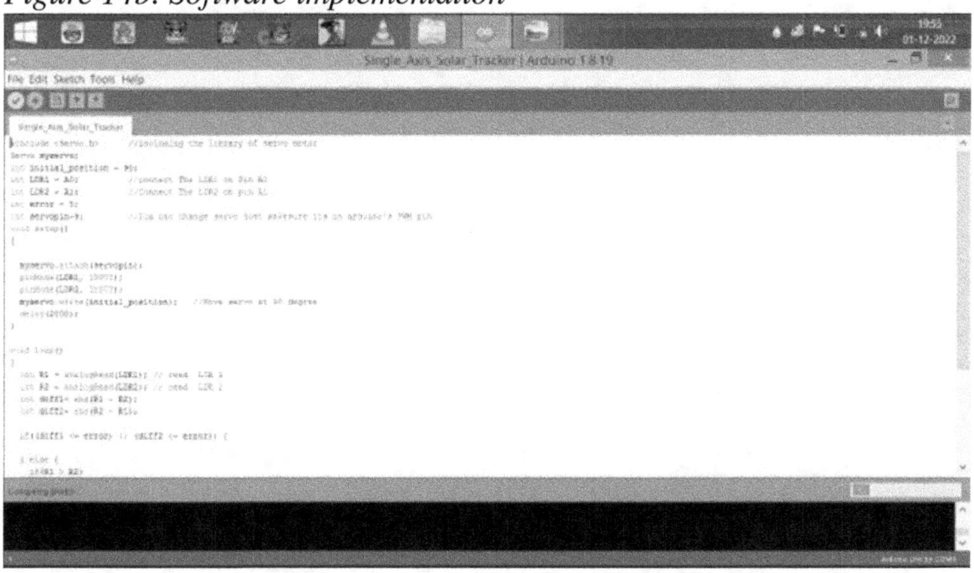

Figure 14c. Software implementation (Execution phase)

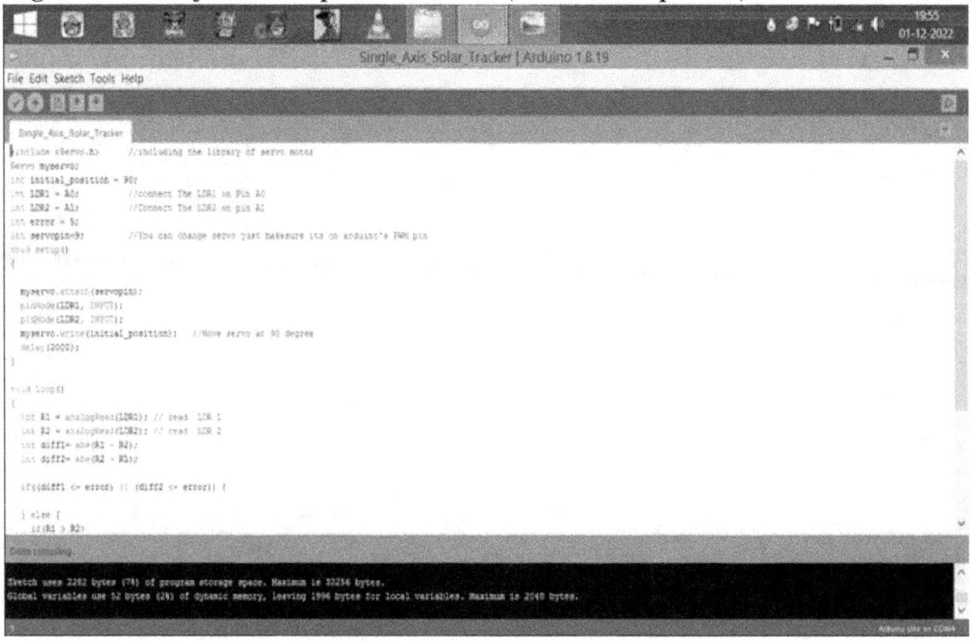

RESULT AND DISCUSSIONS

6.1 Result

Solar tracking output in Arduino IDE:

Figure 15. Final implementation

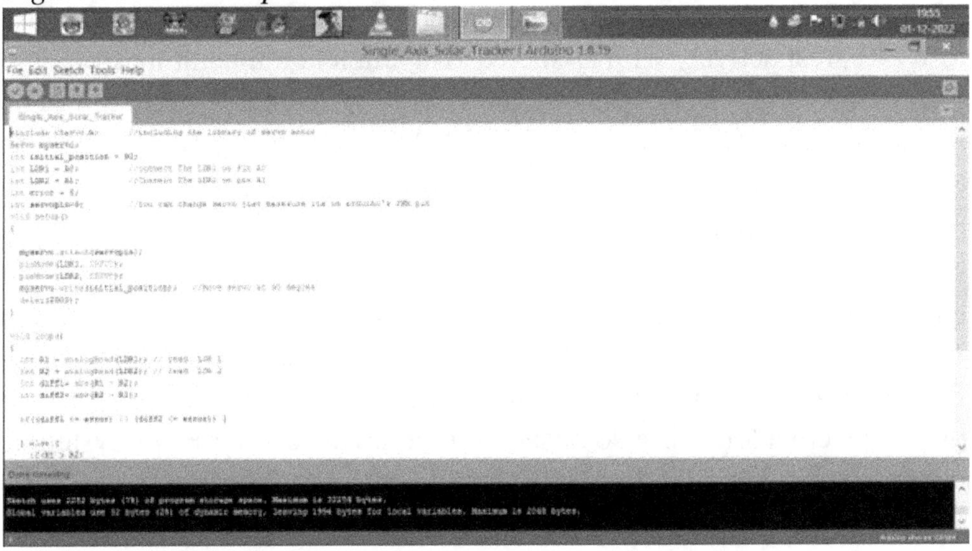

Figure 16. Single axis solar tracker

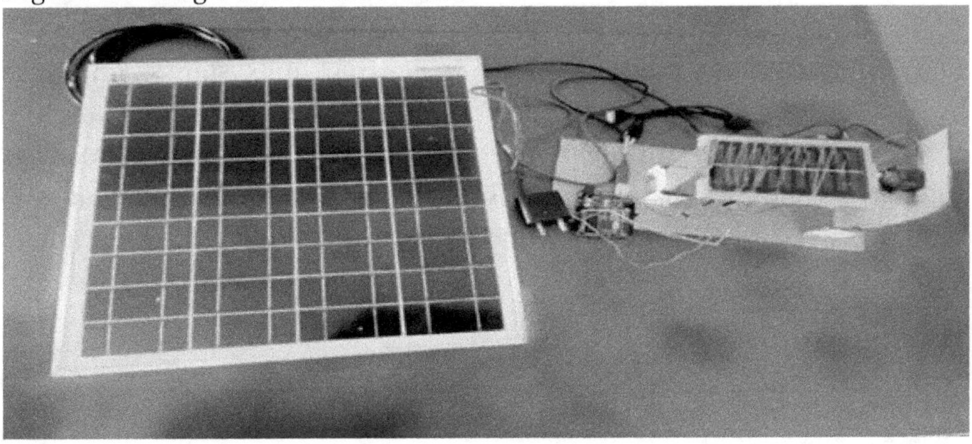

6.2 Discussions

Model has been simulated by using Proteus software to track solar energy. Using the solar tracking the solar energy will be collected in batteries very effectively. The ambient temperature plays an important role in the performance of any system. The energy and energy efficiency of electrical and thermal systems vary with a rise in ambient temperature.

The electrical energy efficiency is seen to be a constant at 9.46% whereas electrical energy efficiency is found to be decreasing from 9.04% to 7.74%, respectively with an increase in ambient temperature from 280 K to 310 K. The thermal energy and energy efficiencies are found to be increasing from 5.89% to 61.65% and 1.28% to 11.6%, respectively with a rise in ambient temperature.

The overall energy and energy efficiencies are found to be increasing with a rise in ambient temperature as displayed. The overall energy and energy efficiencies are found to be increasing from 15.36% to 71.11% and 11.22% to 21.59%, respectively with a rise in ambient temperature. These figures show that a rise in ambient temperature affects the performance of the system a lot. It is also observed that having a solar PV/T system is better than having an individual solar PV or thermal system.

CONCLUSION AND FUTURE ENHANCEMENT

7.1 Conclusion

We predicted that the efficiency of solar tracking system is improved by 30- 40% and it was found that all the parts of the experimental setup are given the good results. Moreover, this tracking system does track the sun in the continues manner. And this system is more efficient and low-cost effective in long run. From the result it is found that, by automatic tracking system, there is 30% gain in increase efficiency when compared with non-tracking system.

Dual Axis Solar Tracker using LDR with Arduino UNO. The use of stepper motor rather than linear actuator helps to improve the overall tracker performance. The architecture assists by monitoring using a dual axis sensor to draw the full power from the solar radiation. This is possible because the solar panel is still correctly aligned with sun's incident rays. This is well adapted from the idea of the solar tracking device for harnessing more energy than a fixed solar panel. It is tried to develop a easy and low-cost tracking system. In recent years, solar radiation tracker has played a critical role in rising the performance of solar panels, thereby proving to be a better technical feat.

A dual axis solar tracker's clinical significance lies in its better efficiency and durability to produce higher performance compared to a fived solar panel or solar tracker with one single axis. The tracking system is planned so that the solar energy can be trapped in any possible direction. In general, the maximum solar energy can't be tracked in a single axis tracker that travels only along a single axis. If the solar rays are perpendicular to the panel over the whole year in the case of dual axis trackers. As a result, it generates much energy as possible than it lost in the day as is throughout the year. Therefore, the performance increases suggesting that the efficiency is greater than a fixed solar panel (around 30-40% more) or a single solar tracker axis (around 6-7% more)

7.2 Future Enhancement

With a modification in the design and development, the paper work can be enhanced further, Real Time Clock (RTC) can be interfaced rather than sensors used for seasonal tracking here. Using more powerful motors, the tracking capability and lifetime can be increased, but it will be a little bit costly. But in place of the microcontroller board, using Arduino will make it cheaper, although it will be complicated. Solar trackers, whether single-axis or dual-axis, will help to achieve the optimum solar energy level. Today, it seems very right when it comes to the future of the solar tracker industry.

The goals of this project were a purposely kept within what was believed to be attainable within the allotted timeline. As such, many advance improvements can be made up of initial design of solar tracker. It is felt this design represents a functioning scale model which could be replicated for a much larger scale.

REFERENCES

Abdalah, S., & Niimeh, S. (2017). Sun tracking device two axes with Arduino. *Power. Energy Conversion and Management*, *45*, 1931–1939. DOI: 10.1016/j.enconman.2003.10.007

Allouhi, A., Rehman, S., & Buker, M. S. (2002). Solar PV system: A review. *Renewable & Sustainable Energy Reviews*, *20*, 35–55. DOI: 10.1016/j.rser.2017.06.001

Allouhi, A., Rehman, S., Buker, M. S., & Said, Z. (2022). Up-to-date literature review on solar PV systems: Technology progress, market status, and R&D. *Journal of Cleaner Production*, *362*, 132339. DOI: 10.1016/j.jclepro.2022.132339

Awasthi, A., Kallioğlu, M.A., Sharma, A., Mohan, A., Chauhan, R. & Singh, T. , (2022). Solar collector tilt angle optimization for solar power plant setup-able sites at Western Himalaya and correlation formulation. *Journal of Thermal Analysis and Calorimetry*, *147*(20), 11417–11431. DOI: 10.1007/s10973-022-11345-0

Chng, K. K., Siew, F. L., Woong, C. W., & Woong, G. S. (2019). Solar tracing device design and installation. *Renewable Energy*, *34*, 1364–1370. DOI: 10.1016/j.renene.2019.03.004

Karthikeyan, V., & Kalidasa Murugavel, K. (2020). Reducing PV module temperature with radiation-based PV module incorporated composite phase change material. *Materials Today: Proceedings*, *33*(Part 7), 4774–4779. DOI: 10.1016/j.matpr.2020.01.389

Karthikeyan, V., & Sirisamphanwong, C. (2020). Reducing PV module temperature with radiation-based PV module incorporated composite phase change material. *Energy Reports*, *6*, 56–64. DOI: 10.1016/j.egyr.2020.10.008

Kim, G. Y., Han, D. S., & Lee, Z. (2020). Solar panel tilt angle optimization using machine learning model: A case study of Daegu City, South Korea. *Energies*, *13*(3), 529. DOI: 10.3390/en13030529

Lee, K., Kim, N., & Kim, K. (2020). Neutral colored transparent crystalline silicon photovoltaics. *Energy Reports*, *6*, 201–207. DOI: 10.1016/j.egyr.2020.09.044

Lee, K., Kim, N., Kim, K., & Seo, K. (2020). Neutral-colored transparent crystalline silicon photovoltaics. *Joule*, *4*(1), 235–246. DOI: 10.1016/j.joule.2019.11.008

Liu, H., Xu, X., Meng, Y., Yu, D., Liu, H., & Shi, K. (2018). A research for the influence of tilt angles of the solar panel on photovoltaic power generation. In *2018 International Conference on Smart Grid and Clean Energy Technologies (ICSGCE)* (pp. 95-100). IEEE. DOI: 10.1109/ICSGCE.2018.8556655

Ma, T., Li, Z., & Zhao, J. (2019). Photovoltaic panel integrated with phase change material technology. *Applied Energy*, *238*, 321–329. DOI: 10.1016/j.apenergy.2018.12.021

Mahmoudinezhad, S., Rezania, A., & Mahmoudinezhad, R. (2018). Behaviour of hybrid concentrated photovoltaic-thermoelectric generator under variable solar radiation. *Energy Conversion and Management*, *164*, 21–33. DOI: 10.1016/j.enconman.2018.03.025

Mamun, M. A. A., Islam, M. M., Hasanuzzaman, M., & Selvaraj, J. (2022). Effect of tilt angle on the performance and electrical parameters of a PV module: Comparative indoor and outdoor experimental investigation. *Energy and Built Environment*, *3*(3), 278–290. DOI: 10.1016/j.enbenv.2021.02.001

Singh, D., Singh, A. K., Singh, S. P., & Poonia, S. (2021). Optimization of tilt angles for solar devices to gain maximum solar energy in Indian climate. In P. V. Baredar, S. Tangellapalli, & C. S. Solanki (Eds.), *Advances in Clean Energy Technologies*. Springer Proceedings in Energy. Springer, Singapore. DOI: 10.1007/978-981-16-0235-1_16

Zhao, J., Ma, T., Yang, H., & Zhang, X. (2019). Experimental study and performance analysis on solar photovoltaic panel integrated with phase change material. *Energy*, *178*, 471–486. DOI: 10.1016/j.energy.2019.04.166

KEY TERMS AND DEFINITIONS

PV System: Solar panels are photovoltaic cells which gives voltage directly if you place them in sunlight.

Time of Use (TOU): Time of Use (TOU) rate plans for solar power, which means the utility will purchase the power generated during the peak time of the day at a higher rate.

Light Dependent Resistor (LDR): light dependent resistor is also known as photo resistor, photocell, photoconductor.

Energy for Opportunity (EFO): developing a strategy for designing a low-precision, high-efficiency PV tracking system mechanism and facilitating the instrumentation and control.

Real Time Clock (RTC): can be interfaced rather than sensors used for seasonal tracking here. Using more powerful motors, the tracking capability and lifetime can be increased

Chapter 8
Advanced Technologies for Sustainability and Environment

Oussama Wali
https://orcid.org/0009-0002-3197-0360
University of Tübingen, Germany

Mohamed Saifeddine Hadj Sassi
IT for Innovative Services Department, Luxembourg Institute of Science and Technology, Luxembourg

ABSTRACT

The pressing challenges of climate change, resource depletion, and environmental degradation necessitate innovative solutions that harness advanced technologies to promote sustainability and mitigate adverse environmental impacts. This article explores the diverse array of advanced technologies that hold promise for addressing key sustainability and environmental challenges. From renewable energy systems and smart grid technologies to sustainable agriculture practices and green manufacturing processes, these cutting-edge technologies offer opportunities to transition towards a more sustainable and resilient future. By leveraging the power of artificial intelligence, Internet of Things (IoT), and advanced materials, these technologies enable more efficient resource utilization, reduce greenhouse gas emissions, and enhance environmental conservation efforts. This article

DOI: 10.4018/979-8-3693-8141-0.ch008

provides an overview of key advanced technologies for sustainability and environment, highlighting their potential benefits, challenges, and implications for addressing pressing global environmental issues.

1. INTRODUCTION

The accelerating pace of global environmental change, driven by factors such as climate change, biodiversity loss, and pollution, underscores the urgent need for innovative solutions to promote sustainability and environmental resilience. These changes pose significant threats to ecosystems, human health, and the global economy, necessitating a concerted effort to develop and implement strategies that can mitigate adverse impacts and support sustainable development.

Advanced technologies play a pivotal role in this endeavor, offering transformative solutions to address pressing environmental challenges. Technologies such as renewable energy systems, smart grids, precision agriculture, and green infrastructure have the potential to revolutionize the way we interact with and manage our natural resources. By harnessing the power of these technologies, we can significantly reduce greenhouse gas emissions, conserve biodiversity, and enhance the resilience of communities to environmental stressors.

Renewable energy technologies, including solar, wind, hydro, and geothermal power, are at the forefront of the transition to a low-carbon economy. These technologies provide clean, sustainable alternatives to fossil fuels, helping to reduce the carbon footprint of energy production and consumption. Smart grid technology, which integrates renewable energy sources with advanced data analytics and grid management systems, further enhances the efficiency and reliability of energy distribution.

In the agricultural sector, precision farming techniques utilize sensors, drones, and data analytics to optimize crop yields, reduce water and fertilizer usage, and minimize environmental impact. This approach not only improves food security but also promotes the sustainable use of agricultural resources, thereby protecting ecosystems and biodiversity.

Green infrastructure, including green roofs, urban forests, and permeable pavements, offers innovative solutions for managing stormwater, reducing urban heat islands, and enhancing urban biodiversity. These nature-based solutions provide multiple ecosystem services, contributing to climate adaptation and improving the quality of life in urban areas.

In addition to these specific technologies, the integration of big data, artificial intelligence, and the Internet of Things (IoT) in environmental monitoring and management enables more accurate and timely decision-making. These technologies facilitate the collection, analysis, and interpretation of vast amounts of environmental data, supporting proactive and adaptive management strategies.

This article provides a comprehensive overview of advanced technologies for sustainability and the environment, examining their applications, benefits, and implications for achieving environmental sustainability and resilience. We explore how these technologies can be effectively deployed to address a wide range of environmental challenges, from mitigating climate change and preserving biodiversity to managing natural resources and promoting sustainable urban development. By highlighting successful case studies and emerging trends, we aim to illustrate the transformative potential of advanced technologies in fostering a sustainable future.

2. RENEWABLE ENERGY SYSTEMS

Renewable energy systems represent a cornerstone of sustainable energy production, offering a clean and inexhaustible alternative to fossil fuels. This section delves into the various types of renewable energy sources and the technologies driving their deployment.

2.1 Solar Energy

Solar energy, derived from sunlight, stands as one of the most abundant and promising renewable energy sources. This subsection explores the various aspects of solar energy utilization, encompassing both PhotoVoltaic (PV) and Concentrating Solar Power (CSP) technologies.

2.1.1 Photovoltaic (PV) Systems

Photovoltaic systems directly convert sunlight into electricity using semiconductor materials, predominantly silicon-based solar cells. Recent advancements in PV technology have significantly enhanced the efficiency and cost-effectiveness of solar panels, driving down the Levelized Cost OfElectricity (LCOE) associated with solar energy generation. Innovations in PV cell design, such as PERC (Passivated Emitter Rear Cell) and bifacial cells, have improved light absorption and energy conversion efficiency, while thin-film and organic photovoltaics offer lightweight and flexible solar panel options suitable for diverse applications[1].

Moreover, emerging PV technologies, including tandem solar cells and perovskite-silicon tandem cells, hold promise for achieving higher efficiencies and overcoming material constraints inherent in traditional silicon-based PV systems. Furthermore, advancements in PV module manufacturing techniques, such as heterojunction and Metal Wrap-Through (MWT) technologies, enable the production of higher-efficiency modules with improved durability and reliability.

The integration of PV systems with energy storage solutions, such as lithium-ion batteries and flow batteries, facilitates the utilization of solar energy during periods of low sunlight intensity or grid outage, enhancing energy resilience and self-consumption. Additionally, grid-tied PV systems with net metering arrangements enable surplus solar electricity to be exported to the grid, providing economic incentives for solar energy adoption and fostering grid stability(ALLOUHI *et al.,*2023).

2.1.2 Concentrating Solar Power (CSP) Systems

Concentrating Solar Power (CSP) systems utilize mirrors or lenses to concentrate sunlight onto a small area, generating high-temperature thermal energy that drives steam turbines or Stirling engines to produce electricity. CSP technologies offer inherent energy storage capabilities through the integration of Thermal Energy Storage (TES) systems, enabling dispatchable and reliable power generation even after sunset or during periods of low solar irradiance(ISLAM *et al.,*2018).

Recent advancements in CSP technology focus on improving the efficiency and scalability of solar thermal power plants, with innovations in receiver designs, heat transfer fluids, and thermal energy storage materials. High-temperature CSP systems, such as molten salt and Phase Change Materials (PCMs), enable higher operating temperatures and thermal efficiencies, enhancing overall system performance and reducing LCOE.

Furthermore, hybrid CSP-PV systems combine the benefits of both PV and CSP technologies, leveraging PV modules for low-cost electricity generation during daylight hours and CSP components for dispatchable power generation and energy storage. Integrated solar power projects, such as Concentrated Photovoltaic-Thermal (CPV-T) systems, offer synergistic energy solutions that maximize land use efficiency and optimize resource utilization.

By elucidating the diverse array of solar energy technologies and their applications, this subsection underscores the pivotal role of solar energy in promoting sustainable energy development, mitigating climate change, and fostering energy independence and resilience.

2.2 Wind Energy

Wind energy, harnessed from the kinetic energy of moving air masses, represents a prominent renewable energy source with significant potential for sustainable electricity generation. This subsection delves into the multifaceted realm of wind energy, encompassing onshore and offshore wind power technologies, as well as recent innovations and emerging trends in wind turbine design and integration.

2.2.1 Onshore Wind Power

Onshore wind power installations involve the deployment of wind turbines on land-based sites with favorable wind conditions, such as plains, ridges, and coastal regions. These wind turbines typically consist of rotor blades mounted on a tall tower, connected to a generator that converts rotational energy into electricity. Advancements in onshore wind turbine technology have led to the development of larger, more efficient turbines capable of capturing greater wind energy and generating higher power outputs.

Recent innovations in onshore wind turbine design focus on enhancing energy capture efficiency, reducing maintenance costs, and minimizing environmental impacts. Aerodynamic enhancements, such as blade curvature optimization and vortex generators, improve turbine performance by increasing lift and reducing drag, thereby enhancing energy conversion efficiency. Additionally, advanced control systems and predictive maintenance algorithms leverage data analytics and machine learning to optimize turbine operation, predict component failures, and preemptively schedule maintenance activities, ensuring optimal performance and reliability.

Furthermore, community wind projects and distributed wind systems empower local communities and landowners to participate in renewable energy production and benefit from the economic and environmental advantages of wind energy. Community-owned wind farms, cooperatives, and small-scale wind turbines offer decentralized energy solutions, promote energy democracy, and foster social acceptance and support for renewable energy development(DARWISH *et al.*,2020).

2.2.2 Offshore Wind Power

Offshore wind power entails the installation of wind turbines in marine environments, typically in shallow or deep waters near the coastline or offshore islands. Offshore wind farms harness the stronger and more consistent wind resources available at sea, enabling higher capacity factors and energy yields compared to onshore wind installations. Moreover, offshore wind projects encounter fewer land use conflicts and aesthetic concerns, while benefiting from proximity to densely populated coastal areas and urban centers.

Recent advancements in offshore wind technology include the development of floating wind turbines, which extend wind energy potential to deeper waters and more remote offshore locations. Floating offshore wind farms utilize Tension-Leg Platforms (TLPs), semi-submersible platforms, or floating spar buoys to support turbines in offshore environments with challenging seabed conditions or significant water depths. These innovative floating wind solutions unlock vast expanses of untapped offshore wind resources, expand the geographical scope of offshore wind development, and accelerate the global transition to renewable energy.

Furthermore, hybrid offshore energy projects integrate wind power with complementary renewable energy sources, such as offshore solar Vhotovoltaic (PV) arrays, wave energy converters, and energy storage systems. Hybrid energy systems leverage synergies between different renewable resources, diversify energy production portfolios, and enhance overall system reliability and resilience(DINH *et al.*,2019).

By elucidating the diverse array of wind energy technologies and their applications, this subsection underscores the pivotal role of wind energy in advancing sustainability goals, decarbonizing the energy sector, and mitigating climate change impacts on a global scale.

2.3 Hydroelectric Power

Hydroelectric power, derived from the gravitational force of flowing or falling water, stands as one of the oldest and most widely utilized renewable energy sources globally. This subsection delves into the multifaceted realm of hydroelectric power generation, encompassing conventional hydroelectric dams, pumped-storage hydroelectricity, and innovative hydrokinetic technologies, along with their respective advantages, challenges, and environmental implications.

2.3.1 Conventional Hydroelectric Dams

Conventional hydroelectric dams harness the potential energy of water stored in reservoirs behind dams, releasing it through turbines to generate electricity. The kinetic energy of flowing water drives turbine blades connected to generators, converting mechanical energy into electrical power. Conventional hydroelectric power plants offer reliable and dispatchable electricity generation, capable of quickly responding to fluctuations in demand and providing grid stability and balancing services.

Large-scale hydroelectric projects, such as the Three Gorges Dam in China and the Hoover Dam in the United States, exemplify the monumental capacity and energy output achievable with conventional hydroelectric installations. These mega-dams boast substantial electricity generation capacities, reservoir storage volumes, and hydrological control capabilities, enabling them to meet significant portions of national energy demand and support economic development and industrial growth (OUALI *et al.*,2024).

Despite their considerable benefits, conventional hydroelectric dams also pose environmental and social challenges, including habitat disruption, alteration of river ecosystems, and displacement of local communities due to reservoir inundation. The construction and operation of large dams can lead to ecological imbalances, sedimentation issues, and downstream flow alterations, impacting aquatic biodiversity and riparian ecosystems. Moreover, concerns regarding dam safety, seismic risks, and climate change-induced hydrological variability underscore the need for robust risk assessment, monitoring, and adaptive management strategies to ensure the sustainability and resilience of hydroelectric projects(KOUGIAS *et al.*,2019).

2.3.2 Pumped-Storage Hydroelectricity

Pumped-storage hydroelectricity represents a versatile and flexible energy storage solution that plays a crucial role in grid stability, load balancing, and renewable energy integration. Pumped-storage facilities consist of two interconnected reservoirs located at different elevations, with reversible turbines and pumps facilitating energy conversion and storage. During periods of low electricity demand or excess renewable energy generation, surplus electricity is used to pump water from a lower reservoir to an upper reservoir, storing potential energy. Conversely, during peak demand periods, water is released from the upper reservoir through turbines to generate electricity, meeting grid demand and supporting system reliability.

Pumped-storage hydroelectric plants exhibit rapid response times and high efficiency levels, making them ideal for providing ancillary services, regulating grid frequency, and mitigating intermittency issues associated with variable renewable energy sources like wind and solar power. Moreover, pumped-storage facilities enable the integration of intermittent renewables, facilitate renewable energy curtailment avoidance, and enhance grid flexibility and resilience(REHMAN *et al.*,2015).

In recent years, advanced pumped-storage technologies, such as closed-loop and seawater pumped-storage systems, have emerged as promising innovations in energy storage and grid optimization. Closed-loop pumped-storage schemes utilize underground caverns or abandoned mines as lower reservoirs, minimizing environmental footprint and land use requirements while maximizing storage capacity and efficiency(see Figure 1). Seawater pumped-storage projects leverage the vast energy potential of ocean tides and currents to store and release renewable energy, harnessing coastal and marine resources for sustainable power generation.

Figure 1. Conceptual Framework of Wind-Powered Pumped Hydroelectric Storage (PHES) System.

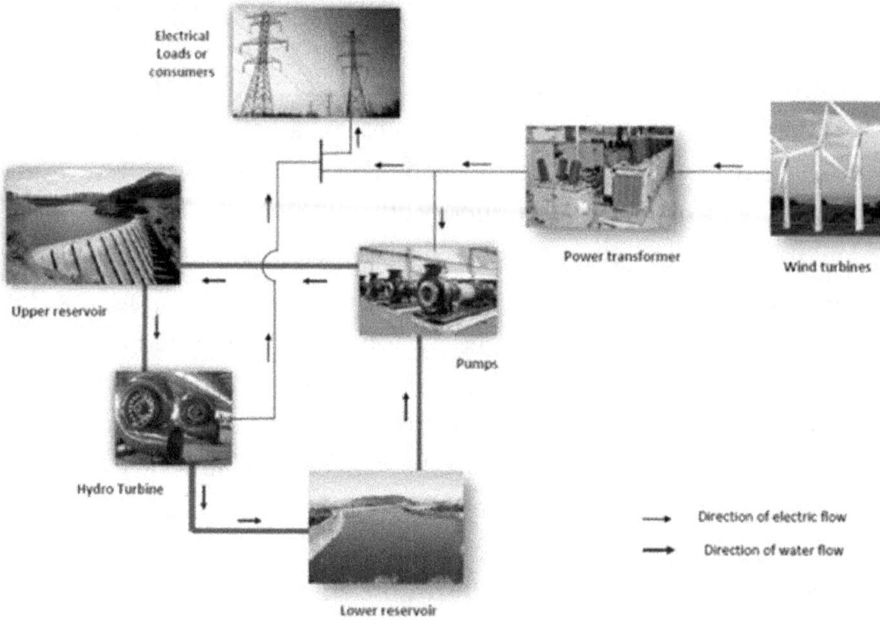

By elucidating the diverse array of hydroelectric power technologies and their applications, this subsection underscores the pivotal role of hydropower in advancing sustainability objectives, fostering energy security, and accelerating the global transition to renewable energy(see Figure 2).

Figure 2. Conceptual Framework of Solar PV-Powered Pumped Hydroelectric Storage (PHES) System.

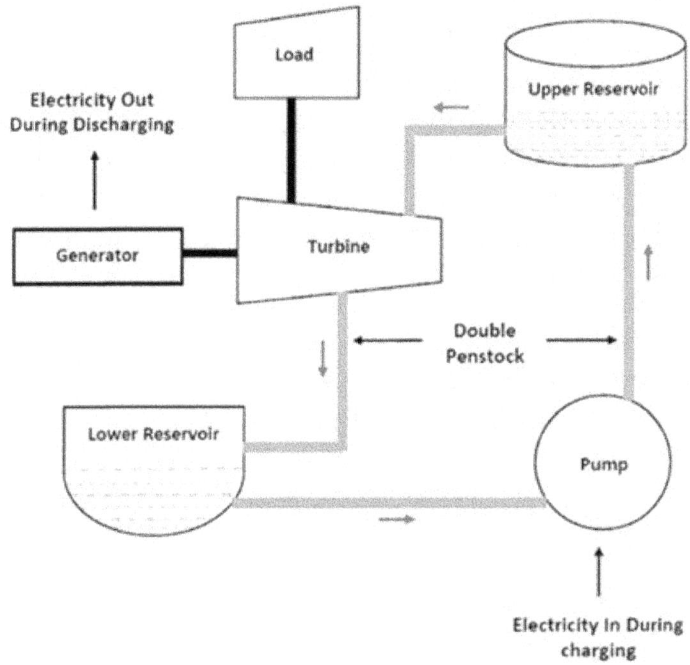

2.4 Biomass Energy

Biomass energy, derived from organic materials such as plants, agricultural residues, forestry residues, and organic waste, constitutes a versatile and renewable energy resource with diverse applications in power generation, heat production, and biofuel synthesis. This subsection elucidates the multifaceted landscape of biomass energy utilization, encompassing biomass power plants, biofuels, and biogas production, along with their respective benefits, challenges, and environmental implications(SABIR *et al.*,2021).

2.4.1 Biomass Power Plants

Biomass power plants utilize organic materials as fuel to generate electricity through combustion or biochemical processes. Biomass combustion facilities employ solid biomass feedstocks, such as wood chips, agricultural residues, and dedicated energy crops, to produce steam, which drives turbines connected to electricity generators(see Figure 3). These biomass-fired power plants offer baseload or dispatchable electricity generation, complementing intermittent renewable energy sources and enhancing grid stability.

Figure 3. Historical and Projected Power Generation Energy Consumption by Region (Quadrillion British Thermal Units)

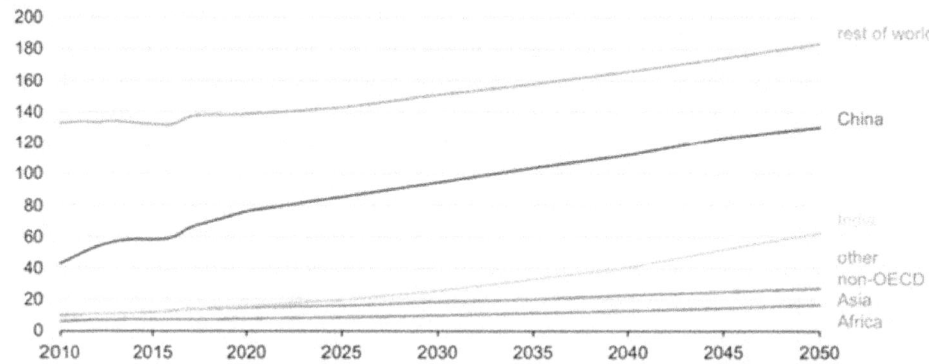

(Source: US Energy Information Administration, International Energy Outlook 2020).

Advanced biomass technologies, including fluidized bed combustion, gasification, and pyrolysis, enable efficient energy conversion, emissions reduction, and resource utilization in biomass power generation(ARBI *et al.*,2018). Fluidized bed combustion systems facilitate the combustion of diverse biomass feedstocks with high moisture content, while gasification processes convert biomass into syngas (synthetic gas), which can be used for power generation, heat production, or biofuel synthesis(see Figure 4). Pyrolysis technologies thermally decompose biomass in the absence of oxygen, yielding bio-oil, biochar, and syngas fractions for energy and chemical applications(MOHAGHEGH *et al.*,2021).

Figure 4. A Schematic Representation of the Hybrid Solar-Biomass Concept for Steam Power Plant.

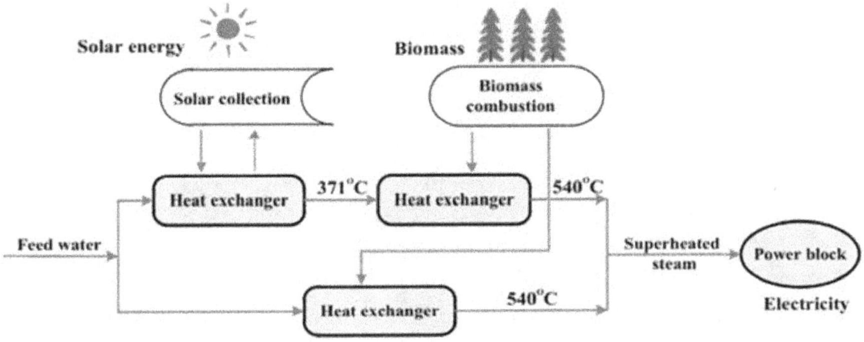

However, biomass combustion for power generation entails environmental and sustainability considerations, including air pollutant emissions, land use impacts, and biomass resource availability. The combustion of biomass fuels releases Carbon diOxide (CO2), Nitrogen Oxides (NOx), SulfurdiOxide (SO2), and Particulate Matter (PM), contributing to air quality degradation and climate change(see Figure 5). Sustainable biomass sourcing practices, forest management strategies, and emissions abatement technologies are essential for mitigating environmental impacts and ensuring the sustainability of biomass energy systems.

Figure 5. Thermodynamic Diagram of the Solar-Biomass Hybrid Power Plant.

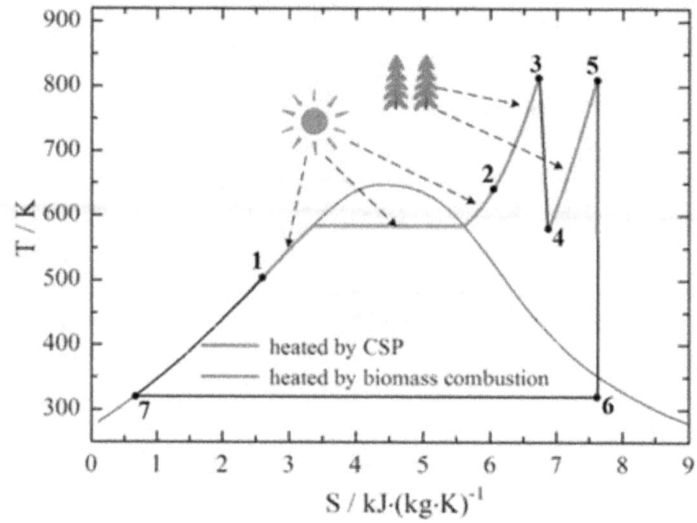

2.4.2 Biofuels Production

Biofuels, derived from biomass feedstocks such as crops, algae, and organic waste, offer renewable alternatives to fossil fuels in the transportation sector. This article examines the production pathways, properties, and sustainability aspects of major biofuel types, including biodiesel, ethanol, and advanced biofuels.

Biodiesel, a renewable diesel substitute, is produced through the transesterification of vegetable oils or animal fats with methanol or ethanol, yielding Fatty Acid Methyl Esters (FAME) or Fatty Acid Ethyl Esters (FAEE). Biodiesel blends can be used in conventional diesel engines with minor modifications, reducing greenhouse gas emissions and dependence on petroleum-derived fuels.

Ethanol, a widely utilized biofuel, is primarily produced through the fermentation of sugars or starches from feedstocks such as corn, sugarcane, and cellulosic biomass. The conversion of biomass into ethanol involves enzymatic hydrolysis of cellulose and hemicellulose to fermentable sugars, followed by microbial fermentation and distillation processes. Ethanol can be blended with gasoline to enhance octane ratings and reduce carbon emissions in spark-ignition engines.

Advanced biofuels, including cellulosic ethanol, renewable diesel, and drop-in biofuels, represent next-generation bioenergy solutions that utilize non-food biomass feedstocks, such as agricultural residues, forestry residues, and energy crops. Advanced biofuel production technologies, such as enzymatic hydrolysis, thermochemical conversion, and microbial fermentation, enable the efficient conversion of lignocellulosic biomass into high-energy-density liquid fuels(KHAN*et al.*,2022).

Sustainable biofuel production entails addressing key challenges, such as feedstock availability, land use competition, and lifecycle environmental impacts. Integrated biorefinery approaches, biomass-to-energy co-production, and techno-economic optimization are essential for enhancing biofuel production efficiency, reducing production costs, and maximizing environmental benefits.

2.4.3 Biogas Generation

Biogas, a renewable gaseous fuel composed primarily of methane (CH4) and Carbon diOxide (CO2), is produced through anaerobic digestion of organic materials in biogas digesters or anaerobic reactors. This subsection explores the process of biogas production, feedstock selection, and utilization options, highlighting its role in waste valorization, energy recovery, and greenhouse gas mitigation.

Anaerobic digestion involves the microbial decomposition of organic matter in the absence of oxygen, yielding biogas as a byproduct. Common biogas feedstocks include agricultural residues, livestock manure, organic waste, and wastewater sludge, which undergo biochemical conversion into biogas through complex microbial consortia. Biogas composition and methane yield depend on feedstock characteristics, reactor conditions, and process optimization parameters.

Biogas utilization encompasses various applications, including electricity generation, heat production, and Renewable Natural Gas (RNG) production. Biogas can be combusted in gas engines or turbines to generate electricity and heat, providing decentralized energy solutions for rural communities, agricultural facilities, and wastewater treatment plants. Moreover, biogas upgrading technologies enable the purification and enrichment of biogas to produce RNG, a renewable substitute for natural gas in heating, transportation, and industrial applications.

Despite its potential benefits, biogas production entails technical, economic, and regulatory challenges, including feedstock variability, process stability, and biogas utilization infrastructure. Technological innovations, policy incentives, and collaborative partnerships are critical for overcoming barriers to biogas deployment and realizing its full potential as a sustainable energy resource(ARCHANA *et al.*,2024).

By examining the diverse array of biomass energy technologies and their applications, this subsection underscores the pivotal role of biomass in advancing sustainability objectives, fostering energy security, and mitigating climate change. Sustainable biomass utilization practices, coupled with technological innovation andpolicy support, are essential for harnessing the full potential of biomass energy and transitioning towards a low-carbon, resilient energy future.

2.5 Emerging Technologies

Emerging technologies in the realm of renewable energy and sustainability offer novel approaches to address pressing environmental challenges and accelerate the transition towards a more sustainable future. This subsection explores cutting-edge advancements and innovative solutions across various domains, including energy generation, storage, and resource management.

2.5.1 Perovskite Solar Cells

Perovskite solar cells represent a revolutionary advancement in photovoltaic technology, offering high efficiency, low-cost fabrication, and versatility in device design. These solar cells utilize organometal halide perovskite materials as light-absorbing layers, exhibiting exceptional optoelectronic properties and tunable bandgap characteristics. Perovskite solar cells have demonstrated rapid efficiency improvements, with lab-scale devices surpassing 25% power conversion efficiency, rivaling traditional silicon-based photovoltaics.

The unique properties of perovskite materials, including high absorption coefficients, long carrier diffusion lengths, and defect tolerance, enable the fabrication of thin-film solar cells with enhanced light harvesting and charge transport properties. Solution-based deposition techniques, such as spin-coating, inkjet printing, and spray coating, facilitate scalable and cost-effective manufacturing processes for perovskite solar modules.

However, perovskite solar cells face challenges related to stability, scalability, and toxicity, necessitating ongoing research efforts to address material degradation mechanisms, device encapsulation techniques, and environmentally friendly fabrication methods. Collaborative research initiatives, industry partnerships, and regulatory support are crucial for advancing perovskite solar technology towards commercialization and widespread deployment(URBINA *et al.*,2020).

2.5.2 Solid-State Batteries

Solid-state batteries represent a paradigm shift in energy storage technology, offering higher energy density, improved safety, and enhanced cycle life compared to conventional lithium-ion batteries. These batteries replace liquid electrolytes with solid electrolytes, eliminating the risk of electrolyte leakage, dendrite formation, and thermal runaway, thereby enhancing battery safety and reliability.

Solid-state battery architectures encompass various electrolyte materials, including ceramic, polymer, and glassy solid electrolytes, each offering distinct advantages in terms of ionic conductivity, mechanical stability, and compatibility with electrode materials. Advanced manufacturing techniques, such as thin-film deposition, ceramic sintering, and ion exchange processes, enable the fabrication of solid-state battery cells with tailored electrochemical properties and form factors.

The development of solid-state battery technology faces challenges related to electrolyte/electrode interfaces, interfacial resistance, and volumetric energy density, necessitating interdisciplinary research efforts in materials science, electrochemistry, and device engineering. Collaborative research consortia, public-private partnerships, and government funding initiatives play a crucial role in accelerating the commercialization and market adoption of solid-state batteries for diverse applications, including electric vehicles, grid energy storage, and portable electronics(WU *et al.,*2023).

2.5.3 Artificial Photosynthesis

Artificial photosynthesis represents a transformative approach to sustainable fuel production, mimicking the natural process of photosynthesis to convert solar energy into chemical fuels such as hydrogen and hydrocarbons(see Figure 6). This technology integrates photoactive materials, catalysts, and reaction chambers to harness sunlight, water, and carbon dioxide as feedstocks for fuel synthesis.

Figure 6. The Role of Artificial Photosynthesis in Advancing Green Chemistry.

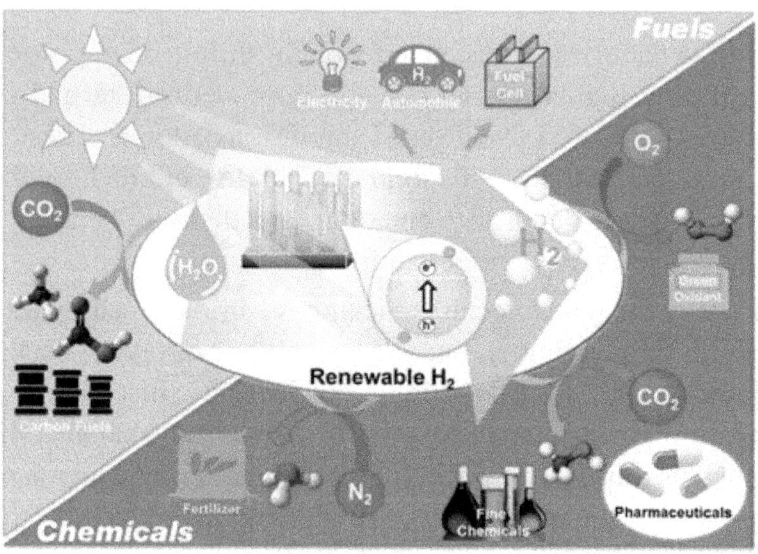

Key components of artificial photosynthesis systems include photoelectrodes, cocatalysts, and membrane separators, which facilitate light absorption, charge separation, and product separation in photochemical reactions. Advanced nanomaterials, such as metal oxides, quantum dots, and molecular catalysts, exhibit tailored optical and electronic properties for efficient light harvesting and catalytic conversion of reactants.

The development of artificial photosynthesis technology requires interdisciplinary collaborations between chemists, physicists, materials scientists, and engineers to optimize device performance, stability, and scalability. Research challenges include improving photoelectrode efficiency, enhancing catalytic activity, and reducing energy losses in multi-step reaction pathways. Technological breakthroughs in artificial photosynthesis hold promise for sustainable fuel production, carbon dioxide mitigation, and renewable energy storage, contributing to a carbon-neutral energy economy.

2.5.4 Smart Grid Technologies

Smart grid technologies integrate advanced communication, control, and monitoring capabilities into electric power systems, enabling dynamic optimization of energy generation, distribution, and consumption. These technologies enhance grid resilience, reliability, and efficiency while facilitating the integration of renewable energy sources, electric vehicles, and demand-side management strategies(LAMNATOU *et al.,*2022).

Key components of smart grid infrastructure include sensors, meters, and automation devices deployed throughout the grid to collect real-time data on electricity flows, voltage levels, and equipment health. Advanced data analytics, machine learning algorithms, and artificial intelligence enable grid operators to forecast demand, optimize generation dispatch, and detect anomalies or faults in the grid.

Smart grid technologies offer numerous benefits, including reduced energy costs, enhanced grid stability, and increased renewable energy integration, but they also present challenges related to cybersecurity, interoperability, and regulatory frameworks. Collaborative research initiatives, demonstration projects, and pilot deployments are essential for validating smart grid solutions, fostering industry adoption, and informing policy development to realize the full potential of smart grid technologies in advancing sustainability and environmental objectives.

2.6 Integration and Grid Stability

The integration of renewable energy sources into the existing grid infrastructure presents significant challenges and opportunities for enhancing grid stability, reliability, and resilience. This subsection delves into key strategies and technologies aimed at facilitating the seamless integration of renewable energy resources while ensuring grid stability and mitigating operational challenges.

2.6.1 Grid Interconnection and Power Electronics

Effective grid integration of renewable energy sources necessitates robust interconnection systems and advanced power electronics solutions to manage variable generation outputs and voltage fluctuations. Grid interconnection standards and protocols facilitate the seamless integration of Distributed Energy Resources (DERs), including solar PhotoVoltaic (PV) systems, wind turbines, and energy storage systems, into the grid infrastructure(TANG*et al.,*2021).

Power electronic devices such as inverters, converters, and voltage regulators play a crucial role in controlling the flow of electricity between renewable energy systems and the grid, ensuring voltage and frequency stability, and enabling grid-tied operation. Advanced power electronics technologies, including Voltage Source Converters (VSCs), multi-level converters, and Flexible AC Transmission Systems (FACTS), offer enhanced controllability, efficiency, and grid compatibility for renewable energy integration.

2.6.2 Energy Storage Systems (ESS)

Energy Storage Systems (ESS) play a pivotal role in enhancing grid stability, balancing supply and demand, and mitigating the intermittency of renewable energy sources. ESS technologies encompass a diverse range of solutions, including lithium-ion batteries, flow batteries, Compressed Air Energy Storage (CAES), and Pumped Hydroelectric Storage (PHS), each offering unique advantages in terms of energy density, response time, and cycle life (RANA*et al.*,2023).

Grid-scale energy storage facilities provide essential services such as frequency regulation, peak shaving, and renewable energy firming, enabling grid operators to manage variability and uncertainty in renewable generation and enhance grid reliability. Advanced control algorithms, predictive analytics, and optimization strategies optimize ESS operation, maximize revenue streams, and minimize system costs while ensuring grid stability and resilience(ARBI *et al.*,2021).

2.6.3 Demand-Side Management (DSM)

Demand-Side Management (DSM) programs leverage advanced technologies and pricing incentives to modify consumer energy consumption patterns, reduce peak demand, and enhance grid flexibility and stability(see Figure 7). DSM strategies include Time-Of-Use (TOU) pricing, Demand Response (DR) programs, and smart home automation systems that enable consumers to adjust their energy usage in response to grid conditions and price signals(see Figure 8).

Figure 7. Framework for Energy Management.

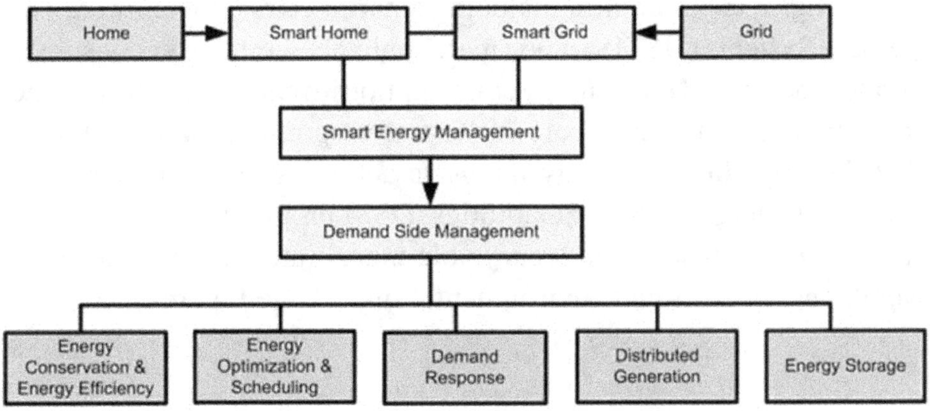

Figure 8. Diverse Smart Home Management Systems.

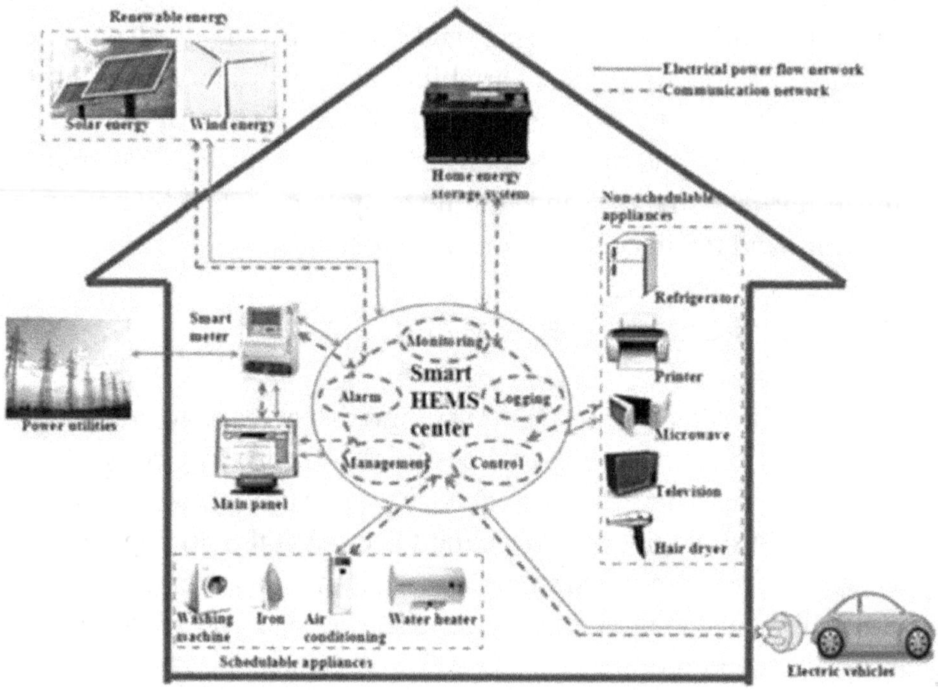

Smart grid technologies, including smart meters, Home Energy Management Systems (HEMS), and smart appliances, empower consumers to monitor and control their energy consumption in real-time, optimize energy usage patterns, and participate in demand response initiatives(IQBAL *et al.*,2021). By shifting energy-intensive activities to off-peak hours and leveraging energy storage capabilities, DSM programs contribute to grid stability, load balancing, and renewable energy integration while reducing overall energy costs and environmental impact(see Figure 9).

Figure 9. Strategic Deployment of Demand-Side Management (DSM).

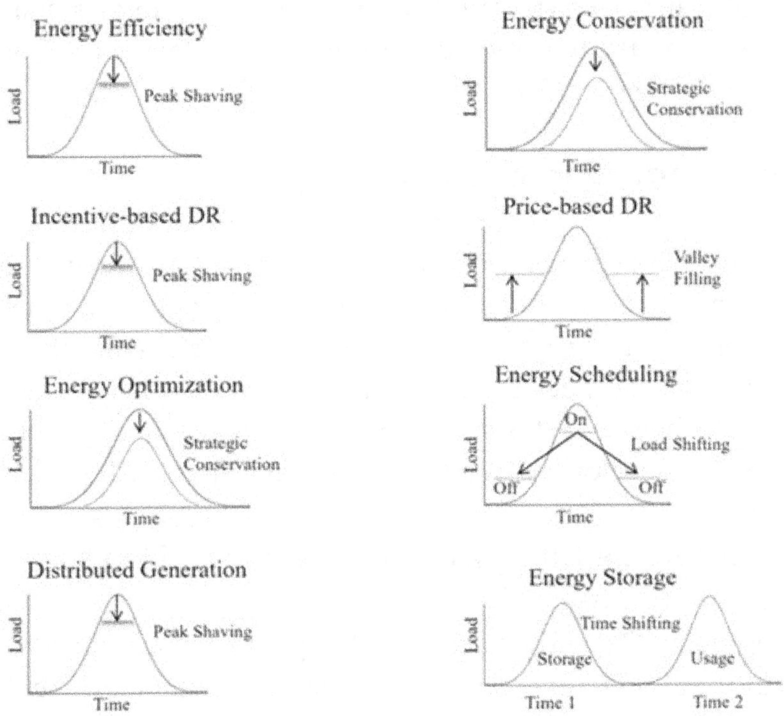

2.6.4 Grid Modeling and Simulation

Grid modeling and simulation tools enable utilities, researchers, and policymakers to assess the impact of renewable energy integration on grid stability, evaluate system performance under different scenarios, and design optimal grid configurations and operating strategies. Advanced modeling techniques, including dynamic system simulations, power flow analysis, and probabilistic forecasting, provide insights into grid behavior, voltage profiles, and transient stability during renewable energy integration.

Real-time monitoring and control systems, combined with advanced data analytics and machine learning algorithms, enable grid operators to anticipate and mitigate potential grid disturbances, optimize generation dispatch, and ensure compliance with grid reliability standards and regulations. Collaborative research efforts, industry partnerships, and open-access grid simulation platforms facilitate knowledge sharing, technology transfer, and best practices dissemination, fostering innovation and accelerating the transition towards a sustainable and resilient energy future(AGUERO *et al.,*2017).

2.7 Policy and Market Dynamics

The dynamics of policies and market mechanisms significantly influence the deployment and adoption of advanced technologies for sustainability and environmental conservation. This subsection examines the multifaceted interactions between governmental policies, regulatory frameworks, market incentives, and stakeholder engagement in shaping the trajectory of sustainable development and environmental stewardship.

2.7.1 Renewable Energy Incentives and Subsidies

Governmental incentives and subsidies play a pivotal role in promoting the widespread adoption of renewable energy technologies and driving investment in sustainable infrastructure. Financial incentives such as Feed-In Tariffs (FITs), Investment Tax Credits (ITCs), and Production Tax Credits (PTCs) incentivize renewable energy project development, reduce financial barriers, and stimulate private sector investment in clean energy deployment.

Policy frameworks that mandate Renewable Portfolio Standards (RPS) and enforce GreenHouseGas (GHG) emissions reduction targets create market demand for renewable energy generation and incentivize utilities to diversify their energy portfolios towards cleaner and more sustainable alternatives. Additionally, renewable energy auctions and competitive procurement processes facilitate cost-effective project deployment, foster competition among developers, and drive down renewable energy costs over time.

2.7.2 Carbon Pricing and Emissions Trading

Carbon pricing mechanisms, including carbon taxes and Emissions Trading Schemes (ETS), internalize the external costs of carbon emissions, incentivize emission reductions, and create market incentives for low-carbon technologies and practices. By assigning a monetary value to carbon pollution, carbon pricing mechanisms encourage businesses and industries to invest in energy efficiency measures, renewable energy deployment, and emissions abatement strategies.

Emissions trading systems establish a cap on total allowable emissions and allocate tradable emission permits to regulated entities, allowing them to buy and sell permits in a secondary market. Through market-driven mechanisms, emissions trading promotes cost-effective emissions reductions, facilitates technology innovation, and fosters international cooperation in addressing climate change challenges(NARASSIMHAN, *et al.,*2018).

2.7.3 Regulatory Frameworks and Environmental Standards

Robust regulatory frameworks and environmental standards play a critical role in ensuring environmental protection, safeguarding public health, and promoting sustainable development practices. Environmental regulations governing air quality, water pollution, waste management, and land use impose compliance requirements on industries and businesses, incentivizing the adoption of cleaner production processes and pollution prevention measures.

Regulatory agencies and environmental authorities enforce environmental laws, conduct monitoring and enforcement activities, and collaborate with stakeholders to develop science-based policies and regulations that address emerging environmental challenges. Regulatory flexibility mechanisms, such as emissions trading programs, pollution taxes, and performance-based standards, provide industries with compliance options and encourage innovation in pollution control technologies and environmental management practices.

2.7.4 International Cooperation and Climate Diplomacy

Global efforts to address climate change and promote sustainable development require coordinated action, multilateral cooperation, and diplomatic engagement among nations, international organizations, and non-state actors. International agreements such as the Paris Agreement provide a framework for collective action, emission reduction commitments, and climate finance mechanisms to support climate mitigation and adaptation efforts worldwide.

Bilateral and multilateral partnerships facilitate technology transfer, capacity building, and knowledge sharing in renewable energy deployment, climate resilience, and sustainable development initiatives. Climate diplomacy efforts aim to build consensus, resolve disputes, and negotiate ambitious climate targets and commitments to limit global warming and mitigate the adverse impacts of climate change on vulnerable communities and ecosystems(LEIJTEN*et al.*,2019).

2.7.5 Market Innovation and Green Finance

Market innovation and financial instruments drive investment in sustainable infrastructure, green technologies, and climate-resilient solutions. Green bonds, environmental funds, and impact investing channels mobilize private capital towards environmentally sustainable projects, renewable energy investments, and climate adaptation initiatives, leveraging market forces to accelerate the transition towards a low-carbon economy.

Financial institutions, including banks, pension funds, and institutional investors, incorporate environmental, social, and governance (ESG) criteria into investment decisions and asset allocation strategies, integrating sustainability considerations into financial risk management and long-term value creation. Innovations in green finance, such as green bonds, carbon pricing mechanisms, and sustainability-linked loans, incentivize businesses to adopt sustainable practices, disclose environmental performance metrics, and align corporate strategies with climate resilience and environmental stewardship objectives(AGHION, *et al.*,2022).

3. SMART GRID TECHNOLOGIES

The evolution of traditional power grids into smart grids represents a transformative shift in the way electricity is generated, transmitted, distributed, and consumed(ARBI *et al.*,2024). Smart grid technologies leverage advanced sensing, communication, Finance (HAMDI et al.2024) and control systems to optimize grid operations, enhance reliability, and integrate renewable energy resources, energy storage systems, and demand-side management strategies(AHSAN *et al.*, 2023). This subsection explores the key components, functionalities, and benefits of smart grid technologies in advancing energy efficiency, grid resilience, and sustainability objectives(see Figure 10).

Figure 10. A Conceptual Framework for Advanced Smart Grid Energy Systems.

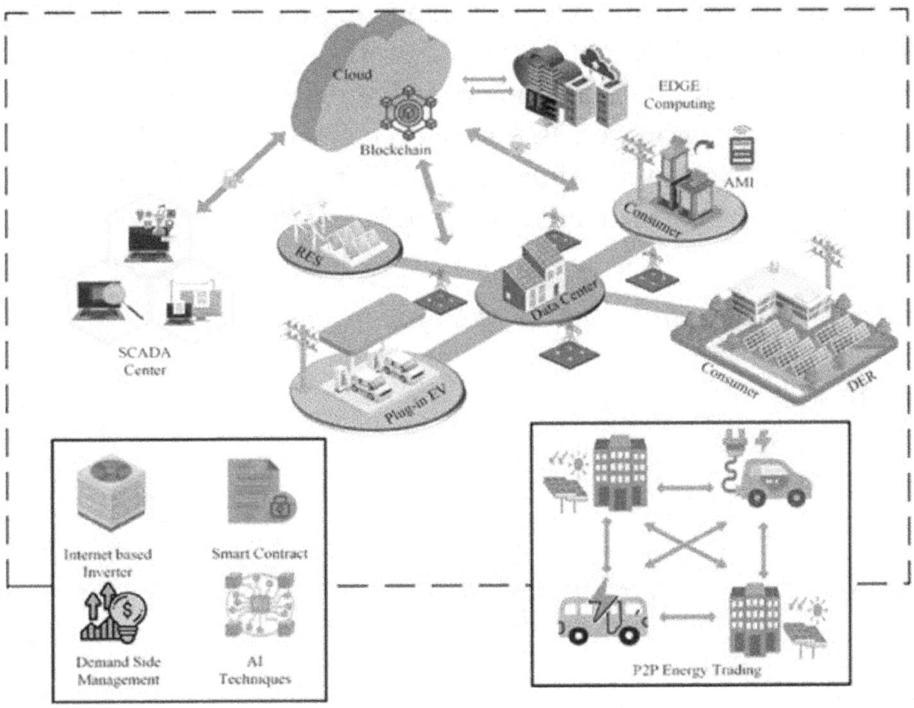

3.1. Advanced Metering Infrastructure (AMI)

Advanced Metering Infrastructure (AMI) enables real-time monitoring, remote meter reading, and two-way communication between utility providers and end-users, facilitating dynamic pricing, demand response programs, and energy consumption feedback mechanisms. Smart meters equipped with AMI functionalities measure electricity consumption at fine-grained intervals, allowing utilities to analyze usage patterns, identify inefficiencies, and optimize grid operations for improved reliability and efficiency(REFAAT*et al.,* 2018).

3.2. Distribution Automation and Self-Healing Networks

Distribution automation technologies enhance grid resilience and reliability by automating fault detection, isolation, and restoration processes, minimizing outage durations, and improving service restoration capabilities(see Figure 11). Self-healing networks utilize intelligent sensors, predictive analytics, and autonomous control algorithms to detect and mitigate grid disturbances, isolate faulty components, and reconfigure distribution circuits in real-time, ensuring continuous power delivery and minimizing disruptions to end-users(see Figure 12).

Figure 11. Architectural Design of an Intelligent Electricity Grid.

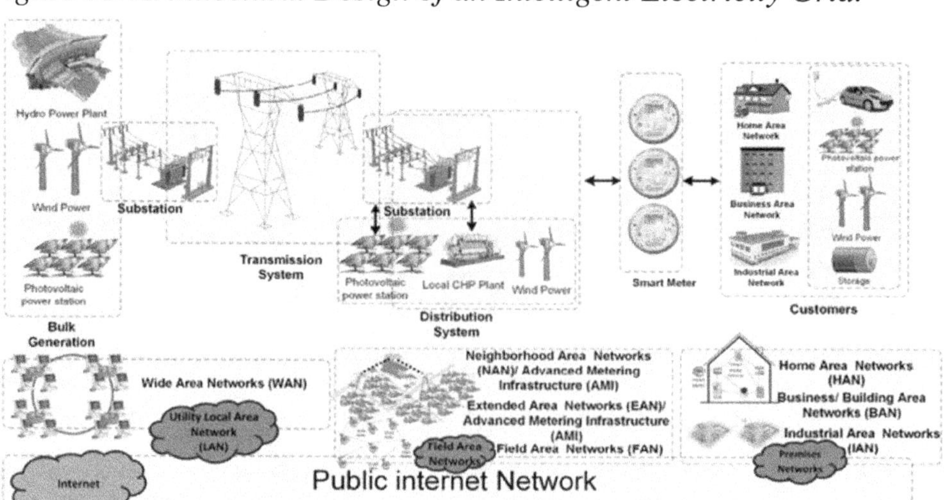

Figure 12. Proposed Flowchart for Self-Healing Mechanism.

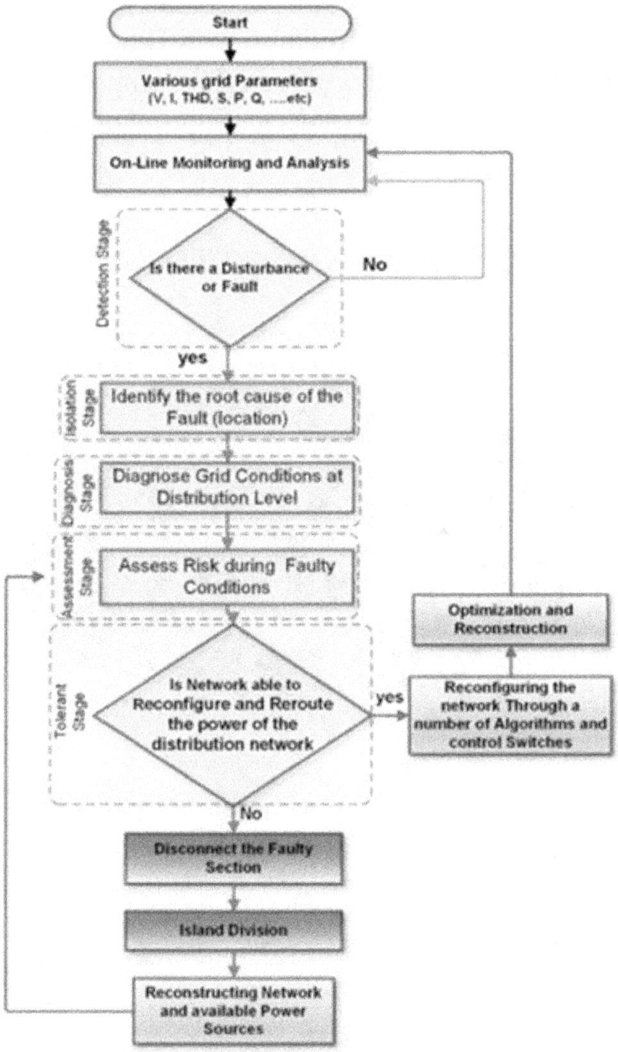

3.3. Grid Edge Intelligence and Decentralized Energy Resources

Grid Edge Intelligence (GEI) refers to the integration of intelligent devices, Distributed Energy Resources (DERs), and decentralized energy management systems at the periphery of the grid, enabling localized control, optimization, and coordination of energy assets(see Figure 13). DERs such as rooftop solar panels, battery storage systems, Electric Vehicles (EVs), and smart appliances contribute to grid flexibility, demand-side management, and renewable energy integration, empowering consumers to actively participate in energy markets and optimize their energy usage patterns(see Figure 14).

Figure 13. Countries Contributing to the Global Smart Grid Market.

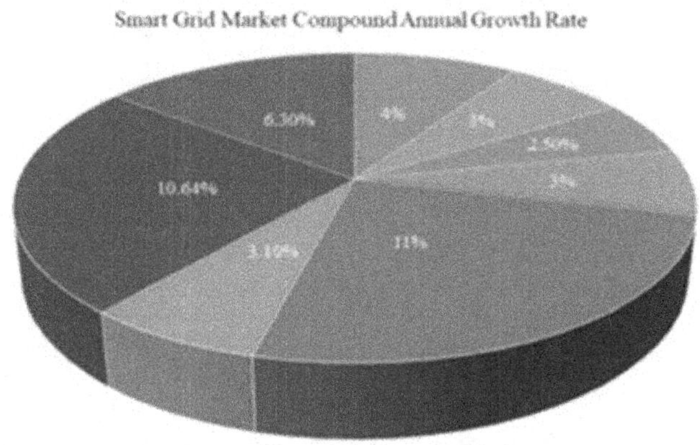

Figure 14. Traditional Architecture of Smart Grid Systems.

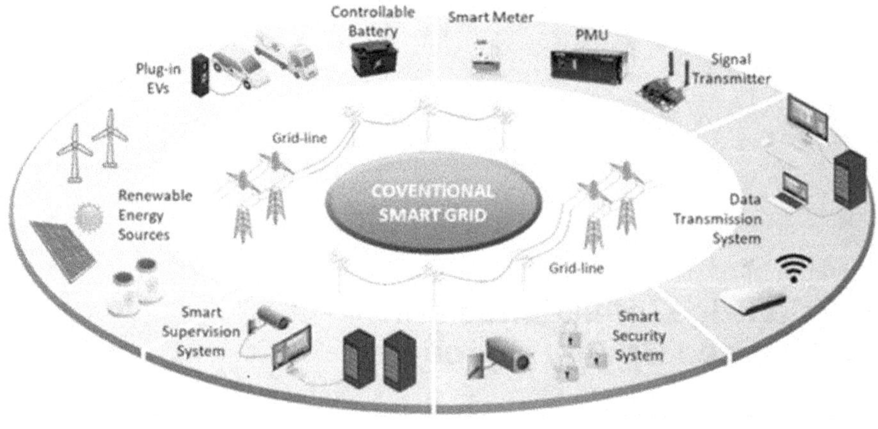

3.4. Demand Response and Energy Management Systems

Demand Response (DR) programs leverage smart grid technologies to incentivize consumers to adjust their electricity consumption patterns in response to grid conditions, price signals, or environmental considerations. Automated Energy Management Systems (EMS) enable dynamic load scheduling, load shedding, and demand-side flexibility measures, reducing peak demand, alleviating grid congestion, and optimizing energy utilization across diverse sectors, including residential, commercial, and industrial facilities(REHMAN *et al.*,2021).

3.5. Cybersecurity and Resilience Frameworks

Cybersecurity and resilience frameworks are essential components of smart grid infrastructure, safeguarding critical assets, data, and communication networks against cyber threats, malicious attacks, and system vulnerabilities. Robust cybersecurity measures, including encryption protocols, authentication mechanisms, and intrusion detection systems, protect against unauthorized access, data breaches, and cyber intrusions, ensuring the integrity, confidentiality, and availability of grid operations and services(ALOTAIBI *et al.*,2020).

3.6. Grid Modernization and Investment Strategies

Grid modernization initiatives require strategic investments in smart grid technologies, grid infrastructure upgrades, and digitalization efforts to enhance system efficiency, reliability, and sustainability. Public-private partnerships, government incentives, and regulatory reforms support grid modernization projects, accelerate technology deployment, and foster innovation in energy management, grid optimization, and distributed energy resource integration(TUBALLA *et al.*,2016).

3.7. Interoperability and Standards Development

Interoperability standards and protocols facilitate seamless integration, interoperability, and compatibility among diverse smart grid components, devices, and systems, enabling plug-and-play functionality, data exchange, and interoperable communications across heterogeneous platforms. Standardization efforts by international organizations, industry consortia, and regulatory bodies ensure vendor neutrality, promote market competition, and drive interoperability in smart grid deployments, fostering innovation, scalability, and interoperability across global energy markets(see Figure 15).

Figure 15. Research Trends in Smart Grid Technologies: A Comprehensive Review.

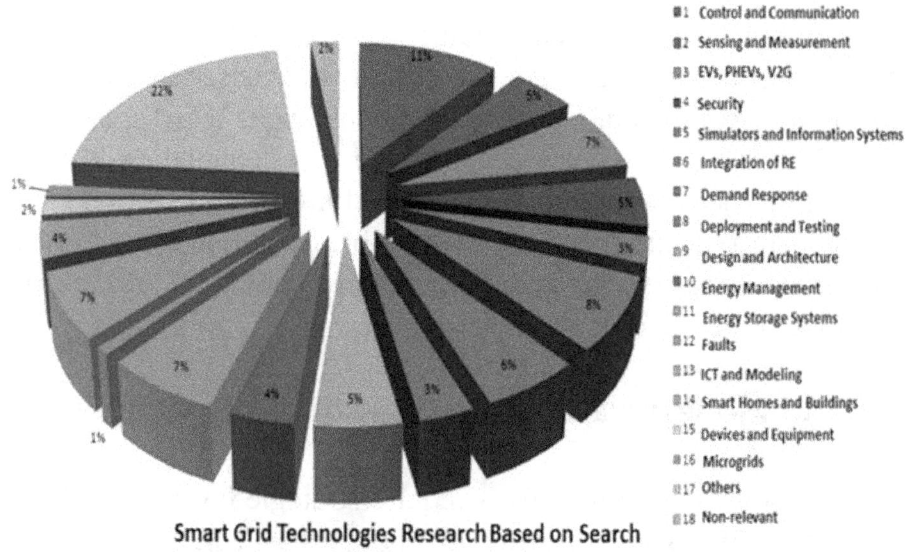

4. SUSTAINABLE AGRICULTURE PRACTICES

Sustainable agriculture practices encompass a range of techniques and methodologies aimed at maximizing agricultural productivity, minimizing environmental impact, and promoting long-term ecological resilience.

This section explores key sustainable agriculture practices and their contributions to enhancing food security, conserving natural resources, and mitigating climate change(OUALI *et al.,*2021).

4.1. Agroecology and Organic Farming

Agroecology principles emphasize the integration of ecological concepts and agricultural practices to optimize resource use efficiency, enhance soil fertility, and promote biodiversity conservation. Organic farming methods prioritize the use of natural inputs, biological pest control, and crop rotation strategies to minimize reliance on synthetic chemicals, pesticides, and fertilizers, reducing environmental pollution and preserving ecosystem integrity(ALTIERI *et al.,*2017).

4.2. Precision Agriculture and Smart Farming

Precision agriculture utilizes advanced technologies, including Geographic Information Systems (GIS), Global Positioning Systems (GPS), and remote sensing tools, to monitor, analyze, and manage agricultural operations with spatial and temporal precision. Smart farming solutions integrate sensor networks, data analytics, and automation systems to optimize irrigation, fertilization, and pest management practices, improving resource efficiency, yield stability, and crop quality(ROY*et al.,*2020).

4.3. Conservation Agriculture and Soil Health Management

Conservation agriculture practices prioritize soil conservation, erosion control, and soil health restoration through minimal soil disturbance, permanent soil cover, and diversified crop rotations(M. TAHAT *et al.,* 2020). Soil health management strategies, such as cover cropping, no-till farming, and organic soil amendments, enhance soil structure, microbial activity, and nutrient cycling, mitigating soil degradation, erosion, and loss of arable land(see Figure 16).

Figure 16. Exploring the Role of Beneficial Soil Microbes in Sustainable Agriculture and Environmental Development: A Conceptual Framework.

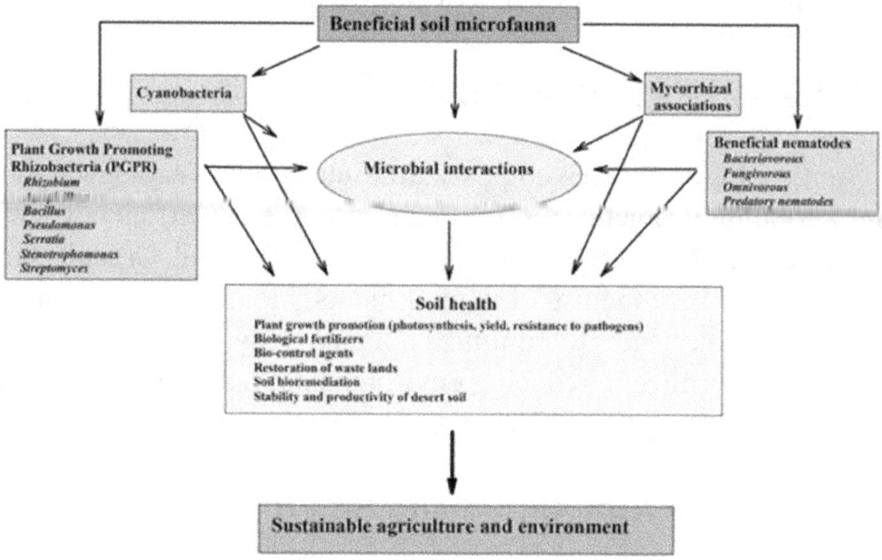

4.4. Agroforestry and Integrated Crop-Livestock Systems

Agroforestry systems integrate trees, shrubs, and woody perennials into agricultural landscapes to enhance ecosystem services, carbon sequestration, and biodiversity conservation while diversifying farm production and income streams. Integrated crop-livestock systems promote synergies between crop cultivation and livestock grazing activities, optimizing nutrient cycling, soil fertility, and biomass production while reducing greenhouse gas emissions and land degradation(NAYAK *et al.,*2019).

4.5. Water Conservation and Irrigation Efficiency

Water conservation practices, such as drip irrigation, micro-sprinklers, and rainwater harvesting systems, optimize water use efficiency, minimize water losses, and mitigate water scarcity challenges in agricultural regions. Adoption of precision irrigation technologies, soil moisture sensors, and automated irrigation scheduling tools enables farmers to apply water precisely where and when needed, reducing water wastage, runoff, and groundwater depletion(VELASCO-MUÑOZ *et al.,*2019).

4.6. Agrobiodiversity and Crop Genetic Resources

Agrobiodiversity conservation efforts aim to preserve and promote genetic diversity within crop species, livestock breeds, and wild relatives to enhance resilience to pests, diseases, and environmental stressors. Seed banks, gene banks, and participatory plant breeding programs facilitate the conservation, evaluation, and utilization of crop genetic resources, ensuring food security, livelihood sustainability, and adaptation to changing climatic conditions (PATHIRANA *et al.,*2022).

4.7. Climate-Smart Agriculture and Adaptation Strategies

Climate-smart agriculture approaches integrate climate resilience, mitigation, and adaptation strategies to enhance agricultural productivity, livelihood resilience, and ecosystem sustainability in the face of climate change impacts. Climate-smart practices, including drought-resistant crop varieties, agroforestry buffers, and soil carbon sequestration techniques, help farmers cope with climate variability, extreme weather events, and shifting climatic patterns while reducing greenhouse gas emissions and enhancing carbon sequestration.

5. GREEN MANUFACTURING PROCESSES

Green manufacturing processes are integral to achieving sustainable production systems that minimize environmental impact, optimize resource utilization, and reduce waste generation across industrial sectors. This section delves into various green manufacturing techniques and innovations aimed at promoting resource efficiency, pollution prevention, and circular economy principles(VENKATRAMANAN *et al.,*2019).

5.1. Lean Manufacturing and Just-in-Time Production

Lean manufacturing principles emphasize the elimination of waste, streamlined production flows, and continuous process improvement to enhance operational efficiency and reduce resource consumption. Just-In-Time (JIT) production strategies minimize inventory stockpiles, reduce lead times, and optimize production schedules to meet customer demand while minimizing excess inventory, storage costs, and material waste.

5.2. Eco-design and Sustainable Product Development

Eco-design methodologies integrate environmental considerations into product development processes, emphasizing lifecycle assessments, material selection criteria, and end-of-life disposal strategies to minimize ecological footprint and enhance product sustainability. Sustainable product design practices prioritize renewable materials, recyclable components, and energy-efficient manufacturing processes to reduce resource depletion, pollution emissions, and environmental degradation(SINGHAL *et al.,*2024).

5.3. Energy-Efficient Technologies and Renewable Resources

Integration of energy-efficient technologies, such as energy management systems, heat recovery systems, and advanced process controls, improves energy productivity, reduces greenhouse gas emissions, and lowers operating costs in manufacturing operations. Adoption of renewable energy sources, including solar photovoltaics, wind turbines, and biomass boilers, further enhances energy independence, resilience, and environmental performance by displacing fossil fuel-based energy sources and mitigating carbon emissions.

5.4. Waste Minimization and Resource Recovery

Implementation of waste minimization strategies, such as material substitution, process optimization, and closed-loop recycling, reduces waste generation, conserves raw materials, and minimizes environmental pollution in manufacturing processes(AWOGBEMI, *et al.*, 2022). Resource recovery technologies, including waste-to-energy systems, anaerobic digestion, and industrial symbiosis networks, transform waste streams into valuable resources, energy sources, and secondary raw materials, promoting resource circularity and waste valorization(see Figure 17).

Figure 17. Regional Waste Generation Projections for 2016, 2030, and 2050 (Millions of Tons).

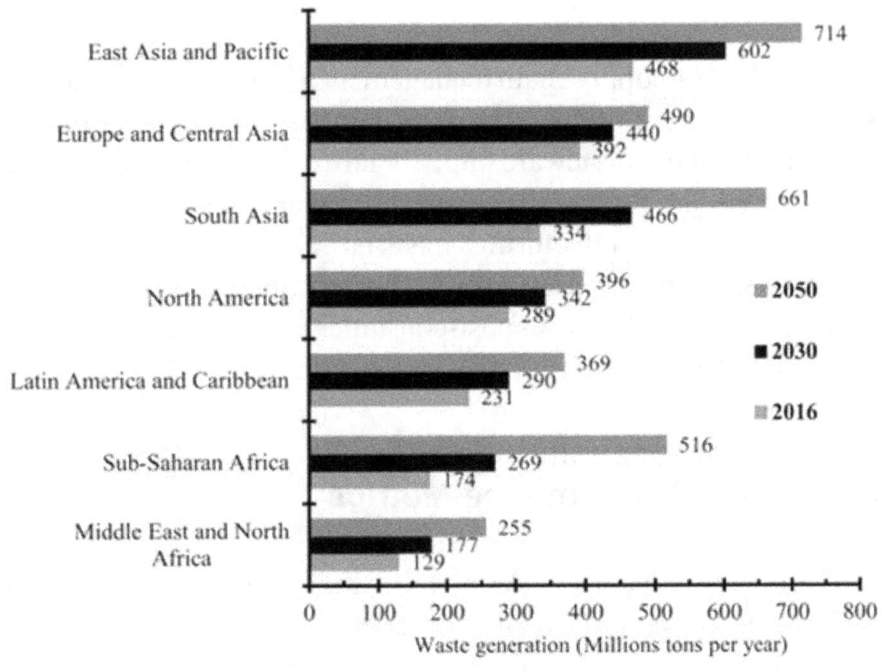

5.5. Water Conservation and Sustainable Water Management

Water conservation measures, such as water reuse systems, water-efficient equipment, and water footprint assessments, optimize water use efficiency, reduce water consumption, and mitigate water pollution risks in manufacturing facilities. Sustainable water management practices, including rainwater harvesting, greywater recycling, and water stewardship initiatives, ensure responsible water usage, protect aquatic ecosystems, and safeguard water quality for surrounding communities and ecosystems(WEERASOORIYA *et al.,*2021).

5.6. Green Supply Chain Management and Circular Economy Practices

Adoption of green supply chain management practices, such as supplier audits, eco-labeling requirements, and sustainable procurement policies, promotes environmental stewardship, social responsibility, and ethical sourcing throughout the supply chain. Circular economy principles, including product remanufacturing, material recovery, and closed-loop supply chains, maximize resource utilization, minimize waste generation, and create economic value from post-consumer and post-industrial waste streams(KARMAKER *et al.,*2023).

5.7. Life Cycle Assessment and Environmental Performance Metrics

Life Cycle Assessment (LCA) methodologies quantify the environmental impacts of manufacturing processes, products, and services across their entire lifecycle, from raw material extraction to end-of-life disposal, enabling informed decision-making and environmental footprint reduction. Environmental performance metrics, such as carbon footprint, water footprint, and energy intensity indicators, assess manufacturing sustainability, track progress towards environmental goals, and drive continuous improvement efforts in resource efficiency and environmental stewardship(TADDESE *et al.,*2020).

6. ENVIRONMENTAL MONITORING AND MANAGEMENT

Environmental monitoring and management play a crucial role in safeguarding natural ecosystems, assessing pollution levels, and ensuring regulatory compliance across various industrial activities. This section explores the importance of robust environmental monitoring systems and effective management strategies in maintaining environmental quality, identifying emerging risks, and fostering sustainable development(ARBI,2018).

6.1. Air Quality Monitoring and Pollution Control

Air quality monitoring systems employ advanced sensors, remote sensing technologies, and atmospheric modeling techniques to assess air pollution levels, track emission sources, and mitigate health risks associated with airborne pollutants. Continuous monitoring of criteria air pollutants, such as particulate matter, nitrogen oxides, sulfur dioxide, volatile organic compounds, and ozone, enables early detection of air quality deterioration and implementation of targeted pollution control measures, including emission reduction strategies, industrial emission standards, and vehicle emissions regulations(SASSI *et al.,*2020b).

6.2. Water Quality Assessment and Remediation

Water quality assessment programs utilize field sampling, laboratory analysis, and hydrological modeling tools to evaluate surface water and groundwater quality, identify contaminant sources, and prioritize remediation actions in aquatic ecosystems(OUALI *et al.,*2022b). Monitoring parameters include physical, chemical, and biological indicators of water quality, such as pH, dissolved oxygen, nutrients, heavy metals, pesticides, pathogens, and aquatic biodiversity. Remediation technologies, such as wastewater treatment plants, constructed wetlands, and in-situ bioremediation, restore water quality, protect aquatic habitats, and ensure safe drinking water supplies for human consumption and ecosystem health(SASSI et al., 2019a).

6.3. Soil Contamination Monitoring and Land Reclamation

Soil contamination monitoring programs assess soil quality, identify contamination hotspots, and assess risks to human health and ecological receptors from exposure to hazardous substances in contaminated soils. Sampling and analysis techniques, including soil sampling grids, soil profiling, and chemical analysis, determine contaminant concentrations and distribution patterns in soil matrices. Remediation strategies, such as soil vapor extraction, soil washing, and phytoremediation, mitigate soil contamination risks, restore soil fertility, and facilitate land reclamation for agricultural, industrial, or recreational land use purposes(UKHURE-BOR*et al.*,2022).

6.4. Ecological Monitoring and Biodiversity Conservation

Ecological monitoring initiatives monitor ecosystem health, biodiversity trends, and habitat conditions to assess ecological resilience, detect species declines, and inform conservation priorities in natural and managed landscapes. Monitoring methods include habitat surveys, species inventories, population monitoring, and ecological modeling techniques to quantify ecosystem services, identify critical habitats, and track species distributions over time. Biodiversity conservation strategies, such as habitat restoration, protected area management, and species reintroduction programs, enhance habitat connectivity, preserve biodiversity hotspots, and promote ecosystem resilience in the face of environmental change(-STEPHENSON *et al.*,2020).

6.5. Environmental Compliance and Regulatory Enforcement

Environmental compliance programs ensure adherence to environmental regulations, permits, and standards through regulatory inspections, compliance audits, and enforcement actions to prevent environmental violations and penalties. Regulatory agencies, such as environmental protection agencies, set emission limits, effluent standards, and waste disposal regulations to safeguard public health and environmental quality. Compliance monitoring measures, such as emissions reporting, pollutant tracking, and environmental impact assessments, verify regulatory compliance, promote pollution prevention, and deter environmental non-compliance through enforcement measures, fines, and penalties(GRAY *et al.*,2011).

7. CHALLENGES AND OPPORTUNITIES

The pursuit of advanced technologies for sustainability and environmental conservation presents both challenges and opportunities that must be addressed to achieve long-term environmental resilience and socio-economic prosperity(see Figure 18). This section delves into the key challenges facing sustainable development efforts and the opportunities for innovation, collaboration, and transformative change to overcome these obstacles(see Figure 19)(NIŽETIĆ*et al.*, 2020).

Figure 18. IoT Technology Market Overview.

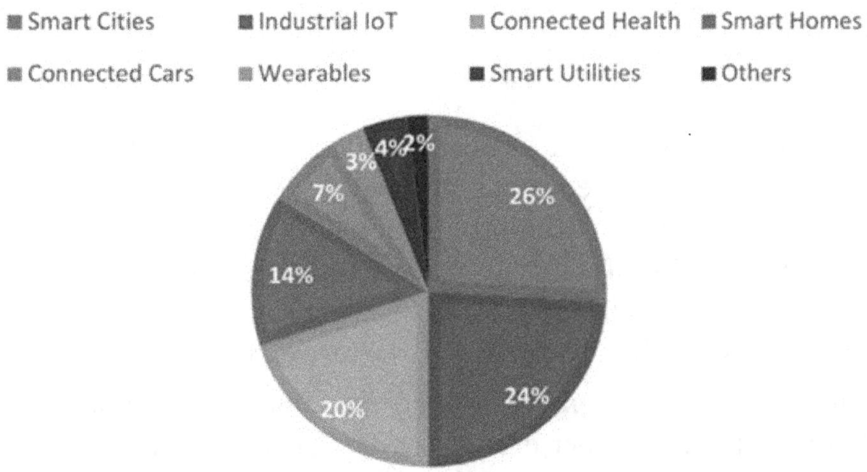

Figure 19. Challenges Encountered in Implementing the Smart City Concept.

7.1. Challenges

Resource Scarcity: The growing demand for natural resources, coupled with finite resource availability and depletion, poses a significant challenge to sustainable development efforts. Addressing resource scarcity requires the adoption of resource-efficient technologies, circular economy principles, and sustainable resource management practices to minimize waste generation and maximize resource recovery and reuse.

Climate Change Impacts: The adverse impacts of climate change, including extreme weather events, sea-level rise, and biodiversity loss, threaten ecosystem integrity, human well-being, and socio-economic stability. Mitigating climate change requires concerted global efforts to reduce greenhouse gas emissions, transition to low-carbon energy systems, and enhance climate resilience through adaptation measures, ecosystem restoration, and climate-smart agricultural practices(NIŽETIĆ*et al.*,2020).

Environmental Degradation: Widespread environmental degradation, such as deforestation, land degradation, water pollution, and habitat destruction, undermines ecosystem services, biodiversity conservation, and human health. Addressing environmental degradation necessitates the adoption of integrated land-use planning, sustainable land management practices, and ecosystem-based approaches to restore degraded landscapes, protect critical habitats, and conserve natural resources(HADJ SASSI *et al.,*2024).

Technological Barriers: The adoption of advanced technologies for sustainability faces various technological barriers, including high costs, limited scalability, and technological complexity. Overcoming technological barriers requires investments in research and development, technology transfer, and capacity-building initiatives to accelerate technology deployment, improve cost-effectiveness, and enhance technology accessibility for developing countries and marginalized communities(SASSI *et al.,*2019b).

Policy and Governance Gaps: Inadequate policy frameworks, regulatory frameworks, and governance mechanisms pose significant barriers to sustainable development and environmental protection. Strengthening policy coherence, institutional capacity, and stakeholder engagement are essential to address policy and governance gaps, enhance regulatory enforcement, and foster multi-stakeholder partnerships for sustainable development goals(SASSI *et al.,*2019c).

7.2. Opportunities

Innovation and Technology: Advances in science, technology, and innovation offer unprecedented opportunities to address environmental challenges, drive sustainable development, and foster green growth. Emerging technologies, such as artificial intelligence, renewable energy, and digitalization, enable transformative solutions for resource efficiency, pollution prevention, and environmental monitoring and management(OUALI *et al.,*2023b).

Circular Economy Transition: The transition to a circular economy model presents opportunities to decouple economic growth from resource consumption, minimize waste generation, and maximize resource efficiency and value retention throughout the product life cycle. Circular economy initiatives, such as product redesign, material recycling, and resource recovery, create new business opportunities, stimulate innovation, and promote sustainable consumption and production patterns.

Policy Innovation: Innovative policy instruments, such as carbon pricing mechanisms, eco-labeling schemes, and green procurement policies, can incentivize sustainable practices, mobilize private sector investments, and facilitate market-driven solutions to environmental challenges. Policy innovation, supported by multi-level governance frameworks and international cooperation, can unlock synergies between environmental protection, economic development, and social equity objectives.

Community Engagement: Empowering local communities, indigenous peoples, and civil society organizations as active participants in sustainable development initiatives enhances social inclusiveness, cultural diversity, and environmental stewardship. Community-based approaches to natural resource management, participatory decision-making processes, and knowledge sharing platforms foster grassroots innovation, local resilience, and adaptive capacity to environmental change.

Global Partnerships: Collaborative partnerships between governments, businesses, academia, and civil society organizations are essential to mobilize resources, share best practices, and scale up sustainable development solutions at the regional, national, and global levels. Global partnerships, such as the United Nations Sustainable Development Goals, the Paris Agreement on climate change, and the Convention on Biological Diversity, provide frameworks for collective action, mutual learning, and shared responsibility for global environmental sustainability(SABIR, *et al.*2020).

By addressing these challenges and seizing opportunities for innovation, collaboration, and transformative change, stakeholders can contribute to the realization of a sustainable and resilient future for current and future generations(REIS *et al.*,2021).

8. CONCLUSION

In conclusion, advanced technologies offer transformative solutions for addressing key sustainability and environmental challenges, providing a pathway to a more sustainable and resilient future. The deployment of renewable energy systems, such as solar, wind, and geothermal power, is crucial in reducing our reliance on fossil fuels and mitigating the impacts of climate change. Smart grid technologies further enhance the efficiency and reliability of energy distribution, integrating renewable sources and enabling more responsive and adaptive energy management(GUO *et al.,*2022).

In agriculture, precision farming techniques optimize resource use and improve crop yields, contributing to food security while minimizing environmental impact. These practices promote the sustainable use of land and water resources, preserving ecosystems and biodiversity for future generations. Similarly, green manufacturing processes reduce waste, lower emissions, and enhance resource efficiency, supporting sustainable industrial development(OUALI *et al.,*2023a).

Green infrastructure solutions, including green roofs, urban forests, and permeable pavements, provide multiple ecosystem services, improving urban resilience to climate change and enhancing the quality of life in cities. These nature-based approaches help manage stormwater, reduce urban heat islands, and promote urban biodiversity, demonstrating the value of integrating natural systems into urban planning and development.

Furthermore, the integration of big data, artificial intelligence, and the Internet of Things (IoT) in environmental monitoring and management enables more accurate, timely, and informed decision-making. These technologies facilitate the collection, analysis, and interpretation of vast amounts of environmental data, supporting proactive and adaptive management strategies that can respond to emerging challenges and opportunities(OUALI et al., 2022a).

The potential of advanced technologies to foster sustainability is immense, but realizing this potential requires innovation, collaboration, and a commitment to ethical and responsible development. Policymakers, businesses, researchers, and communities must work together to create an enabling environment for technological adoption and innovation. This includes investing in research and development, fostering public-private partnerships, and ensuring equitable access to technological benefits(OUA-LI *et al.*,2022c).

By harnessing the power of innovation and collaboration, we can leverage these technologies to build a more sustainable and resilient future for generations to come. This will involve preserving our planet's precious resources, safeguarding the health and well-being of all living beings, and creating a world where economic growth and environmental stewardship go hand in hand. As we move forward, it is imperative that we adopt a holistic and integrated approach to sustainability, recognizing the interconnectedness of social, economic, and environmental systems and striving to achieve balance and harmony between them.

REFERENCES

Aghion, P., Antonin, C., & Bunel, S. (2022). Financial markets and green innovation. *NBER Working Paper Series.* DOI: 10.3386/w30374

Aguero, J. R., Takayesu, M., & Lawrence, C. (2017). Modernizing the grid: Challenges and opportunities for a sustainable future. *IEEE Power & Energy Magazine*, *15*(3), 74–83. DOI: 10.1109/MPE.2017.2660819

Ahsan, F., Dana, N. H., Sarker, S. K., Li, L., Muyeen, S. M., Ali, M. F., & Das, P., (2023). Data-driven next-generation smart grid towards sustainable energy evolution: Techniques and technology review. *Protection and Control of Modern Power Systems*, *8*(3), 1–42. DOI: 10.1186/s41601-023-00319-5

Allouhi, A., Rehman, S., Buker, M. S., & Said, Z., (2023). Recent technical approaches for improving energy efficiency and sustainability of PV and PV-T systems: A comprehensive review. *Sustainable Energy Technologies and Assessments*, *56*, 103026. DOI: 10.1016/j.seta.2023.103026

Alotaibi, I., Abido, M.A., Khalid, M. & Savkin, A.V., (2020). A comprehensive review of recent advances in smart grids: A sustainable future with renewable energy resources. *Energies*, *13*(23), 6269. DOI: 10.3390/en13236269

Altieri, M. A., Nicholls, C. I., & Montalba, R. (2017). Technological approaches to sustainable agriculture at a crossroads: An agroecological perspective. *Sustainability (Basel)*, *9*(3), 349. DOI: 10.3390/su9030349

Arbi, A., Cao, J. and Alsaedi, A.,, (2018). Dynamics of BAM neural networks with mixed delays and leakage time-varying delays in the weighted pseudo-almost periodic on time-space scales. *Mathematical Methods in the Applied Sciences*, *41*(3), 1230–1255. DOI: 10.1002/mma.4661

Arbi, A., & Chen, Z. (2018). Improved synchronization analysis of competitive neural networks with time-varying delays. *Nonlinear Analysis (Vilnius)*, *23*(1), 82–107. DOI: 10.15388/NA.2018.1.7

Arbi, A., & Tahri, N., (2024). Synchronization analysis of novel delayed dynamical Clifford-valued neural networks on timescales. *Journal of Algorithms & Computational Technology, 18*, 17483026241241492. DOI: 10.1177/17483026241241492

Arbi, A., Guo, Y. & Cao, J., (2021). Convergence analysis on time scales for HOBAM neural networks in the Stepanov-like weighted pseudo-almost automorphic space. *Neural Computing & Applications, 33*(8), 3567–3581. DOI: 10.1007/s00521-020-05183-0

Archana, K., Visckram, A.S., Kumar, P.S., Manikandan, S., Saravanan, A. and Natrayan, L., (2024). A review on recent technological breakthroughs in anaerobic digestion of organic biowaste for biogas generation: Challenges towards sustainable development goals. *Fuel, 358*, 130298. DOI: 10.1016/j.fuel.2023.130298

Awogbemi, O., Kallon, D.V.V. & Bello, K.A., (2022). Resource recycling with the aim of achieving zero-waste manufacturing. *Sustainability (Basel), 14*(8), 4503. DOI: 10.3390/su14084503

Darwish, A.S. & Al-Dabbagh, R., (2020). Wind energy state of the art: Present and future technology advancements. *Renewable Energy and Environmental Sustainability, 5*, 7. DOI: 10.1051/rees/2020003

Dinh, V.N. and McKeogh, E. (2019). Offshore wind energy: Technology opportunities and challenges. In *Proceedings of the 1st Vietnam Symposium on Advances in Offshore Engineering: Energy and Geotechnics* (pp. 3–22). Springer Singapore. DOI: 10.1007/978-981-13-2306-5_1

Gray, Wayne B., & Jay P. Shimshack, (2011). The effectiveness of environmental monitoring and enforcement: A review of the empirical evidence. *Review of Environmental Economics and Policy, 5*(1), 3–24. DOI: 10.1093/reep/req017

Guo, Y., Ge, S.S. & Arbi, A., (2022). Stability of traveling wave solutions for nonlinear cellular neural networks with distributed delays. *Journal of Systems Science and Complexity, 35*(1), 18–31. DOI: 10.1007/s11424-021-0180-7

Hadj Sassi, M.S. & Chaari Fourati, L., (2024). Design cognitive IoT architecture framework for immersive visual technologies of air quality monitoring systems. *Multimedia Tools and Applications*, *83*(17), 51615–51646. DOI: 10.1007/s11042-023-17249-x

Hamdi, M., Mestiri, S. & Arbi, A., (2024). Artificial intelligence techniques for bankruptcy prediction of Tunisian companies: An application of machine learning and deep learning-based models. *Journal of Risk and Financial Management*, *17*(4), 132. DOI: 10.3390/jrfm17040132

Iqbal, S., Sarfraz, M., Ayyub, M., Tariq, M., Chakrabortty, R.K., Ryan, M.J. & Alamri, B., (2021). A comprehensive review on residential demand-side management strategies in smart grid environments. *Sustainability (Basel)*, *13*(13), 7170. DOI: 10.3390/su13137170

Islam, M.T., Huda, N., Abdullah, A.B. & Saidur, R., (2018). A comprehensive review of state-of-the-art concentrating solar power (CSP) technologies: Current status and research trends. *Renewable & Sustainable Energy Reviews*, *91*, 987–1018. DOI: 10.1016/j.rser.2018.04.097

Karmaker, C.L., Al Aziz, R., Ahmed, T., Misbauddin, S.M. & Moktadir, M.A., (2023). Impact of industry 4.0 technologies on sustainable supply chain performance: The mediating role of green supply chain management practices and circular economy. *Journal of Cleaner Production*, *419*, 138249. DOI: 10.1016/j.jclepro.2023.138249

Khan, S., Naushad, M., Iqbal, J., Bathula, C. & Al-Muhtaseb, A.A.H., (2022). Challenges and perspectives on innovative technologies for biofuel production and sustainable environmental management. *Fuel*, *325*, 124845. DOI: 10.1016/j.fuel.2022.124845

Kougias, I., Aggidis, G., Avellan, F., Deniz, S., Lundin, U., Moro, A., Muntean, S., Novara, D., Pérez-Díaz, J.I., Quaranta, E. & Schild, P., (2019). Analysis of emerging technologies in the hydropower sector. *Renewable & Sustainable Energy Reviews*, *113*, 109257. DOI: 10.1016/j.rser.2019.109257

Lamnatou, C., Chemisana, D., & Ortega, E. (2022). Smart grids and smart technologies in relation to photovoltaics, storage systems, buildings and the environment. *Renewable Energy, 185*, 1376–1391. DOI: 10.1016/j.renene.2021.11.019

Leijten, J., Edler, J., & Boekholt, P. (2019). Innovation policy and international relations: Directions for EU diplomacy. *European Journal of Futures Research, 7*(1), 4. DOI: 10.1186/s40309-019-0156-1

Mohaghegh, S., Niknam, H., & Alishah, R. S. (2021). Latest advances on hybrid solar–biomass power plants. *Energy Sources. Part A, Recovery, Utilization, and Environmental Effects*, •••, 1–24. DOI: 10.1080/15567036.2021.1919484

Narassimhan, E., Gallagher, K. S., Koester, S., & Rivera Alejo, J. (2018). Carbon pricing in practice: A review of existing emissions trading systems. *Climate Policy, 18*(8), 967–991. DOI: 10.1080/14693062.2018.1467827

Nayak, A., & Singh, S. (2019). Crop-livestock-agroforestry based integrated farming system: An eco-efficient sustainable practice for food and nutritional security.

Nižetić, S., & Kovačić, T. (2020). Internet of Things (IoT): Opportunities, issues, and challenges towards a smart and sustainable future. *Journal of Cleaner Production, 274*, 122877. DOI: 10.1016/j.jclepro.2020.122877 PMID: 32834567

Ouali, I., & Benotmane, M. (2024). Text recuperated using ontology with stable marriage optimization technique and text visualization using AR. *Multimedia Tools and Applications, 83*(41), 1–28. DOI: 10.1007/s11042-024-18795-8

Ouali, I., & Boudoukhane, A. (2022). Real-time application for recognition and visualization of Arabic words with vowels based deep learning and augmented reality. In *2022 International Wireless Communications and Mobile Computing (IWCMC)* (pp. 678-683). IEEE.

Ouali, I., & Boudoukhane, A. (2022). Augmented reality for scene text recognition, visualization and reading to assist visually impaired people. *Procedia Computer Science, 207*, 158–167. DOI: 10.1016/j.procs.2022.09.048

Ouali, I., & Sassi, H. (2021). Architecture for real-time visualizing Arabic words with diacritics using augmented reality for visually impaired people. In *International Conference on Advanced Information Networking and Applications* (pp. 285-296). Cham: Springer International Publishing. DOI: 10.1007/978-3-030-75100-5_25

Ouali, I., & Sassi, H. (2022). Text detection and recognition using augmented reality and deep learning. In *International Conference on Advanced Information Networking and Applications* (pp. 13-23). Cham: Springer International Publishing. DOI: 10.1007/978-3-030-99584-3_2

Ouali, I., & Sassi, H. (2023). An augmented reality for an Arabic text reading and visualization assistant for the visually impaired. *Multimedia Tools and Applications*, *82*(28), 43569–43597. DOI: 10.1007/s11042-023-14880-6

Ouali, I., & Zhang, W. (2023). A novel method for Arabic text detection with interactive visualization. In *2023 IEEE Symposium on Computers and Communications (ISCC)* (pp. 1046-1050). IEEE. DOI: 10.1109/ISCC58397.2023.10218141

Pathirana, M. R., & Silva, P. (2022). Management and utilization of plant genetic resources for a sustainable agriculture. *Plants*, *11*(15), 2038. DOI: 10.3390/plants11152038 PMID: 35956515

Rana, M. M., Akhter, S., & Uddin, S. (2023). Applications of energy storage systems in power grids with and without renewable energy integration—A comprehensive review. *Journal of Energy Storage*, *68*, 107811. DOI: 10.1016/j.est.2023.107811

Refaat, M., Zhang, W., & El-Sharkawi, M. A. (2018). Self-healing control strategy: Challenges and opportunities for distribution systems in smart grid. In *2018 IEEE 12th International Conference on Compatibility, Power Electronics and Power Engineering (CPE-POWERENG 2018)* (pp. 1-6). IEEE.

Rehman, F., Shah, S. M., & Ali, M. (2021). An efficient energy management in smart grid considering demand response program and renewable energy sources. *IEEE Access : Practical Innovations, Open Solutions*, *9*, 148821–148844. DOI: 10.1109/ACCESS.2021.3124557

Rehman, S., Al-Hadhrami, L. M., & Alam, M. M. (2015). Pumped hydro energy storage system: A technological review. *Renewable & Sustainable Energy Reviews*, *44*, 586–598. DOI: 10.1016/j.rser.2014.12.040

Reis, A., & Silva, J. (2021). Striding towards sustainability: A framework to overcome challenges and explore opportunities through industry 4.0. *Sustainability (Basel)*, *13*(9), 5232. DOI: 10.3390/su13095232

Roy, D., Kaur, A., & Meena, M. (2020). Precision farming: A step towards sustainable, climate-smart agriculture. In *Global climate change: Resilient and smart agriculture* (pp. 199-220). DOI: 10.1007/978-981-32-9856-9_10

Sabir, M., & Ahmad, I. (2021). Neuro-swarms intelligent computing using Gudermannian kernel for solving a class of second order Lane-Emden singular nonlinear model. *AIMS Mathematics*, *6*(3), 2468–2485. DOI: 10.3934/math.2021150

Sabir, Z., Saoud, S., Raja, M.A.Z., Wahab, H.A. and Arbi, A., (2020). Heuristic computing technique for numerical solutions of nonlinear fourth order Emden–Fowler equation. *Mathematics and Computers in Simulation*, *178*, 534–548. DOI: 10.1016/j.matcom.2020.06.021

Sassi, H., & Ouali, I. (2019). Multi-oriented real-time Arabic scene text detection with deep fully convolutional networks. In *2019 IEEE/ACS 16th International Conference on Computer Systems and Applications (AICCSA)* (pp. 1-6). IEEE. DOI: 10.1109/AICCSA47632.2019.9035340

Sassi, H., & Ouali, I. (2019). Business information architecture for big data and Internet of Things. In *2019 15th International Wireless Communications & Mobile Computing Conference (IWCMC)* (pp. 1749-1756). IEEE.

Sassi, H., & Ouali, I. (2019). Computer-aided software engineering (CASE) tool for big data and IoT architecture. In *2019 15th International Wireless Communications & Mobile Computing Conference (IWCMC)* (pp. 1403-1410). IEEE.

Sassi, H., & Ouali, I. (2020). Investigation on deep learning methods for privacy and security challenges of cognitive IoV. In *2020 International Wireless Communications and Mobile Computing (IWCMC)* (pp. 714-720). IEEE. DOI: 10.1109/IWCMC48107.2020.9148417

Singhal, A., & Garg, R. (2024). Environmental sustainability consideration with just-in-time practices in Industry 4.0 era: A state of the art. *Operations Management Research*, 1-24.

Stephenson, S. S., & Sherwin, J. (2020). Technological advances in biodiversity monitoring: Applicability, opportunities, and challenges. *Current Opinion in Environmental Sustainability*, *45*, 36–41. DOI: 10.1016/j.cosust.2020.08.005

Taddese, S., & Mekonnen, K. (2020). Sustainability performance indicators for additive manufacturing: A literature review based on product life cycle studies. *International Journal of Advanced Manufacturing Technology*, *107*(7-8), 3109–3134. DOI: 10.1007/s00170-020-05249-2

Tahat, M., Ahmad, A., & Daka, A. (2020). Soil health and sustainable agriculture. *Sustainability*, *12*(12), 4859. DOI: 10.3390/su12124859

Tang, Y., Sun, Y., & Liu, H. (2021). Power electronics: The enabling technology for renewable energy integration. *CSEE Journal of Power and Energy Systems*, *8*(1), 39–52. DOI: 10.17775/CSEEJPES.2021.00170

Tuballa, M. T., & Olasimbo, F. (2016). A review of the development of smart grid technologies. *Renewable & Sustainable Energy Reviews*, *59*, 710–725. DOI: 10.1016/j.rser.2016.01.011

Ukhurebor, K. E., & Usman, S. (2022). An overview of the emergence and challenges of land reclamation: Issues and prospects. *Applied and Environmental Soil Science*, *2022*, 1–14. DOI: 10.1155/2022/5889823

Urbina, A., Ballesteros, D., & Cabanillas, A. (2020). The balance between efficiency, stability and environmental impacts in perovskite solar cells: A review. *Journal of Physics: Energy*, *2*(2), 022001. DOI: 10.1088/2515-7655/ab5eee

Velasco-Muñoz, J. F., & López, A. M. (2019). Sustainable irrigation in agriculture: An analysis of global research. *Water (Basel)*, *11*(9), 1758. DOI: 10.3390/w11091758

Venkatramanan, S., & Elango, A. (2019). Climate-smart agriculture technologies for environmental management: The intersection of sustainability, resilience, wellbeing and development. In *Sustainable green technologies for environmental management* (pp. 29-51).

Weerasooriya, P., & Mahadevan, S. (2021). Industrial water conservation by water footprint and sustainable development goals: A review. *Environment, Development and Sustainability*, *23*(9), 12661–12709. DOI: 10.1007/s10668-020-01184-0

Wu, J., Zhang, Y., & Lin, Y. (2023). Toward sustainable all solid-state Li–metal batteries: Perspectives on battery technology and recycling processes. *Advanced Materials*, *35*(51), 2301540. DOI: 10.1002/adma.202301540 PMID: 37191036

Chapter 9
Low-Cost Computing to Automate Appliances Across an IoT Network for Efficient Energy Utilization

Renuka Devi Saravanan
Vellore Institute of Technology, Chennai, India

Soham Bhattacharyya
Vellore Institute of Technology, Chennai, India

Hritibroto Sanyal
Vellore Institute of Technology, Chennai, India

Riddhirup Bera
Vellore Institute of Technology, Chennai, India

ABSTRACT

This chapter focuses on building a smart environment that can preserve energy on its own. The proposed model incorporates a bidirectional visitor counter that adjusts power supply based on peoples' presence or absence. In the case of a living room, this system will identify the amount

DOI: 10.4018/979-8-3693-8141-0.ch009

of people in the room and switch on electricity to specified equipment. When the number of individuals within a closed space, the system turns off the power supply. The deployed appliances will be controlled by one or more programmed microcontrollers, which will instruct them to work efficiently based on need, drawing just the necessary amount of electricity and conserving power in the process. The majority of appliances may be handled from a single location, thereby increasing convenience. There will be greater energy efficiency. The intelligent design of interconnected appliances allows the user to remotely manage and monitor their operation even when they are far away from them.

1. INTRODUCTION

Home/ workspace automation is a technology that allows the user to remotely monitor and control the devices which are connected to the Internet. Automation works on three levels:

- **Monitoring**: The users can make use of the mobile applications to remotely monitor the critical parameters of the devices that are connected to the network.
- **Control**: The users can control or manage the devices remotely based on the observed (monitored) information.
- **Automation**: It involves in triggering a device based on some event.

Thus, automation makes our life more convenient and can preserve critical resources like water, electricity, etc. The core requirement for automation is connecting a network of devices so that they can be monitored and accessed. A central hub or a router is required to connect all the devices to the Internet. Also a device orchestrating every other connected device is required. One such central device is our smart phones with the controller App installed. There are a variety of protocols to connect to a hub such as WiFi, Bluetooth, Zigbee, Z-Wave and then the hub bridges their connection to the internet.

Home automation has several useful applications (Kathiria et al. (2017), Han and Lim (2010)). The most important are energy management, communication, convenience, accessibility. Energy management involves in conserving energy by avoiding waste. This in turn results in energy efficiency. Through home automation, it is possible to communicate with the devices and control them remotely. It also makes it possible to automate repetitive and routine tasks in the devices connected to the Internet thereby providing convenience and security. It also guarantees universal accessibility in any environment. Cloud computing plays a predominant role in automation. Instead of relying on multiple high-end computers to upload and process the data, cloud based solution is considered more affordable and convenient to use.

2. NEED FOR AUTOMATION

At a time when fossil fuels are reaching depletion and society is shifting toward the usage of alternative energy sources such as solar energy, wind energy, tidal energy, and so on. Energy conservation has arisen as a critical issue in society. The government and environmental groups are conducting campaigns, events, and awareness initiatives in schools and offices, as well as promoting them through the media. As a result, our concept may be commercially executed on a wide scale and reach the market as smart appliances aimed at reducing wasteful power waste.

There is the possibility of implementing the project inside any building, such as rooms, hallways, or any type of workplace. The system is high-performing and has low maintenance expenses. It is incredibly simple and efficient to use. As unwanted usage of electricity is reduced, there will be less waste of resources, whether deliberately or inadvertently. If built on a wide scale, the project can be implemented in campuses, companies, and complexes, as well as individual houses (Rizman et al. (2013), Vaibhav and Gavish (2013), O'Reilly (2005)) .

This chapter attempts to create a smart environment in the home or workplace that can preserve energy on its own. In current culture, energy waste is seen as a major issue. Because most energy sources are non-renewable, wasting precious energy might have serious consequences in the future. Every home in the United States spends an average of $1,368.36 per year on energy. And 35% of the energy utilized is really wasted. So, in addition to the environmental consequences, considerable monetary losses may be averted if we can properly preserve energy.

Due to this issue, India wastes 20% of all renewable energy generated in a 24-hour period. Electricity is currently controlled manually by the user in current systems. Human mistake is highly prevalent in such instances, and a lot of energy is lost every day as a result of such blunders. Our System is designed to handle this issue while also conserving energy.

3. LITERATURE SURVEY

Sharif et al. (2022) proposed a home automation system which makes use of different sensors and controllers to monitor and control the home appliances which are used in our day-to-day life. The devices to be monitored must be connected to the Internet in order to access, monitor, manage, and control it remotely. The proposed method seems to be cost-effective and flexible. An android based application was developed for remote monitoring and control. In order to achieve reliability and robustness, edge computing platform was incorporated during the computation offloading process. The proposed system is fully automatic and it is driven based on the environmental conditions and home occupant's need. The proposed model ensures complete home automation and also it reduces the power consumption significantly via optimum utilization.

Gondkar et al. (2022) proposed a model to build a home automation system by assembling Ardino board and bluetooth together. The entire system can be monitored and controlled using Android smartphone. Perni et al. (2023) proposed a model which involves designing a power management system to monitor and control the electronic devices through a mobile/web dashboard. Unlike traditional methods, this model uses wireless communication in order to make the model flexible and reliable. The model proposed is cost effective, involves minimal manpower and conserves electricity. Iyappan et al. (2022) proposed a system which includes a central processing module to control the devices that are connected to the Internet via home Wi-Fi connection. This system mainly focuses on increasing the system performance and reliability. It also enables the user to create, install and customize additional features via mobile application.

Hassan et al. (2022) proposed a smart kitchen in which the users can control devices like air conditioners, ovens and freezers remotely through their mobile phones. This system is capable of detecting gas leaks in the kitchen by deploying a built-in gas detection sensor. Also, it notifies the user whenever the gas pressure exceeds certain threshold. In addition, system automatically detects the room temperature and humidity level in the kitchen. They used ESP32, DHT11 Sensor, 5V relay X8, and MQ-135 gas sensors to detect and control the temperature, humidity, and detecting gas leakage. The hardware was integrated and programmed using an Arduino. The experimental results revealed that the system has a significant impact on electricity consumption and cost.

Willoughby and Alexander (2022) proposed an IoT based home automation and weather monitoring system. The components used are ESP32 which acts as a network gateway, a relay module, DHT11 sensor to monitor temperature and humidity and two protocols for creating interface: HTTP and MQTT. The data with respect to house hold appliances and weather are collected and stored periodically. Based on the observed value, the devices can be controlled remotely in a cost effective manner.

Yar et al. (2021) suggested an integrated system residence built on top of IoT and edge-computing model. Raspberry Pi (RPI) device acts as a controlling unit, offering an economical solution for connecting different devices connected through the internat. Both local and remote control is possible with this system. Moreover, the edge computing model is employed to store confidential information in the cloud thereby preserving the privacy of the consumer. This model was proven efficient in terms of power usage, bandwidth utilization, and response time and cost effectiveness. Maragatham et al. (2021) also proposed a similar model with WLAN module (Wireless Local Area Network) to remotely control home appliances. A relay module is used to switch on/off the devices.

Stolojescu-Crisan et al. (2022) proposed qToggle with a more flexible network design. The functionalities of qToggle include automation, control, monitoring, and security. qToggle system is made user friendly and customizable with the help of the mobile apps and add-ons. Sahrab

(2021) proposed a model which focuses on home security and automation. Home security is achieved by antitheft mechanism where laser source, light-dependent resistor and infrared sensors are used to detect and alarm the user. In home automation, fire and gas leakage is detected using flame sensor and MQ-05 sensor respectively. In addition, servo motor, LCD and bluetooth module are incorporated to have a complete reliable system.

Baqir and Zahraa (2022) proposed a cost effective and energy efficient alert system in which the devices to be monitored are linked to the I/O ports of the ESP32 microcontroller board. The devices can be controlled using mobile app or web server. Wireless communication exists between the microcontroller and smart phone. Motion sensors are incorporated to set the action of the system. Jain et al.'s framework (2022) focuses on the development of home automation, enabling the user to computerize all of their household appliances and combine them to provide consistent control over every area of their house. The data received from the sensors is sent to WiFi module using cloud and the decision is made using decision tree.

Flamini et. al. (2023) proposed a cost-effective automation and monitoring system. A typical home with smart devices installed for equipment control and widespread electrical and thermal energy consumption monitoring has been used as the reference for their work. The primary environmental factors that impact energy are also tracked, including the windows' open or closed positions, the air temperature and humidity in each area, the amount of light present in the rooms and the building as a whole, and the presence of people. The open-source SCADA Home Assistant was then updated to include these components, and a very basic dashboard that could be accessed locally from any web browser was made available.

Mustofa et al (2023) proposed an home automation system named SECHA which is considered to be energy-efficient and cost-effective. Regardless of the type of home, it enables users to automate their homes with IoT. With the help of an Android app, SECHA has created an affordable smart home automation system that combines Wi-Fi and GSM technology are used for remote monitoring and control. An ESP32 microcontroller with Wi-Fi and a GSM SIM800 has been used to create this automation system.

Balan et al. (2023) proposed an Android-based IoT-based electric meter surveillance system. The electric analyzer pulse is recorded using an optical sensor and an Arduino Uno. A low-cost wireless network of sensors for digital energy meters is used in conjunction with a smartphone application that can read the unit's meter on its own. The proposed model includes three major components namely, the controller, NB-IoT connection module, and cloud. This system involves in less human intervention.

4. PROPOSED SYSTEM

The goal of this chapter is to build a system of smart appliances that will work according to environmental circumstances and will eliminate electricity wastage, hence aiding in energy conservation. Current methods include user-controlled electricity. Human mistake is highly prevalent in such situations, and a lot of energy is squandered every day as a result of such blunders. The proposed system is designed to handle this issue while also conserving energy. The objectives of the model proposed are

- To delegate management of energy-consuming equipment from people to pre-programmed systems that turn off electricity to appliances when the room/structure is empty.
- To redirect optimal electricity to appliances based on demands and environmental circumstances.
- To promote the use and development of smart appliances in order to solve the concerns of energy conservation, global warming, and the transition to renewable energy sources.

The proposed system incorporates a bidirectional visitor counter that adjusts power supply based on people's presence or absence. This technique may be utilized efficiently in both public and private settings. In the case of a living room, this system will identify the amount of people in the room and switch on electricity to specified equipment. When the number of individuals within a closed space, such as a hall/ office/ room, reaches zero, the system turns off the power supply. The deployed appliances will be controlled by one or more programmed microcontrollers, which will instruct them to work efficiently based on need, drawing just the necessary amount of electricity and conserving power in the process. A ceiling fan, for example, will be part of the system and will spin at a speed determined by the temperature of the area. As a result, this method will significantly cut energy usage on a broad scale.

The majority of appliances may be handled from a single location, increasing convenience. There will be greater energy efficiency, which means that based on how one uses the linked appliances around the clock, one may make one's area energy-efficient. Making a person's life easier is a big selling point, and our initiative focuses on this. The intelligent design of interconnected appliances allows the user to remotely manage and monitor their operation even when he is far away from them. This even protects the safety of other items and equipment in the event of a breakdown at any end.

4.1 System Design

The proposed model consists of a network of smart appliances that react to external environmental conditions and then operate accordingly to reduce wasteful consumption. When no one is there, a system would turn off all of the electrical appliances in the room. This would decrease energy waste produced when individuals forget to turn off electrical appliances in a room and leave, and the electric appliance continues to run for no one, generating excessive power waste. When individuals enter the room, the electrical appliances, such as smart lighting and smart fans, begin to work.

Smart lights would only turn on when the ambient light intensity fell below a specified threshold and turn off when the ambient light intensity rose over that threshold. The brightness of the light would change depending on the strength of the ambient light in between. If the ambient light intensity is high, the brightness of the light will be low; if the ambient light intensity is low, the brightness of the light will be high; and so on. This would solve the issue of lights being turned on when there is enough sunshine and we do not require artificial lighting, hence reducing wasteful energy waste.

Smart fans would operate only above a specified external temperature and would be turned off below that temperature, with the intervals varying according to the external temperature. If the external temperature is low, the fan speed will become low and will be turned off below a particular temperature; if the temperature is high, the fan speed will become high up to a given limit. To put the aforementioned notion into action, a pre-programmed controller unit that regulates the power output and has output ports for electrical appliances as well as a manual control option would be necessary.

4.2 Core Components and their working principle

Entry/Leave Detector

A mechanism will be in place to keep track of the number of persons in a room. This would be accomplished by employing two sensors, one within the room and one outside the room. When there is no one within the room, i.e. when the number of persons inside the room is zero, all electrical appliances are turned off, and when the number of people inside the room is more than zero, all electrical appliances are turned on.

Smart Light

There will be a lighting system in which the brightness of the smart light is determined by the intensity of the ambient light. If the ambient light intensity is strong, the brightness of the smart light will be low, and it will turn off if the ambient light intensity exceeds a certain threshold. If the ambient light intensity is low, the brightness of the smart light will rise automatically. This will be accomplished with the help of photo resistors and an Arduino.

Smart Fan

There will be a fan system whose speed will be determined by the temperature of the area. If the ambient temperature is low, the fan's speed will increase up to a particular limit; if the ambient temperature is high, the fan's speed will drop, and below a given temperature, it will turn off. As a result, we would not have to wake up in the middle of the night or leave work to alter the fan speed, while also reducing wasteful power waste.

Working Pronciple

The Entry/Leave Detector determines if the appliances are turned on or off. The Entry/Leave Detector operates on the following principle: There would be two PIR sensors on either side of the door or at the room's entry. When a person enters the room, the first sensor outside the room detects movement, and when the person exits, the sensor within the room senses movement. Only when the sensors detect movement in this specific sequence is the entry into the room detected, and the count of the number of persons within the room grows, and the electrical appliances turn on and begin to work. The block diagram and entire work flow of the proposed model are shown in Figure1 and Figure 2 respectively.

Figure 1. Block diagram of proposed system

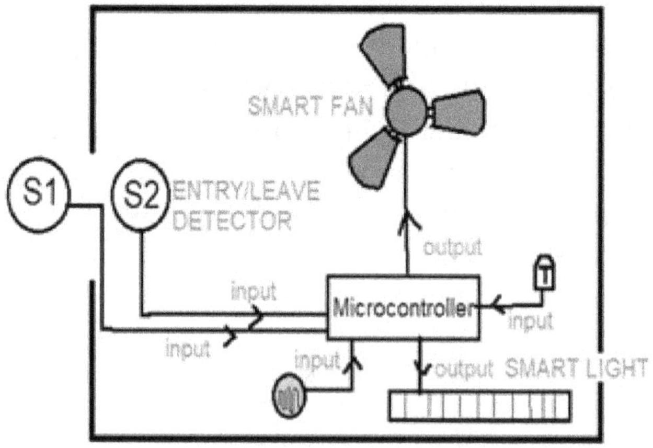

Figure 2. Work flow of proposed system

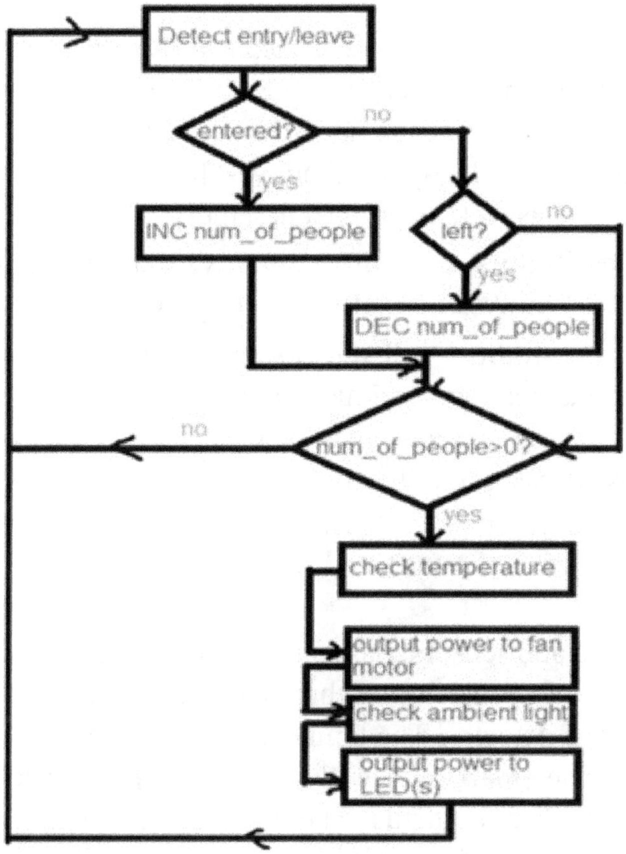

When the Entry/Leave Detector detects that a person has entered the room and the electrical appliances are turned on, the smart light begins to function; if the ambient light intensity is high, the brightness of the smart light is low; if the ambient light intensity is low, the brightness of the smart light is automatically increased up to a certain intensity. Above a certain level of ambient light intensity, the light will turn off. The smart fan is also activated, and if the ambient temperature is low, the fan's speed will increase up to a set limit; if the ambient temperature is high, the fan's speed will drop, and below a particular temperature, it will be turned off.

4.3 Feasibility study

Economic Feasibility - In theory, the idea is fairly possible. All electronic components used in the project (say, the fan and light) are inexpensive and widely accessible. The manufacturing of such a system will not be prohibitively expensive. However, there will be an extra payment for the integrated software as well as product assembly.

Technical Feasibility - All of the necessary electronic components are readily available. The system's software and code are straightforward.

Operational Feasibility - All sensors are extremely reactive and can easily measure changes. This technique can function flawlessly with very little variation. All sensors are extremely sensitive. By modifying the code, the project may be easily modified.

4.4 Overview of Software

Using Arduino and sensors, our team is developing a smart household system. The project is made up of three parts: a smart light, a smart fan, and an entry-leave detector. The temperature will allow the smart fan to alter its speed. The smart light will shine in proportion to the amount of light flowing in from outside. The entry-leave detector will identify whether or not a person is present in the room. The electrical devices in the room will only function if someone is there.

4.5 Hardware Specification

Figure 3 shows the circuit design of the proposed work. The components used are

1. PIR Sensor
2. Temperature sensor
3. NPN transistor
4. DC motor
5. Resistors
6. LCD screen

7. Arduino UNO
8. Light bulb
9. Power supply
10. Photo resistor
11. Breadboard
12. Connecting wires

Figure 3. Complete circuit

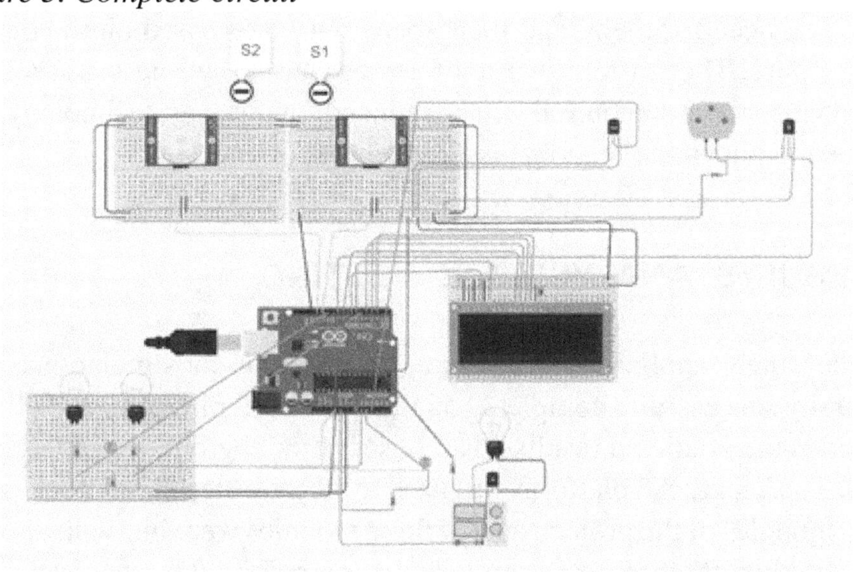

4.6 Software Requirements

The project was created using Tinkercad software and was emulated online. Tinkercad includes all of the components required for simulating hardware projects on software. The Arduino UNO was used for programming, and the code was created in C++. The Arduino UNO board has a number of digital and analogue input/output (I/O) pins that may be used to connect to various expansion boards and other devices. The board features 14 digital I/O pins (six of which are capable of PWM output), 6 analog I/O pins, and is programmable through a type B USB cable using the

Arduino IDE (Integrated Development Environment). It may be powered by a USB connection or an external 9-volt battery, and it handles voltages ranging from 7 to 20 volts.

As a result, the initiative will eliminate wasteful power waste by restricting the operation of equipment to just when they are needed. Electric appliances will only operate when there are humans in the room and will turn off when there aren't. Smart lights will adjust their brightness based on the intensity of the ambient light and will turn off when not in use, saving a significant amount of energy. Smart fans will only turn on when there is a need for them, and their speed will vary based on the outside temperature. The wasteful waste of power caused by rotating at a faster speed when it is not required will be reduced. In this way, technology may be used to alleviate the global issue of energy waste.

5 RESULTS, ANALYSIS AND TESTING

The smart appliances with energy conservation simulations were generally successfully completed on the Tinkercad platform, and all tests provided the predicted results on all observational grounds and test cases used. The Tinkercad platform was used to step-by-step simulate the three main modules of the project, and all three modules were individually built and tested on three different projects before being integrated as a single project where a single simulated Arduino UNO board programmatically controlled each of the project's main components, namely, the Smart Fan, Smart Light, and Entry/Leave Detector.

The three different project components were also simulated separately by mounting the various sensors and actuators as needed, onto four separate, simulated Arduino boards on three different simulated circuit files on Tinkercad, where all three components were experimented with to see if they could work independently, as this would reduce the chances of cluttering the final integrated circuit simulation with unmanageable logical, runtime, and syntactic errors. Thus, the three members of our team worked individually, keeping in mind how the final circuit would be generated by integrating the various modules into the final version's restricted number of input ports, output ports, analogue, digital, and PWM ports of the Arduino UNO board.

As with other simulation-based projects, this one had some constraints that had to be overcome, such as some errors caused by glitches in the simulated platform's software, such as simulating a timer for the ELD module that did not simulate the correct passage of time in milliseconds with respect to the real-world clock. The experimental configuration of the three primary modules, as well as the final, integrated circuit module, is detailed below.

5.1 Smart Fan Module

The smart fan module was built and tested independently on an independently simulated circuit containing a single Arduino UNO board on which the essential components only required for implementing the smart fan were mounted, such as the temperature sensor, which acts as a sensor feeding data to the Arduino microcontroller, based on which the DC motor, another essential component required solely for this module, representing the fan, functions. Figure 4 shows the Smart fan test and the oobservations on independent smart fan module are shown in Table 1. The amount of pulse-width-modulated current provided to the DC motor via the PWM interface of the ATMega328p microcontroller on Arduino determines its speed. When the simulation began, the temperature sensor linked to the Arduino read the ambient temperature as 25°C, Tinkercad's default ambient temperature setting.

When a PWM signal of 85 was given to the NPN transistor controlling the motor at 25°C, the fan speed varied throughout a range of values between 126rpm and 142rpm, a range size of 15rpm. The temperature remained at 25°C unless manually changed by using the slider supplied by Tinkercad's UI. The motor maintained the same range of speeds recorded for 25°C across the 20°C to 30°C temperature range, since a PWM value of 85 was provided to the motor during this temperature range. When the temperature control slider was adjusted below 20°C, the motor's speed decreased and nearly instantly stopped at 0rpm.

Because the PWM value provided was 0, the motor stayed static at 0rpm for all temperatures ranging from 0°C to 20°C. When the temperature was increased to a value more than 30°C but less than 35°C, the motor spun at varying speeds ranging from 274rpm to 289rpm, a range size of 15rpm, with a PWM value of 180 provided. Because a PWM value of 225 was given to the motor, it indicated a fixed rotation speed of 400rpm for all temperature values over 35°C.

Figure 4. Smart Fan test

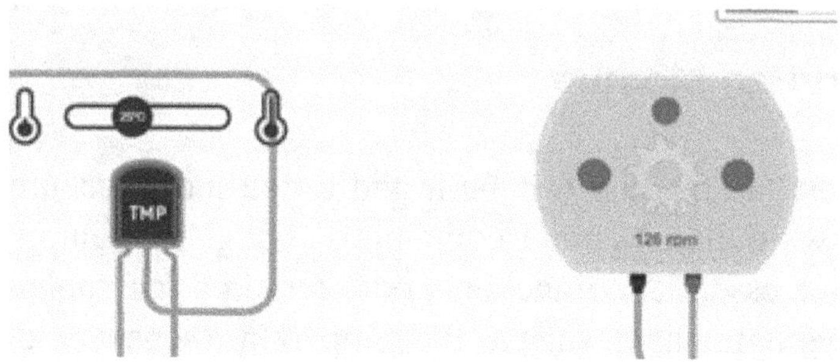

Table 1. Observations on independent smart fan module

Supplied Temperature (°C)	In programmed temperature range (°C)	Observed DC motor speed range (RPM)
12	<=20	0
25	>20, <=30	126~142
32	>30, <=35	274~289
39	>35	400

5.2 Smart Light Module

The smart light module was also first constructed and implemented individually on two distinct, mutually exclusive Arduino boards in the same Tinkercad circuit file. The two systems were tested individually to see if they operated as expected in terms of adjusting brightness through analogue and digital signals. In the first device, which used two bulbs as actuator components, the photo resistor's input value caused the brightness of the lights to alter almost exactly as expected. However, at maximum minimum ambient light intensity, the variable-brightness bulbs did not glow to their full potential, as we concluded. This was due to the fact that both bulbs drew power from the 5V output of the Arduino boards, which was all the power they had to operate, preventing them from glowing at maximum brightness. Figure 5 and 6 shows the Smart light test with variable and noon-variable brightness respectively. Table 2 shows the oobservations on independent smart light module.

The pair of bulbs responded differently and in harmony to produce changeable brightness dependent on the environmental luminosity circumstances as provided by Tinkercad as the ambient light intensity was gradually changed from least intensity to maximum intensity incrementally. The bulb on the right faded from its maximum brightness at a certain input of ambient luminosity, matching to the respective PWM signals, until both stopped shining. The non-variable light bulb, on the other hand, worked as intended: when the ambient light input value was altered from less than 500 to more than 500, the bulb's output went from shining at maximum brightness to shutting off, with no brightness in between.

Figure 5. Variable brightness smart light test

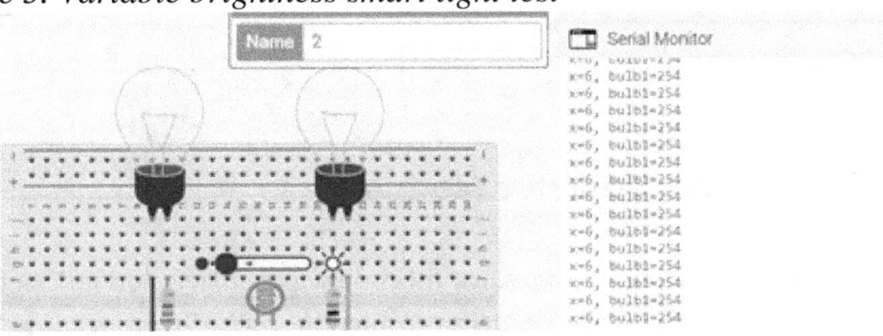

Figure 6. Non-variable brightness smart light test

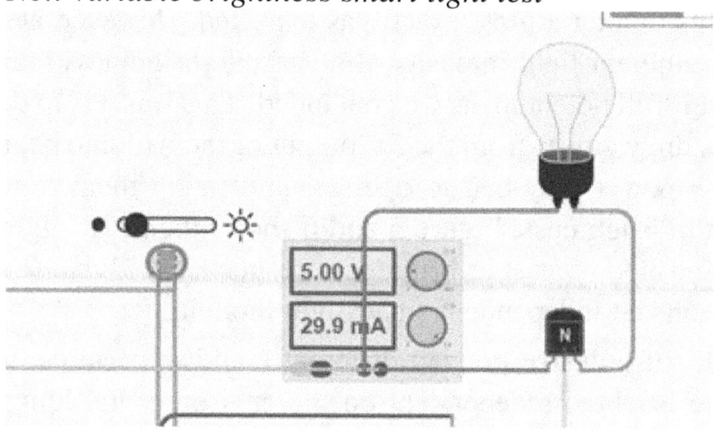

Table 2. Observations on independent smart light module

Supplied Ambient Light	PWM signal supplied to left bulb	PWM signal supplied to right bulb
6	254	254
158	254	150
343	254	0
452	100	0
567	0	0

5.3 Entry/Leave detector Module

Initially, the entry/leave detector module was constructed independently on Tinkercad with little contribution to the overall project other than keeping track of the number of persons in the room, as updated by the two PIR sensors installed on either side of the room's entrance doorway. The PIR sensors were marked by S1—which is assumed to be within the room—and S2—which is imagined to be outside the room. For the algorithm to recognize that someone had entered, S2 had to detect movement first, followed by S1 as shown in Figure 7. The software increased the counter variable by one when this occurred.

When S2 sensed movement immediately after S1, on the other hand, the counter variable was decremented by one, indicating that someone had gone. However, because there is a check for this, the counter never dipped below 0. For simplicity of use, there is an LCD panel that displays the counter's value at all times. Instead of the outputs of the smart fan and light components connected to the Arduino, the separately designed Entry/ Leave detector has two LEDs that indicate whether the room is inhabited or not. When the red LED lights up, the room is inhabited; when the green LED lights up, the room is unoccupied.

Figure 7. S2, then S1, picked up movement

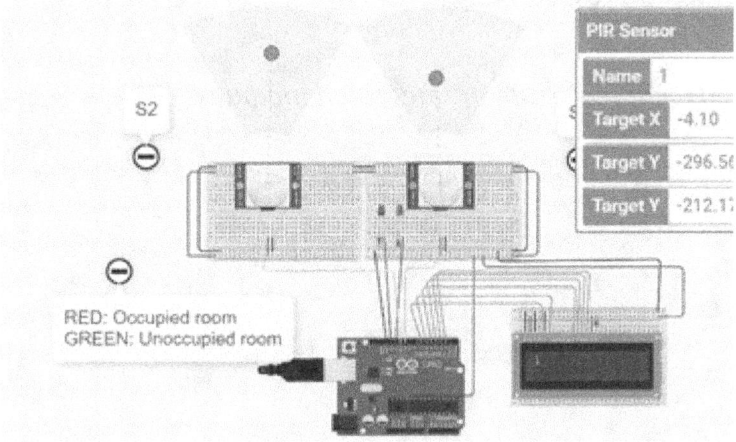

5.4 Integrated Modules

The three major modules of the project were combined onto a single Arduino board to mimic the operation of all components simultaneously. Except for the green and red LEDs from module 5.3, all prior hardware components were re-attached to other Arduino ports in this final version of the project. As a result, the final integration lost the ability to alert the user through LEDs whether or not the fictitious room is inhabited. All of the other hardware components, on the other hand, were able to function together and achieve the intended outcomes. First and foremost, as demonstrated by module 5.3, when S1 and S2 sensed movement within 1.5 seconds of each other, the counter of the number of persons within the room grew by one. Second, the fan and light began to operate as soon as the number of individuals exceeded or equaled one, which is one of the final circuit arrangement's two extra features. In the same manner as explained in section 5.1, the fan (DC motor) began rotating at a speed according to the PWM signal sent to it, which in turn related to the temperature supplied to the temperature sensor. This occurred when the counter reached a value greater than one. Also, when the counter exceeded one, the smart light module began to work as indicated in section 5.2. Figure 8 and 9 depicts the occupied and unoccupied states of integrated modules. Table 3 and Table 4 shows the observations recorded on integrated Smart fan and light module respectively.

Figure 8. 'Occupied' state of integrated modules

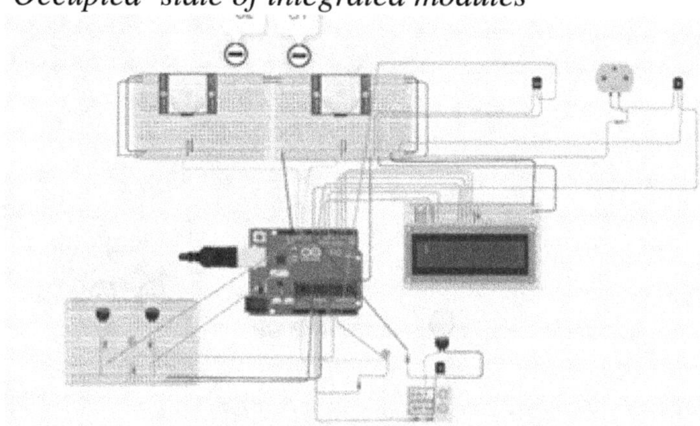

Figure 9. 'Unoccupied' state of integrated modules

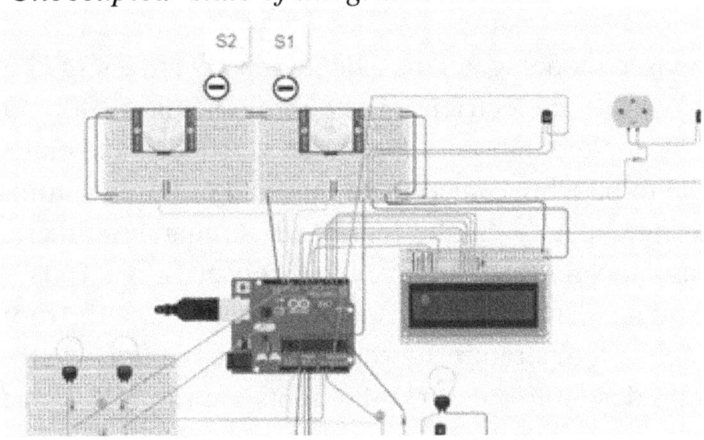

Table 3. Observations on integrated smart fan module

Supplied Temperature (°C)	In programmed temperature range (°C)	Observed DC motor speed range (RPM)
18	<=20	0
23	>20, <=30	126~142
31	>30, <=35	274~289
37	>35	400

Table 4. Observations on integrated smart light module

Supplied Ambient Light	PWM signal supplied to left bulb	PWM signal supplied to right bulb
6	254	254
145	254	150
322	254	0
463	100	0
582	0	0

6 CONCLUSION AND FUTURE WORK

Our proposed model would be a huge step toward energy conservation by reducing wasteful electricity waste through automation. Our project, which can be applied in homes, businesses, schools, and enterprises, has the potential to be a huge success in the field of home automation. If its manufacturing capacity can be increased, its market attractiveness will skyrocket as it tackles the issue of energy conservation. Thus, in the commercial version, we have two sensors on either side of the room to detect entry and exit, a temperature sensor to operate the fans via the MCU, an ambient light detector to control the lights via the MCU, and all of the other components described. This entire system will be installed at the customer's preferred location. The fans and lights are optional, since they may be put at a later date with the assistance of another provider. We intend to physically execute it so that consumers may utilize it and it can help to energy saving and the improvement of our environment and society.

REFERENCES

Balan, R. S., Gouri, M. S., Senthilnathan, T., Gondkar, S. R., Gondar, R. R., Zeema, J. L., & Jothikumar, R. (2023). Development of smart energy monitoring using NB-IOT and cloud. *Measurement. Sensors*, *29*, 100884. DOI: 10.1016/j.measen.2023.100884

Baqir, Z. (2023). IoT based automation of a home and alert system. *Computer Information*, *3*(1), 1–8.

Bhatia, V., & Bhatia, G. (2013). Room temperature based Fan Speed Control System using Pulse Width Modulation Technique. *International Journal of Computer Applications*, *81*(5), 35–40. DOI: 10.5120/14011-2067

Flamini, A., Ciurluini, L., Loggia, R., Massaccesi, A., Moscatiello, C., & Martirano, L. (2023). A prototype of low-cost home automation system for energy savings and living comfort. *IEEE Transactions on Industry Applications*, *59*(4), 4931–4941. DOI: 10.1109/TIA.2023.3271618

Gondkar, S. S., William, P., & Pardeshi, D. B. (2022, May). Design of a novel IoT framework for home automation using google assistant. In 2022 6th International conference on intelligent computing and control systems (ICICCS) (pp. 451-454). IEEE.

Han, D.-M., & Lim, J.-H. (2010). Design and implementation of smart home energy management systems based on zigbee. *IEEE Transactions on Consumer Electronics*, *56*(3), 1417–1425. DOI: 10.1109/TCE.2010.5606278

Hassan, C. A. U., Iqbal, J., Khan, M. S., Hussain, S., Akhunzada, A., Ali, M., Gani, A., Uddin, M., & Ullah, S. S. (2022). Design and Implementation of Real-Time Kitchen Monitoring and Automation System Based on Internet of Things. *Energies*, *15*(18), 6778. DOI: 10.3390/en15186778

Iyappan, P., Loganathan, J., Verma, M. K., Dumka, A., Singh, R., Gehlot, A., Akram, S. V., Kaur, S., & Joshi, K. (2022). A generic and smart automation system for home using internet of things. *Bulletin of Electrical Engineering and Informatics*, *11*(5), 2727–2736. DOI: 10.11591/eei.v11i5.3785

Jain, R., Bekuma, Y., Pattanaik, B., Assebe, A., & Bayisa, T. (2022). Design of a smart wireless home automation system using fusion of iot and machine learning over cloud environment. In 2022 3rd international conference on intelligent engineering and management (ICIEM), pp. 840-847. IEEE. DOI: 10.1109/ICIEM54221.2022.9853116

Kathiria, P., Vadgama, B., Shah, D., Ashishdeep, A., Agrawal, S. (2017). IoT Based approach for controlling electrical peripheral devices of auditorium. Int. J. Adv. Res. Comput. Sci. vol. 8, no. 5

Maragatham, T., Balasubramanie, P., & Vivekanandhan, M. (2021). IoT Based Home Automation System using Raspberry Pi 4. *IOP Conference Series: Materials Science and Engineering*. p. 1055. DOI: 10.1088/1757-899X/1055/1/012081

Mustofa, A. A., Dagnew, Y. A., Gantela, P., & Idrisi, M. J. (2023). SE-CHA: A Smart Energy-Efficient and Cost-Effective Home Automation System for Developing Countries. *Journal of Computer Networks and Communications*, *1*, 8571506. DOI: 10.1155/2023/8571506

O'Reilly, F., & Buckley, J. (2005). Use of wireless sensor networks for fluorescent lighting control with daylight substitution. *Proceedings of the Workshop on Real-World Wireless Sensor Networks (REANWSN).*

Perni, D. D. S., Suneetha, M., Kantamneni, M., & Revalamadugu, R. V. (2023). Mobile based Automation of Electrical Appliances. In 2023 7th International Conference on Computing Methodologies and Communication (ICCMC), pp. 1517-1522. IEEE. DOI: 10.1109/ICCMC56507.2023.10083685

Rizman, Z. I., Yeap, K. H., Ismail, N., Mohamad, N., & Husin, N. H. (2013). Design an automatic temperature control system for smart electric fan using PIC. *International Journal of Scientific Research*, *2*(9), 1–4.

Sahrab, A. A., & Marhoon, H. M. (2022). Design and Fabrication of a Low-Cost System for Smart Home Applications. *Journal of Robotics and Control*, *3*(4), 409–414. DOI: 10.18196/jrc.v3i4.15413

Sharif, Z., Jung, L. T., Ayaz, M., Yahya, M., & Khan, D. (2022). Smart home automation by internet-of-things edge computing platform. *International Journal of Advanced Computer Science and Applications, 13*(4), •••. DOI: 10.14569/IJACSA.2022.0130455

Stolojescu-Crisan, C., Crisan, C., & Butunoi, B. P. (2021). An IoT-based smart home automation system. *Sensors (Basel), 21*(11), 3784. DOI: 10.3390/s21113784 PMID: 34070717

Willoughby, A. A., Soge, A. O., Adeleke, M. A., & Ilori, O. A. (2022). An IoT-based home automation and weather monitoring system. [IJRIAS]. *Int. J. Res. Innov. Appl. Sci., 7*(3), 26–29. DOI: 10.51584/IJRIAS.2022.7302

Yar, H., Imran, A. S., Khan, Z. A., Sajjad, M., & Kastrati, Z. (2021). Towards smart home automation using IoT-enabled edge-computing paradigm. *Sensors (Basel), 21*(14), 4932. DOI: 10.3390/s21144932 PMID: 34300671

Compilation of References

Abdalah, S., & Niimeh, S. (2017). Sun tracking device two axes with Arduino. *Power. Energy Conversion and Management*, *45*, 1931–1939. DOI: 10.1016/j.enconman.2003.10.007

Abdelhalim, A., Saleh, M., & Hussein, A. (2022). Artificial intelligence, healthcare, clinical genomics, and pharmacogenomics approaches in precision medicine. *Frontiers in Genetics*, *13*, 929736. DOI: 10.3389/fgene.2022.929736 PMID: 35873469

Aghion, P., Antonin, C., & Bunel, S. (2022). Financial markets and green innovation. *NBER Working Paper Series.* DOI: 10.3386/w30374

Aguero, J. R., Takayesu, M., & Lawrence, C. (2017). Modernizing the grid: Challenges and opportunities for a sustainable future. *IEEE Power & Energy Magazine*, *15*(3), 74–83. DOI: 10.1109/MPE.2017.2660819

Ahsan, M. T., Dutta, S., & Hasan, M. (2023). Data-driven next-generation smart grid towards sustainable energy evolution: Techniques and technology review. *Protection and Control of Modern Power Systems*, *8*(3), 1–42. DOI: 10.1186/s41601-023-00319-5

Akter, S., & Wamba, S. F. (2016). Big data analytics in E-commerce: A systematic review and agenda for future research. *Electronic Markets*, *26*(2), 173–194. DOI: 10.1007/s12525-016-0219-0

Alahi, M. E. E., Sukkuea, A., Tina, F. W., Nag, A., Kurdthongmee, W., Suwannarat, K., & Mukhopadhyay, S. C. (2023). Integration of IoT-enabled technologies and artificial intelligence (AI) for smart city scenario: Recent advancements and future trends. *Sensors (Basel)*, *23*(11), 5206. DOI: 10.3390/s23115206 PMID: 37299934

Alanazi, H. O., Khan, M., & Alazzam, M. B. (2022). Using machine learning for healthcare challenges and opportunities. *Informatics in Medicine Unlocked*, *30*, 100924. DOI: 10.1016/j.imu.2022.100924

Albarella, N., Lui, D. G., Petrillo, A., & Santini, S. (2023). A Hybrid Deep Reinforcement Learning and Optimal Control Architecture for Autonomous Highway Driving. *Energies*, *16*(8), 3490. Advance online publication. DOI: 10.3390/en16083490

Ali, T., Irfan, M., Alwadie, A. S., & Glowacz, A. (2020). IoT-based smart waste bin monitoring and municipal solid waste management system for smart cities. *Arabian Journal for Science and Engineering*, *45*(12), 10185–10198. DOI: 10.1007/s13369-020-04637-w

Allouhi, A., Kousksou, T., Jamil, A., El Rhafiki, T., Zeraouli, Y., & Mourad, Y. (2023). Recent technical approaches for improving energy efficiency and sustainability of PV and PV-T systems: A comprehensive review. *Sustainable Energy Technologies and Assessments*, *56*, 103026. DOI: 10.1016/j.seta.2023.103026

Allouhi, A., Rehman, S., & Buker, M. S. (2002). Solar PV system: A review. *Renewable & Sustainable Energy Reviews*, *20*, 35–55. DOI: 10.1016/j.rser.2017.06.001

Allouhi, A., Rehman, S., Buker, M. S., & Said, Z. (2022). Up-to-date literature review on solar PV systems: Technology progress, market status, and R&D. *Journal of Cleaner Production*, *362*, 132339. DOI: 10.1016/j.jclepro.2022.132339

Alotaibi, M. F., & Islam, S. M. (2020). A comprehensive review of recent advances in smart grids: A sustainable future with renewable energy resources. *Energies*, *13*(23), 6269. DOI: 10.3390/en13236269

Alowais, F., Alharthi, M., & Alshehri, S. (2023). Revolutionizing healthcare: The role of artificial intelligence in clinical practice. *BMC Medical Education, 23*(1), 689. DOI: 10.1186/s12909-023-04698-z PMID: 37740191

Altieri, M. A., Nicholls, C. I., & Montalba, R. (2017). Technological approaches to sustainable agriculture at a crossroads: An agroecological perspective. *Sustainability (Basel), 9*(3), 349. DOI: 10.3390/su9030349

Annapurani, . (2021). Healthcare Data Analytics Using Business Intelligence Tool. In *Machine Learning and Analytics in Healthcare Systems* (pp. 191–212). CRC Press. DOI: 10.1201/9781003185246-10

Anshari, , Almunawar, M. N., Lim, S. A., & Al-Mudimigh, A. (2019). Customer relationship management and big data enabled: Personalization & customization of services. *Applied Computing and Informatics, 15*(2), 94–101. DOI: 10.1016/j.aci.2018.05.004

Apostolova, E., Willis, M., Whitfill, T., & Henry, J. (2017). Open globe injury patient identification in warfare clinical notes. *AMIA Annual Symposium Proceedings*, 403.

Arbi, A. (2018). Dynamics of BAM neural networks with mixed delays and leakage time-varying delays in the weighted pseudo–almost periodic on time-space scales. *Mathematical Methods in the Applied Sciences, 41*(3), 1230–1255. DOI: 10.1002/mma.4661

Arbi, , Cao, J., & Alsaedi, A. (2018). Improved synchronization analysis of competitive neural networks with time-varying delays. *Nonlinear Analysis (Vilnius), 23*(1), 82–107. DOI: 10.15388/NA.2018.1.7

Arbi, , Guo, Y., & Cao, J. (2021). Convergence analysis on time scales for HOBAM neural networks in the Stepanov-like weighted pseudo almost automorphic space. *Neural Computing & Applications, 33*(8), 3567–3581. DOI: 10.1007/s00521-020-05183-0

Arbi, , & Tahri, N. (2024). Synchronization analysis of novel delayed dynamical Clifford-valued neural networks on timescales. *Journal of Algorithms & Computational Technology, 18*, 17483026241241492. DOI: 10.1177/17483026241241492

Archana, M., Arunkumar, C., Ramasamy, S., & Kandasamy, S. (2024). A review on recent technological breakthroughs in anaerobic digestion of organic biowaste for biogas generation: Challenges towards sustainable development goals. *Fuel*, *358*, 130298. DOI: 10.1016/j.fuel.2023.130298

Atitallah, S. B., Driss, M., Boulila, W., & Ghézala, H. B. (2020). Leveraging Deep Learning and IoT big data analytics to support the smart cities development: Review and future directions. *Computer Science Review*, *38*, 100303. DOI: 10.1016/j.cosrev.2020.100303

Awasthi, A., Kallioğlu, M. A., Sharma, A., & Kumar, A. (2022). Solar collector tilt angle optimization for solar power plant setup-able sites at Western Himalaya and correlation formulation. *Journal of Thermal Analysis and Calorimetry*, *147*(20), 11417–11431. DOI: 10.1007/s10973-022-11345-0

Awogbemi, O., & Alabi, O. (2022). Resource recycling with the aim of achieving zero-waste manufacturing. *Sustainability (Basel)*, *14*(8), 4503. DOI: 10.3390/su14084503

Ayankoya, . (2014),Intrinsic relations between data science, big data, business analytics and datafication. In: *Proceedings of the Southern African Institute for Computer Scientist and Information Technologists Annual Conference 2014 on SAICSIT 2014 Empowered by Technology*. p. 192-198. DOI: 10.1145/2664591.2664619

Baby, C. J., Singh, H., Srivastava, A., & Dhawan, R.; Mahalakshmi, P. (2017). Smart bin: An intelligent waste alert and prediction system using machine learning approach. International Conference on Wireless Communications, Signal Processing and Networking (WiSPNET), pp. 771–774. DOI: 10.1109/WiSPNET.2017.8299865

Balachandran, , & Prasad, S. (2017). Challenges and benefits of deploying big data analytics in the cloud for business intelligence. *Procedia Computer Science*, *112*, 1112–1122. DOI: 10.1016/j.procs.2017.08.138

Balan, R. S., Gouri, M. S., Senthilnathan, T., Gondkar, S. R., Gondar, R. R., Zeema, J. L., & Jothikumar, R. (2023). Development of smart energy monitoring using NB-IOT and cloud. *Measurement. Sensors*, *29*, 100884. DOI: 10.1016/j.measen.2023.100884

Baqir, Z. (2023). IoT based automation of a home and alert system. *Computer Information*, *3*(1), 1–8.

Baxter, S. L., Saseendrakumar, B. R., & Wang, Y. (2019). Machine learning-based predictive modeling of surgical intervention in glaucoma using systemic data from electronic health records. *American Journal of Ophthalmology*, *208*, 30–40. DOI: 10.1016/j.ajo.2019.07.005 PMID: 31323204

Belhadi, A., Zkik, K., Cherrafi, A., & Sha'ri, M. Y. (2019). Understanding big data analytics for manufacturing processes: Insights from literature review and multiple case studies. *Computers & Industrial Engineering*, *137*, 106099. DOI: 10.1016/j.cie.2019.106099

Bhatia, V., & Bhatia, G. (2013). Room temperature based Fan Speed Control System using Pulse Width Modulation Technique. *International Journal of Computer Applications*, *81*(5), 35–40. DOI: 10.5120/14011-2067

Bhattacharya, K., Hazra, M., Dutta, D., Roy, K., Islam, F., & Basak, S. (2021). Smart dustbin utility system using iot. *International Journal for Research in Applied Science and Engineering Technology*, *9*(7), •••.

Bhattarai, B. P., Paudyal, S., Luo, Y., Mohanpurkar, M., Cheung, K., Tonkoski, R., Hovsapian, R., Myers, K. S., Zhang, R., Zhao, P., Manic, M., Zhang, S., & Zhang, X. (2019). Big data analytics in smart grids: State-of-the-art, challenges, opportunities, and future directions. *IET Smart Grid*, *2*(2), 141–154. DOI: 10.1049/iet-stg.2018.0261

Bibri, S. E. (2018). The IoT for smart sustainable cities of the future: An analytical framework for sensor-based big data applications for environmental sustainability. *Sustainable Cities and Society*, *38*, 230–253. DOI: 10.1016/j.scs.2017.12.034

Bibri, S. E., Krogstie, J., Kaboli, A., & Alahi, A. (2024). Smarter eco-cities and their leading-edge artificial intelligence of things solutions for environmental sustainability: A comprehensive systematic review. *Environmental Science and Ecotechnology, 19*, 100330. DOI: 10.1016/j.ese.2023.100330 PMID: 38021367

Bratton, B. (2021). AI urbanism: A design framework for governance, program, and platform cognition. *AI & Society, 36*(4), 1307–1312. DOI: 10.1007/s00146-020-01121-9

Calzada, I. (2018). (Smart) citizens from data providers to decision-makers? The case study of Barcelona. *Sustainability (Basel), 10*(9), 3252. DOI: 10.3390/su10093252

Chaganti, S., Wong, T. Y., & Ting, D. S. (2017). Phenotype analysis of early risk factors from electronic medical records improves image-derived diagnostic classifiers for optic nerve pathology. In *Medical Imaging 2017: Imaging Informatics for Healthcare, Research, and Applications* (pp. 99-105). SPIE. https://doi.org/DOI: 10.1117/12.2255739

Chan, C. Y. (2017). Advancements, prospects, and impacts of automated driving systems. *International Journal of Transportation Science and Technology, 6*(3), 208–216. DOI: 10.1016/j.ijtst.2017.07.008

Chand, R. P., Sri, V. B., Lakshmi, P. M., Chakravathi, S. S., Veerendra, O. D. M., & Rao, C. V. (2021, December). Arduino based smart dustbin for waste management during Covid-19. In 2021 5th International Conference on Electronics, Communication and Aerospace Technology (ICECA) (pp. 492-496). IEEE.

Chaudhary, . (2022). *Big data analytics: applications in business and marketing*. Auerbach Publications. DOI: 10.1201/9781003307761

Chen, C. P., & Zhang, C. Y. (2014). Data-intensive applications, challenges, techniques and technologies: A survey on Big Data. *Information Sciences, 275*, 314–347. DOI: 10.1016/j.ins.2014.01.015

Chng, K. K., Siew, F. L., Woong, C. W., & Woong, G. S. (2019). Solar tracing device design and installation. *Renewable Energy*, *34*, 1364–1370. DOI: 10.1016/j.renene.2019.03.004

Choe, C., Choe, M., & Jung, S. (2023). Run Your 3D Object Detector on NVIDIA Jetson Platforms:A Benchmark Analysis †. *Sensors (Basel)*, *23*(8), 4005. Advance online publication. DOI: 10.3390/s23084005 PMID: 37112347

Darwish, M. A., Alharthi, M. R., & Rahman, S. M. (2020). Wind energy state of the art: Present and future technology advancements. *Renewable Energy and Environmental Sustainability*, *5*, 7. DOI: 10.1051/rees/2020003

De Fine Licht, K., & Folland, A. (2019). Defining "social sustainability": Towards a sustainable solution to the conceptual confusion. *Etikk i Praksis*, *13*(2), 21–39. DOI: 10.5324/eip.v13i2.2913

Dinh, T. V., Tran, D. D., Hoang, T. H., & Bui, T. Q. (2019). Offshore wind energy: Technology opportunities and challenges. In *Proceedings of the 1st Vietnam Symposium on Advances in Offshore Engineering: Energy and Geotechnics* (pp. 3–22). Springer Singapore. DOI: 10.1007/978-981-13-2306-5_1

Erevelles, S., Fukawa, N., & Swayne, L. (2016). Big Data consumer analytics and the transformation of marketing. *Journal of Business Research*, *69*(2), 897–904. DOI: 10.1016/j.jbusres.2015.07.001

Esmaeilzadeh, P., Mirzaei, T., & Abdekhoda, M. (2020). Use of AI-based tools for healthcare purposes: A survey study from consumers' perspectives. *BMC Medical Informatics and Decision Making*, *20*(1), 1–19. DOI: 10.1186/s12911-020-01191-1 PMID: 32698869

Farooq, M. S., Khalid, H., Arooj, A., Umer, T., Asghar, A. B., Rasheed, J., Shubair, R. M., & Yahyaoui, A. (2023). A Conceptual Multi-Layer Framework for the Detection of Nighttime Pedestrian in Autonomous Vehicles Using Deep Reinforcement Learning. *Entropy (Basel, Switzerland)*, *25*(1), 135. Advance online publication. DOI: 10.3390/e25010135 PMID: 36673276

Flamini, A., Ciurluini, L., Loggia, R., Massaccesi, A., Moscatiello, C., & Martirano, L. (2023). A prototype of low-cost home automation system for energy savings and living comfort. *IEEE Transactions on Industry Applications*, *59*(4), 4931–4941. DOI: 10.1109/TIA.2023.3271618

Fraccaro, P., Nicolo, M., & Molinari, M. (2015). Combining macula clinical signs and patient characteristics for age-related macular degeneration diagnosis: A machine learning approach. *BMC Ophthalmology*, *15*(1), 1–9. DOI: 10.1186/1471-2415-15-10 PMID: 25623470

Gad-Elrab, A. A. (2021). Modern business intelligence: Big data analytics and artificial intelligence for creating the data-driven value. In *E-Business-Higher Education and Intelligence Applications*. IntechOpen.

Gaskin, J. C., Pershing, S., & Shah, N. (2016). Predictive modeling of risk factors and complications of cataract surgery. *European Journal of Ophthalmology*, *26*(4), 328–337. DOI: 10.5301/ejo.5000706 PMID: 26692059

Gondkar, S. S., William, P., & Pardeshi, D. B. (2022, May). Design of a novel IoT framework for home automation using google assistant. In 2022 6th International conference on intelligent computing and control systems (ICICCS) (pp. 451-454). IEEE.

Gray, D. L., & Reynolds, G. (2011). The effectiveness of environmental monitoring and enforcement: A review of the empirical evidence. *Review of Environmental Economics and Policy*, *5*(1), 3–24. DOI: 10.1093/reep/req017

Grayned, J. (n.d.). *SAE INTERNATIONAL LEVELS OF AUTONOMOUS DRIVING/ SENSOR PACKAGES*. DOI: 10.4271/J3016_201401

Guo, , Ge, S. S., & Arbi, A. (2022). Stability of traveling waves solutions for nonlinear cellular neural networks with distributed delays. *Journal of Systems Science and Complexity*, *35*(1), 18–31. DOI: 10.1007/s11424-021-0180-7

Hadj Sassi, M. S., & Chaari Fourati, L. (2024). Design cognitive IoT architecture framework for immersive visual technologies of air quality monitoring systems. *Multimedia Tools and Applications*, *83*(17), 51615–51646.

Hamdi, , Mestiri, S., & Arbi, A. (2024). Artificial intelligence techniques for bankruptcy prediction of tunisian companies: An application of machine learning and deep learning-based models. *Journal of Risk and Financial Management, 17*(4), 132. DOI: 10.3390/jrfm17040132

Han, D.-M., & Lim, J.-H. (2010). Design and implementation of smart home energy management systems based on zigbee. *IEEE Transactions on Consumer Electronics, 56*(3), 1417–1425. DOI: 10.1109/TCE.2010.5606278

Hassan, C. A. U., Iqbal, J., Khan, M. S., Hussain, S., Akhunzada, A., Ali, M., Gani, A., Uddin, M., & Ullah, S. S. (2022). Design and Implementation of Real-Time Kitchen Monitoring and Automation System Based on Internet of Things. *Energies, 15*(18), 6778. DOI: 10.3390/en15186778

Hazen, , Boone, C. A., Ezell, J. D., & Jones-Farmer, L. A. (2014). Data quality for data science, predictive analytics, and big data in supply chain management: An introduction to the problem and suggestions for research and applications. *International Journal of Production Economics, 154*, 72–80. DOI: 10.1016/j.ijpe.2014.04.018

Ho, E. (2017). Smart subjects for a Smart Nation? Governing (smart) mentalities in Singapore. *Urban Studies (Edinburgh, Scotland), 54*(13), 3101–3118. DOI: 10.1177/0042098016664305

Hussain, M. A., Nikhil, K., & Kalyan, K. Y. P. (2019). IOT Based Smart Dustbin Monitoring With Tracking System Using ATMega 2560 Microcontroller. *Fifteenth International Conference on Information Processing (ICINPRO)*, pp. 1–6. DOI: 10.1109/ICInPro47689.2019.9092295

Iqbal, S., Javed, M. A., & Mahmood, A. (2021). A comprehensive review on residential demand-side management strategies in smart grid environments. *Sustainability (Basel), 13*(13), 7170. DOI: 10.3390/su13137170

Iqbal, S., Khan, M. U., & Ali, H. (2021). Clinical applications of artificial intelligence and machine learning in cancer diagnosis: Looking into the future. *Cancer Cell International, 21*(1), 270. DOI: 10.1186/s12935-021-01981-1 PMID: 34020642

Islam, M. R., Hasanuzzaman, M., Rahim, N. A., Nahar, A., & Hosenuzzaman, M. (2018). A comprehensive review of state-of-the-art concentrating solar power (CSP) technologies: Current status and research trends. *Renewable & Sustainable Energy Reviews*, *91*, 987–1018. DOI: 10.1016/j.rser.2018.04.097

Iyappan, P., Loganathan, J., Verma, M. K., Dumka, A., Singh, R., Gehlot, A., Akram, S. V., Kaur, S., & Joshi, K. (2022). A generic and smart automation system for home using internet of things. *Bulletin of Electrical Engineering and Informatics*, *11*(5), 2727–2736. DOI: 10.11591/eei.v11i5.3785

Jain, R., Bekuma, Y., Pattanaik, B., Assebe, A., & Bayisa, T. (2022). Design of a smart wireless home automation system using fusion of iot and machine learning over cloud environment. In 2022 3rd international conference on intelligent engineering and management (ICIEM), pp. 840-847. IEEE. DOI: 10.1109/ICIEM54221.2022.9853116

Johnson, J. A., Williams, S., & Smith, M. (2021). Precision medicine, AI, and the future of personalized health care. *Clinical and Translational Science*, *14*(1), 86–93. DOI: 10.1111/cts.12884 PMID: 32961010

Kaginalkar, A., Kumar, S., Gargava, P., & Niyogi, D. (2021). Review of urban computing in air quality management as smart city service: An integrated IoT, AI, and cloud technology perspective. *Urban Climate*, *39*, 100972. DOI: 10.1016/j.uclim.2021.100972

Kalis, B., Ohno-Machado, L., & Patel, V. (2018). 10 promising AI applications in health care. *Harvard Business Review*, •••, 2–5.

Kanade, P., Alva, P., Prasad, J. P., & Kanade, S. (2021) Smart Garbage Monitoring System using Internet of Things(IoT), *5th International Conference on Computing Methodologies and Communication (ICCMC)*, pp. 330-335, DOI: 10.1109/ICCMC51019.2021.9418359

Kannan, D., Khademolqorani, S., Janatyan, N., & Alavi, S. (2024). Smart waste management 4.0: The transition from a systematic review to an integrated framework. *Waste Management (New York, N.Y.)*, *174*, 1–14. DOI: 10.1016/j.wasman.2023.08.041 PMID: 37742441

Karmaker, S., & Ali, M. (2023). Impact of industry 4.0 technologies on sustainable supply chain performance: The mediating role of green supply chain management practices and circular economy. *Journal of Cleaner Production*, *419*, 138249. DOI: 10.1016/j.jclepro.2023.138249

Karthikeyan, V., & Kalidasa Murugavel, K. (2020). Reducing PV module temperature with radiation-based PV module incorporated composite phase change material. *Materials Today: Proceedings*, *33*(Part 7), 4774–4779. DOI: 10.1016/j.matpr.2020.01.389

Karthikeyan, V., & Sirisamphanwong, C. (2020). Reducing PV module temperature with radiation-based PV module incorporated composite phase change material. *Energy Reports*, *6*, 56–64. DOI: 10.1016/j.egyr.2020.10.008

Kasula, A., Singh, D., & Verma, P. (2023). AI-driven machine learning solutions for sustainable development in healthcare—Pioneering efficient, equitable, and innovative health service. *International Journal of Sustainable Development Through AI. ML and IoT*, *2*(2), 1–7.

Kathiria, P., Vadgama, B., Shah, D., Ashishdeep, A., Agrawal, S. (2017). IoT Based approach for controlling electrical peripheral devices of auditorium. Int. J. Adv. Res. Comput. Sci. vol. 8, no. 5

Keshavarz, H., Mahdzir, A. M., Talebian, H., Jalaliyoon, N., & Ohshima, N. (2021). The value of big data analytics pillars in telecommunication industry. *Sustainability (Basel)*, *13*(13), 7160. DOI: 10.3390/su13137160

Khan, M. T., Rafat, S., & Rashid, T. (2022). Challenges and perspectives on innovative technologies for biofuel production and sustainable environmental management. *Fuel*, *325*, 124845. DOI: 10.1016/j.fuel.2022.124845

Kim, G. Y., Han, D. S., & Lee, Z. (2020). Solar panel tilt angle optimization using machine learning model: A case study of Daegu City, South Korea. *Energies*, *13*(3), 529. DOI: 10.3390/en13030529

Kougias, I., Monforti-Ferrario, F., Szabó, S., & Jäger-Waldau, A. (2019). Analysis of emerging technologies in the hydropower sector. *Renewable & Sustainable Energy Reviews*, *113*, 109257. DOI: 10.1016/j.rser.2019.109257

Krasic., ... (2021), Big data and business intelligence: research and challenges in telecom industry. In: *Annals of DAAAM and Proceedings of the International DAAAM Symposium*, p. 339-348. DOI: 10.2507/32nd.daaam.proceedings.050

Kumar, N. S., Vuayalakshmi, B., Prarthana, R. J., & Shankar, A. (2016, November). IOT based smart garbage alert system using Arduino UNO. In 2016 IEEE region 10 conference (TENCON) (pp. 1028-1034). IEEE.

Lamnatou, C., Chemisana, D., & Ortega, E. (2022). Smart grids and smart technologies in relation to photovoltaics, storage systems, buildings and the environment. *Renewable Energy, 185*, 1376–1391. DOI: 10.1016/j.renene.2021.11.019

Larson, , & Chang, V. (2016). A review and future direction of agile, business intelligence, analytics and data science. *International Journal of Information Management, 36*(5), 700–710. DOI: 10.1016/j.ijinfomgt.2016.04.013

Lee, C. S., Baughman, D. M., & Lee, A. Y. (2017). Deep learning is effective for classifying normal versus age-related macular degeneration OCT images. *Ophthalmology Retina, 1*(4), 322–327. DOI: 10.1016/j.oret.2016.12.009 PMID: 30693348

Lee, K., Kim, N., & Kim, K. (2020). Neutral colored transparent crystalline silicon photovoltaics. *Energy Reports, 6*, 201–207. DOI: 10.1016/j.egyr.2020.09.044

Lee, K., Kim, N., Kim, K., & Seo, K. (2020). Neutral-colored transparent crystalline silicon photovoltaics. *Joule, 4*(1), 235–246. DOI: 10.1016/j.joule.2019.11.008

Leijten, J., Edler, J., & Boekholt, P. (2019). Innovation policy and international relations: Directions for EU diplomacy. *European Journal of Futures Research, 7*(1), 4. DOI: 10.1186/s40309-019-0156-1

Li, D., & Okhrin, O. (2023). Modified DDPG car-following model with a real-world human driving experience with CARLA simulator. *Transportation Research Part C, Emerging Technologies*, *147*, 103987. Advance online publication. DOI: 10.1016/j.trc.2022.103987

Lincy, F. A., & Sasikala, T. (2021). Smart dustbin management using IOT and Blynk application. In *5th International Conference on Trends in Electronics and Informatics (ICOEI)*, pp. 429-434. IEEE. DOI: 10.1109/ICOEI51242.2021.9452988

Lin, H., Long, E., & Chen, W. (2020). Applications of artificial intelligence to electronic health record data in ophthalmology. *Translational Vision Science & Technology*, *9*(2), 13–13. DOI: 10.1167/tvst.9.2.13 PMID: 32704419

Lin, Z., Liu, Y., & Zhang, J. (2018). Prediction of myopia development among Chinese school-aged children using refraction data from electronic medical records: A retrospective, multicentre machine learning study. *PLoS Medicine*, *15*(11), e1002674. DOI: 10.1371/journal.pmed.1002674 PMID: 30399150

Litman, T. A., & Litman, T. (2013). www.vtpi.org*Info@vtpi.org Phone 250-508-5150 Autonomous Vehicle Implementation Predictions Implications for Transport Planning*. www.vtpi.org/avip.docx

Liu, H., Xu, X., Meng, Y., Yu, D., Liu, H., & Shi, K. (2018). A research for the influence of tilt angles of the solar panel on photovoltaic power generation. In *2018 International Conference on Smart Grid and Clean Energy Technologies (ICSGCE)* (pp. 95-100). IEEE. DOI: 10.1109/ICSGCE.2018.8556655

Luan, H., Geczy, P., Lai, H., Gobert, J., Yang, S. J., Ogata, H., Baltes, J., Guerra, R., Li, P., & Tsai, C. C. (2020). Challenges and future directions of big data and artificial intelligence in education. *Frontiers in Psychology*, *11*, 580820. DOI: 10.3389/fpsyg.2020.580820 PMID: 33192896

Maddileti, T., & Kurakula, H. (2020). IOT based smart dustbin. International Journal of Science and Technoly. *Res*, *9*(2), 1297–1302.

Mahaur, B., Mishra, K. K., & Kumar, A. (2023). An improved lightweight small object detection framework applied to real-time autonomous driving. *Expert Systems with Applications*, *234*, 121036. Advance online publication. DOI: 10.1016/j.eswa.2023.121036

Mahmoudinezhad, S., Rezania, A., & Mahmoudinezhad, R. (2018). Behaviour of hybrid concentrated photovoltaic-thermoelectric generator under variable solar radiation. *Energy Conversion and Management*, *164*, 21–33. DOI: 10.1016/j.enconman.2018.03.025

Mamun, M. A. A., Islam, M. M., Hasanuzzaman, M., & Selvaraj, J. (2022). Effect of tilt angle on the performance and electrical parameters of a PV module: Comparative indoor and outdoor experimental investigation. *Energy and Built Environment*, *3*(3), 278–290. DOI: 10.1016/j.enbenv.2021.02.001

Manzoor, S., An, Y. C., In, G. G., Zhang, Y., Kim, S., & Kuc, T. Y. (2023). SPT: Single Pedestrian Tracking Framework with Re-Identification-Based Learning Using the Siamese Model. *Sensors (Basel)*, *23*(10), 4906. Advance online publication. DOI: 10.3390/s23104906 PMID: 37430819

Maragatham, T., Balasubramanie, P., & Vivekanandhan, M. (2021). IoT Based Home Automation System using Raspberry Pi 4. *IOP Conference Series: Materials Science and Engineering*. p. 1055. DOI: 10.1088/1757-899X/1055/1/012081

Ma, T., Li, Z., & Zhao, J. (2019). Photovoltaic panel integrated with phase change material technology. *Applied Energy*, *238*, 321–329. DOI: 10.1016/j.apenergy.2018.12.021

Medeiros, , Hoppen, N., & Maçada, A. C. G. (2020). Data science for business: Benefits, challenges and opportunities. *The Bottom Line (New York, N.Y.)*, *33*(2), 149–163. DOI: 10.1108/BL-12-2019-0132

Mohaghegh, S., Niknam, H., & Alishah, R. S. (2021). Latest advances on hybrid solar–biomass power plants. *Energy Sources. Part A, Recovery, Utilization, and Environmental Effects*, •••, 1–24. DOI: 10.1080/15567036.2021.1919484

Mohapatra, B. N., & Shirapuri, P. (2020). Arduino based smart dustbin for waste management system. *Perspectives in Communication, Embedded-systems and Signal-processing-PiCES*, *4*(3), 8–11.

Morabito, V. (2015). Big data and analytics. Strategic and organisational impacts.

Mustofa, A. A., Dagnew, Y. A., Gantela, P., & Idrisi, M. J. (2023). SE-CHA: A Smart Energy-Efficient and Cost-Effective Home Automation System for Developing Countries. *Journal of Computer Networks and Communications*, *1*, 8571506. DOI: 10.1155/2023/8571506

Narassimhan, E., Gallagher, K. S., Koester, S., & Rivera Alejo, J. (2018). Carbon pricing in practice: A review of existing emissions trading systems. *Climate Policy*, *18*(8), 967–991. DOI: 10.1080/14693062.2018.1467827

Nayak, A., & Singh, S. (2019). Crop-livestock-agroforestry based integrated farming system: An eco-efficient sustainable practice for food and nutritional security.

Niu, Y., Ying, L., Yang, J., Bao, M., & Sivaparthipan, C. B. (2021). Organizational business intelligence and decision making using big data analytics. *Information Processing & Management*, *58*(6), 102725. DOI: 10.1016/j.ipm.2021.102725

Nižetić, S., Šolić, P., Gonzalez-De, D. L. D. I., & Patrono, L. (2020). Internet of Things (IoT): Opportunities, issues and challenges towards a smart and sustainable future. *Journal of Cleaner Production*, *274*, 122877. DOI: 10.1016/j.jclepro.2020.122877 PMID: 32834567

Nor, M. K. M. M., Asis, I., & Saidin, M. A. (2022). Intelligent Smart Dustbin (i-SMARTBiN). *Politeknik & Kolej Komuniti Journal of Engineering and Technology*, *7*(1), 101–107.

O'Reilly, F., & Buckley, J. (2005). Use of wireless sensor networks for fluorescent lighting control with daylight substitution. *Proceedings of the Workshop on Real-World Wireless Sensor Networks (REANWSN).*

Ortega-Fernández, A., Martín-Rojas, R., & García-Morales, V. J. (2020). Artificial intelligence in the urban environment: Smart cities as models for developing innovation and sustainability. *Sustainability (Basel), 12*(19), 7860. DOI: 10.3390/su12197860

Ouali, I., & Boudoukhane, A. (2022). Real-time application for recognition and visualization of Arabic words with vowels based deep learning and augmented reality. In *2022 International Wireless Communications and Mobile Computing (IWCMC)* (pp. 678-683). IEEE.

Ouali, I., Halima, M. B., & Ali, W. A. L. I. (2022b, May). Real-time application for recognition and visualization of arabic words with vowels based dl and ar. In 2022 International Wireless Communications and Mobile Computing (IWCMC) (pp. 678-683). IEEE.

Ouali, . (2021), Architecture for real-time visualizing arabic words with diacritics using augmented reality for visually impaired people. In: *International conference on advanced information networking and applications*. Cham: Springer International Publishing, p. 285-296. DOI: 10.1007/978-3-030-75100-5_25

Ouali, . (2022a), Text detection and recognition using augmented reality and deep learning. In: *International conference on advanced information networking and applications*. Cham: Springer International Publishing, p. 13-23. DOI: 10.1007/978-3-030-99584-3_2

Ouali, . (2022b). *Real-time application for recognition and visualization of arabic words with vowels based dl and ar. In: 2022 International Wireless Communications and Mobile Computing (IWCMC).* IEEE. DOI: 10.1109/IWCMC55113.2022.9825089

Ouali., ... (2023b), A novel method for arabic text detection with interactive visualization. In: *2023 IEEE Symposium on Computers and Communications (ISCC)*. IEEE, 2023. p. 1046-1050. DOI: 10.1109/ISCC58397.2023.10218141

Ouali, , Ben Halima, M., Masmoudi, N., Ayadi, M., Almuqren, L., & Wali, A. (2024). Text recuperated using ontology with stable marriage optimization technique and text visualization using AR. *Multimedia Tools and Applications*, *83*(41), 1–28. DOI: 10.1007/s11042-024-18795-8

Ouali, , Halima, M. B. E. N., & Wali, A. (2022c). Augmented reality for scene text recognition, visualization and reading to assist visually impaired people. *Procedia Computer Science*, *207*, 158–167. DOI: 10.1016/j.procs.2022.09.048

Ouali, , Halima, M. B., & Wali, A. (2023a). An augmented reality for an arabic text reading and visualization assistant for the visually impaired. *Multimedia Tools and Applications*, *82*(28), 43569–43597. DOI: 10.1007/s11042-023-14880-6

Ouali, I., Fourati, R., Halima, M. B., & Wali, A. (2023, July). A novel method for arabic text detection with interactive visualization. In *2023 IEEE Symposium on Computers and Communications (ISCC)* (pp. 1046-1050). IEEE.

Pathirana, M. R., & Silva, P. (2022). Management and utilization of plant genetic resources for a sustainable agriculture. *Plants*, *11*(15), 2038. DOI: 10.3390/plants11152038 PMID: 35956515

Peissig, P. L., White, T., & McCarty, C. A. (2012). Importance of multi-modal approaches to effectively identify cataract cases from electronic health records. *Journal of the American Medical Informatics Association : JAMIA*, *19*(2), 225–234. DOI: 10.1136/amiajnl-2011-000456 PMID: 22319176

Perni, D. D. S., Suneetha, M., Kantamneni, M., & Revalamadugu, R. V. (2023). Mobile based Automation of Electrical Appliances. In 2023 7th International Conference on Computing Methodologies and Communication (ICCMC), pp. 1517-1522. IEEE. DOI: 10.1109/ICCMC56507.2023.10083685

Phillips-Wren, G., Daly, M., & Burstein, F. (2021). Reconciling business intelligence, analytics and decision support systems: More data, deeper insight. *Decision Support Systems*, *146*, 113560. DOI: 10.1016/j.dss.2021.113560

Radmehr, E., & Bazmara, M. (2017). A Survey of Business Intelligence Solutions in Banking Industry and Big Data Applications.

Rahimi, M., Songhorabadi, M., & Kashani, M. H. (2020). Fog-based smart homes: A systematic review. *Journal of Network and Computer Applications*, *153*, 102531. DOI: 10.1016/j.jnca.2020.102531

Ramírez, J., Patel, D., & Singh, K. (2024). AI in healthcare: Revolutionizing patient care with predictive analytics and decision support systems. [JAIGS]. *Journal of Artificial Intelligence General Science*, *1*(1), 31–37.

Rana, M. M., Akhter, S., & Uddin, S. (2023). Applications of energy storage systems in power grids with and without renewable energy integration—A comprehensive review. *Journal of Energy Storage*, *68*, 107811. DOI: 10.1016/j.est.2023.107811

Rana, S., Gupta, R., & Kumar, N. (2024). AI in healthcare: Transforming patient care through predictive analytics and decision support systems. [JAIGS]. *Journal of Artificial Intelligence General Science*, *1*(1). Advance online publication. DOI: 10.60087/jaigs.v1i1.30

Refaat, M., Zhang, W., & El-Sharkawi, M. A. (2018). Self-healing control strategy: Challenges and opportunities for distribution systems in smart grid. In *2018 IEEE 12th International Conference on Compatibility, Power Electronics and Power Engineering (CPE-POWERENG 2018)* (pp. 1-6). IEEE.

Rehman, A., Naz, S., & Razzak, I. (2022). Leveraging big data analytics in healthcare enhancement: Trends, challenges and opportunities. *Multimedia Systems*, *28*(4), 1339–1371.

Rehman, F., Shah, S. M., & Ali, M. (2021). An efficient energy management in smart grid considering demand response program and renewable energy sources. *IEEE Access : Practical Innovations, Open Solutions, 9*, 148821–148844. DOI: 10.1109/ACCESS.2021.3124557

Rehman, S., Al-Hadhrami, L. M., & Alam, M. M. (2015). Pumped hydro energy storage system: A technological review. *Renewable & Sustainable Energy Reviews, 44*, 586–598. DOI: 10.1016/j.rser.2014.12.040

Reis, A., & Silva, J. (2021). Striding towards sustainability: A framework to overcome challenges and explore opportunities through industry 4.0. *Sustainability (Basel), 13*(9), 5232. DOI: 10.3390/su13095232

Richardson, S., Brown, K., & Carter, M. (2021). Patient apprehensions about the use of artificial intelligence in healthcare. *NPJ Digital Medicine, 4*(1), 140. DOI: 10.1038/s41746-021-00509-1 PMID: 34548621

Rizman, Z. I., Yeap, K. H., Ismail, N., Mohamad, N., & Husin, N. H. (2013). Design an automatic temperature control system for smart electric fan using PIC. *International Journal of Scientific Research, 2*(9), 1–4.

Roy, D., Kaur, A., & Meena, M. (2020). Precision farming: A step towards sustainable, climate-smart agriculture. In *Global climate change: Resilient and smart agriculture* (pp. 199-220). DOI: 10.1007/978-981-32-9856-9_10

Russom, P. (2011). Big data analytics. *TDWI best practices report, fourth quarter, 19*(4), 1-34.

Saad, A. M., Jul, B. O., Basalamah, A., & Sayuti, S. (2023). IoT-Based Smart Dustbin Prototype. PROtek J. *Ilm. Tek. Elektro, 10*(2), 120.

Sabir, , Raja, M. A. Z., Arbi, A., Altamirano, G. C., & Cao, J. (2021). Neuro-swarms intelligent computing using Gudermannian kernel for solving a class of second order Lane-Emden singular nonlinear model. *AIMS Mathematics, 6*(3), 2468–2485. DOI: 10.3934/math.2021150

Sabir, , Saoud, S., Raja, M. A. Z., Wahab, H. A., & Arbi, A. (2020). Heuristic computing technique for numerical solutions of nonlinear fourth order Emden–Fowler equation. *Mathematics and Computers in Simulation*, *178*, 534–548. DOI: 10.1016/j.matcom.2020.06.021

Sahrab, A. A., & Marhoon, H. M. (2022). Design and Fabrication of a Low-Cost System for Smart Home Applications. *Journal of Robotics and Control*, *3*(4), 409–414. DOI: 10.18196/jrc.v3i4.15413

Sakshi, J., Hardika, L., Ishika, A., & Lodha, G. M. (2019). Smart Dustbin Management System. *Journal of Advancement in Software Engineering and Testing*, *2*(2), 1–4.

Sassi, H., & Ouali, I. (2019). Business information architecture for big data and Internet of Things. In *2019 15th International Wireless Communications & Mobile Computing Conference (IWCMC)* (pp. 1749-1756). IEEE.

Sassi, H., & Ouali, I. (2019). Computer-aided software engineering (CASE) tool for big data and IoT architecture. In *2019 15th International Wireless Communications & Mobile Computing Conference (IWCMC)* (pp. 1403-1410). IEEE.

Sassi, M. S. H., & Fourati, L. C. (2020, June). Investigation on deep learning methods for privacy and security challenges of cognitive IoV. In 2020 International Wireless Communications and Mobile Computing (IWCMC) (pp. 714-720). IEEE.

Sassi, M. S. H., Beltaief, I., Zekri, M., & Yahia, S. B. (2019, November). Multi-oriented real-time arabic scene text detection with deep fully convolutional networks. In 2019 IEEE/ACS 16th International Conference on Computer Systems and Applications (AICCSA) (pp. 1-6). IEEE.

Sassi, M. S. H., Fourati, L. C., & Jedidi, F. G. (2019, June). Business information architecture for big data and Internet of Things. In 2019 15th International Wireless Communications & Mobile Computing Conference (IWCMC) (pp. 1749-1756). IEEE.

Sassi, M. S. H., Fourati, L. C., & Jedidi, F. G. (2019b, June). Business information architecture for big data and Internet of Things. In *2019 15th International Wireless Communications & Mobile Computing Conference (IWCMC)* (pp. 1749-1756). IEEE.

Sassi, M. S. H., Jedidi, F. G., & Fourati, L. C. (2019, June). Computer-aided software engineering (CASE) tool for big data and IoT architecture. In 2019 15th International wireless communications & mobile computing conference (IWCMC) (pp. 1403-1410). IEEE.

Sassi, M. S. H., Jedidi, F. G., & Fourati, L. C. (2019a, June). Computer-aided software engineering (CASE) tool for big data and IoT architecture. In *2019 15th International wireless communications & mobile computing conference (IWCMC)* (pp. 1403-1410). IEEE.

Sassi, . (2019a). *Computer-aided software engineering (CASE) tool for big data and IoT architecture. In: 2019 15th International wireless communications & mobile computing conference (IWCMC)*. IEEE.

Sassi, . (2019b). *Business information architecture for big data and Internet of Things. In: 2019 15th International Wireless Communications & Mobile Computing Conference (IWCMC)*. IEEE.

Sassi, . (2020b). *Investigation on deep learning methods for privacy and security challenges of cognitive IoV. In: 2020 International Wireless Communications and Mobile Computing (IWCMC)*. IEEE. DOI: 10.1109/IWCMC48107.2020.9148417

Sassi., ... (2019c), Multi-Oriented Real-Time Arabic Scene Text Detection with Deep Fully Convolutional Networks. In: *2019 IEEE/ACS 16th International Conference on Computer Systems and Applications (AICCSA)*. IEEE, 2019. p. 1-6. DOI: 10.1109/AICCSA47632.2019.9035340

Sedkaoui, S., & Khelfaoui, M. (2019). Understand, develop and enhance the learning process with big data. *Information Discovery and Delivery*, *47*(1), 2–16. DOI: 10.1108/IDD-09-2018-0043

Shaheen, H., Ali, B., & Khan, N. (2021). Applications of artificial intelligence (AI) in healthcare: A review. *ScienceOpenPreprints*.

Sharif, Z., Jung, L. T., Ayaz, M., Yahya, M., & Khan, D. (2022). Smart home automation by internet-of-things edge computing platform. *International Journal of Advanced Computer Science and Applications*, *13*(4), •••. DOI: 10.14569/IJACSA.2022.0130455

Shashaani, S., Teshnehlab, M., Khodadadian, A., Parvizi, M., Wick, T., & Noii, N. (2023). Using Layer-Wise Training for Road Semantic Segmentation in Autonomous Cars. *IEEE Access : Practical Innovations, Open Solutions*, *11*, 46320–46329. DOI: 10.1109/ACCESS.2023.3255988

Sheng, T. J., Islam, M. S., Misran, N., Baharuddin, M. H., Arshad, H., Islam, M. R., & Islam, M. T. (2020). An internet of things based smart waste management system using LoRa and tensorflow deep learning model. *IEEE Access : Practical Innovations, Open Solutions*, *8*, 148793–148811.

Silva, . (2018). Analytical intelligence in processes: Data science for business. *Revista IEEE América Latina*, *16*(8), 2240–2247. DOI: 10.1109/TLA.2018.8528241

Simić, M., Perić, M., Popadić, I., Perić, D., Pavlović, M., Vučetić, M., & Stanković, M. S. (2020). Big Data and development of Smart City: System architecture and practical public safety example. *Serbian Journal of Electrical Engineering*, *17*(3), 337–355. DOI: 10.2298/SJEE2003337S

Simon., ... (2001),*Data warehousing and business intelligence for e-commerce*. Elsevier, 2001.

Singh, D., Singh, A. K., Singh, S. P., & Poonia, S. (2021). Optimization of tilt angles for solar devices to gain maximum solar energy in Indian climate. In P. V. Baredar, S. Tangellapalli, & C. S. Solanki (Eds.), *Advances in Clean Energy Technologies*. Springer Proceedings in Energy. Springer, Singapore. DOI: 10.1007/978-981-16-0235-1_16

Singhal, A., & Garg, R. (2024). Environmental sustainability consideration with just-in-time practices in Industry 4.0 era: A state of the art. *Operations Management Research*, 1-24.

Sinthiya, N. J., Chowdhury, T. A., & Bahalul Haque, A. K. M. (2022). *Artificial intelligence based Smart Waste Management—a systematic review*. Computational Intelligence Techniques for Green Smart Cities. DOI: 10.1007/978-3-030-96429-0_3

Skevofilakas, M., Fotiadis, D. I., & Likas, A. (2010). A hybrid decision support system for the risk assessment of retinopathy development as a long-term complication of Type 1 Diabetes Mellitus. In *2010 Annual International Conference of the IEEE Engineering in Medicine and Biology* (pp. 6713-6716). IEEE. https://doi.org/DOI: 10.1109/IEMBS.2010.5626245

Spangenberg, J. H. (2005). Economic sustainability of the economy: Concepts and indicators. *International Journal of Sustainable Development*, *8*(1–2), 47–64. DOI: 10.1504/IJSD.2005.007374

Sramka, M., Patel, P., & Varadarajan, A. (2019). Improving clinical refractive results of cataract surgery by machine learning. *PeerJ*, *7*, e7202. https://doi.org/10.xxxx. DOI: 10.7717/peerj.7202 PMID: 31304064

Stephenson, S. S., & Sherwin, J. (2020). Technological advances in biodiversity monitoring: Applicability, opportunities, and challenges. *Current Opinion in Environmental Sustainability*, *45*, 36–41. DOI: 10.1016/j.cosust.2020.08.005

Stolojescu-Crisan, C., Crisan, C., & Butunoi, B. P. (2021). An IoT-based smart home automation system. *Sensors (Basel)*, *21*(11), 3784. DOI: 10.3390/s21113784 PMID: 34070717

Sun, , Sun, L., & Strang, K. (2018). Big data analytics services for enhancing business intelligence. *Journal of Computer Information Systems*, *58*(2), 162–169. DOI: 10.1080/08874417.2016.1220239

Syed, A. S., Sierra-Sosa, D., Kumar, A., & Elmaghraby, A. (2021). IoT in smart cities: A survey of technologies, practices and challenges. *Smart Cities*, *4*(2), 429–475. DOI: 10.3390/smartcities4020024

Taddese, S., & Mekonnen, K. (2020). Sustainability performance indicators for additive manufacturing: A literature review based on product life cycle studies. *International Journal of Advanced Manufacturing Technology*, *107*(7-8), 3109–3134. DOI: 10.1007/s00170-020-05249-2

Tahat, M., Ahmad, A., & Daka, A. (2020). Soil health and sustainable agriculture. *Sustainability*, *12*(12), 4859. DOI: 10.3390/su12124859

Tang, Y., Sun, Y., & Liu, H. (2021). Power electronics: The enabling technology for renewable energy integration. *CSEE Journal of Power and Energy Systems*, *8*(1), 39–52. DOI: 10.17775/CSEEJPES.2021.00170

Tuballa, M. L., & Abundo, M. L. (2016). A review of the development of Smart Grid technologies. *Renewable & Sustainable Energy Reviews*, *59*, 710–725. DOI: 10.1016/j.rser.2016.01.011

Ukhurebor, K. E., & Usman, S. (2022). An overview of the emergence and challenges of land reclamation: Issues and prospects. *Applied and Environmental Soil Science*, *2022*, 1–14. DOI: 10.1155/2022/5889823

Ullah, I., Adhikari, D., Su, X., Palmieri, F., Wu, C., & Choi, C. (2024). Integration of data science with the intelligent IoT (IIoT): Current challenges and future perspectives. *Digital Communications and Networks*.

Urbina, A., Ballesteros, D., & Cabanillas, A. (2020). The balance between efficiency, stability and environmental impacts in perovskite solar cells: A review. *Journal of Physics: Energy*, *2*(2), 022001. DOI: 10.1088/2515-7655/ab5eee

Velasco-Muñoz, J. F., & López, A. M. (2019). Sustainable irrigation in agriculture: An analysis of global research. *Water (Basel)*, *11*(9), 1758. DOI: 10.3390/w11091758

Venkatramanan, S., & Elango, A. (2019). Climate-smart agriculture technologies for environmental management: The intersection of sustainability, resilience, wellbeing and development. In *Sustainable green technologies for environmental management* (pp. 29-51).

Wan, C., Wang, W., Yang, C., Xiang, C., & Li, Y. (2022, September). Fast Parking Slot Detection in the Bird's Eye View. In International Conference on Autonomous Unmanned Systems (pp. 1183-1193). Singapore: Springer Nature Singapore.

Wang, L., Yang, S., Yuan, K., Huang, Y., & Chen, H. (2023). A Combined Reinforcement Learning and Model Predictive Control for Car-Following Maneuver of Autonomous Vehicles. [English Edition]. *Chinese Journal of Mechanical Engineering*, *36*(1), 80. Advance online publication. DOI: 10.1186/s10033-023-00904-7

Wang, , Omar, A. H., Alotaibi, F. M., Daradkeh, Y. I., & Althubiti, S. A. (2022). Business intelligence ability to enhance organizational performance and performance evaluation capabilities by improving data mining systems for competitive advantage. *Information Processing & Management*, *59*(6), 103075. DOI: 10.1016/j.ipm.2022.103075

Weerasooriya, P., & Mahadevan, S. (2021). Industrial water conservation by water footprint and sustainable development goals: A review. *Environment, Development and Sustainability*, *23*(9), 12661–12709. DOI: 10.1007/s10668-020-01184-0

Willoughby, A. A., Soge, A. O., Adeleke, M. A., & Ilori, O. A. (2022). An IoT-based home automation and weather monitoring system. [IJRIAS]. *Int. J. Res. Innov. Appl. Sci.*, *7*(3), 26–29. DOI: 10.51584/IJRIAS.2022.7302

Wu, J., Zhang, Y., & Lin, Y. (2023). Toward sustainable all solid-state Li–metal batteries: Perspectives on battery technology and recycling processes. *Advanced Materials*, *35*(51), 2301540. DOI: 10.1002/adma.202301540 PMID: 37191036

Wu, S., Hadachi, A., Lu, C., & Vivet, D. (2023). Transformer for multiple object tracking: Exploring locality to vision. *Pattern Recognition Letters*, *170*, 70–76. DOI: 10.1016/j.patrec.2023.04.016

Xing, T., Wang, X., Ding, K., Ni, K., & Zhou, Q. (2023). Improved Artificial Potential Field Algorithm Assisted by Multisource Data for AUV Path Planning. *Sensors (Basel)*, *23*(15), 6680. Advance online publication. DOI: 10.3390/s23156680 PMID: 37571463

Yadav, D., Pandey, A., Mishra, D., Bagchi, T., Mahapatra, A., Chandrasekhar, P., & Kumar, A. (2022). IoT enabled smart dustbin with messaging alert system. *International Journal of Information Technology : an Official Journal of Bharati Vidyapeeth's Institute of Computer Applications and Management*, *14*(7), 3601–3609. DOI: 10.1007/s41870-022-00947-4

Yang, P. P., & Yamagata, Y. (2020). Urban systems design: Shaping smart cities by integrating urban design and systems science. In *Urban Systems Design* (pp. 1–22). Elsevier. DOI: 10.1016/B978-0-12-816055-8.00001-4

Yar, H., Imran, A. S., Khan, Z. A., Sajjad, M., & Kastrati, Z. (2021). Towards smart home automation using IoT-enabled edge-computing paradigm. *Sensors (Basel)*, *21*(14), 4932. DOI: 10.3390/s21144932 PMID: 34300671

Yigitcanlar, T., Mehmood, R., & Corchado, J. M. (2021). Green artificial intelligence: Towards an efficient, sustainable and equitable technology for smart cities and futures. *Sustainability (Basel)*, *13*(16), 8952. DOI: 10.3390/su13168952

Yildiz, G., Ulu, A., Dizdaroglu, B., & Yildiz, D. (2023). Hybrid Image Improving and CNN (HIICNN) Stacking Ensemble Method for Traffic Sign Recognition. *IEEE Access : Practical Innovations, Open Solutions*, *11*, 69536–69552. DOI: 10.1109/ACCESS.2023.3292955

Ylusoy, U., Eren, O., & Demirhan, A. (2023). Development of an obstacle avoiding autonomous vehicle by using stereo depth estimation and artificial intelligence based semantic segmentation. *Engineering Applications of Artificial Intelligence*. https://doi.org/https://doi.org/10.1016/j.engappai.2023.106808

Zhang, G., Peng, Y., & Wang, H. (2023). Road Traffic Sign Detection Method Based on RTS R-CNN Instance Segmentation Network. *Sensors (Basel)*, *23*(14), 6543. Advance online publication. DOI: 10.3390/s23146543 PMID: 37514837

Zhao, J., Ma, T., Yang, H., & Zhang, X. (2019). Experimental study and performance analysis on solar photovoltaic panel integrated with phase change material. *Energy*, *178*, 471–486. DOI: 10.1016/j.energy.2019.04.166

Ziaul, I. M., & Shuwei, W. (n.d.). ENVIRONMENTAL SUSTAINABILITY: A MAJOR COMPONENT OF. *Sustainable Development*.

About the Contributors

Adnène Arbi is an Associate Professor at the National Institute of Applied Sciences and Technology (INSAT). His current research activities are in the field of Applied Mathematics and Artificial Intelligence (AI). Major research projects include modelling of mathematical neural networks and model predictive control. He published more than 34 papers in peer-reviewed international journals since 2014. He edited two books on Neural Networks, Iot, AI, and Data-driven control published in 2025-2026. He is a member of the editorial board of the journals: Journal of Algorithms & Computational Technology, Innovative Applied Mathematics and Computational Sciences, Frontiers in Applied Mathematics and Statistics and Karshi Multidisciplinary International Scientific Journal. He served as a reviewer for more than 100 papers for international journals such as the IMA Journal of Mathematical Control and Information, Mathematics and Computers in Simulation, Chaos, Solitons & Fractals, Journal of Intelligent & Fuzzy Systems, Computational and Applied Mathematics. American Association for Sciences and Technology, Mathematical Methods in the Applied Sciences, Neural Networks, Asian Journal of Control, Neural processing letters, International Journal of Statistical Distributions and Applications, IEEE Transactions on Neural Networks and Learning Systems, IMA Journal of Mathematical Control and Information, JCAS: International Journal of Control, Automation and Systems. He is an Expert/Consultant for the Science for Africa Foundation (2023). He has co-organized two international workshops and conferences since 2022. He is a member of the Laboratory of Engineering Mathematics at Tunisia Polytechnic School, University of Carthage, Tunisia. Besides, he is a member of international member of laboratoire Artificial Intelligence Research and Applications (AIRA), Hassan I University, Settat, Morocco. H-index: 19; Total citations: 721; Expertise: Time scales, Dynamical Systems, Time delay systems, Neural Networks, Model Predictive Control.

Imene Ouali is a researcher in Computer Science with a specialization in signal and image processing technologies. Her work spans multiple advanced fields, including Artificial Intelligence (AI), Augmented Reality (AR), and Ontology. She has contributed to cutting-edge research and development, integrating these technologies to solve complex problems in various domains. With a strong academic background and extensive experience in AI-driven applications, Dr. Ouali focuses on developing innovative solutions that bridge theoretical advancements and practical implementations. Her expertise also extends to interdisciplinary projects, where she explores the synergy between intelligent systems, data analysis, and emerging technologies.

Achraf Wali is a doctoral student in Computer Science at the University of Sfax. His research focuses on the Internet of Things (IoT), artificial intelligence (AI), and business intelligence (BI) applications. He earned a bachelor's degree in Computer Science and Multimedia, followed by a research master's degree in Big Data, both from the University of Sfax. Additionally, he completed exchange programs at the University of Riga (Latvia) and the University of Palma de Mallorca (Spain), where he achieved distinguished academic results and gained practical experience in various research areas. Furthermore, he has completed several internships with national and international companies. He has also presented his work at international conferences. In addition, he is proficient in multiple languages, including English.

***

Jaafar Abouchabaka obtained two doctorates in Computer Sciences applied to mathematics from Mohammed V University, Rabat, Morocco. Currently, he is a Professor at Department of computer Sciences, Ibn Tofail University, Kenitra, Morocco. His research interests are in concurrent and parallel programming, distributed systems, multi agent systems, genetics algorithms, big data and cloud computing. He can be contacted at email: jaafar.abouchabaka@uit.ac.ma

Mohamed Saifeddine Hadj Sassi is a Postdoc in MR at the Luxembourg Institute of Science and Technology. He holds two PhDs in distinct fields. His first PhD in Applied Electronics from University Roma Tre in Italy focused on augmented and virtual reality systems used in operational control rooms, a study conducted as part of the Marie Skłodowska-Curie Innovative Training Network and the ImmerSAFE Project1 which he completed his milestones successfully. His second PhD is in Computer Systems Engineering from the University of Sfax in Tunisia, where he specialized in developing IoT systems for indoor air quality assessment and monitoring. His dual expertise encompasses using IoT sensors and UWB systems for positioning and tracking, critical in operational environments. Dr. Sassi has led significant projects, including RISARX and CACTUS, applying AR in complex environments such as emergency training for firefighters and operational control rooms. His work, published in high-impact journals and presented internationally, demonstrates his capability to innovate rehabilitation practices using sophisticated AI-enhanced AR platforms, ideally positioning him to advance home-based rehabilitation for stroke survivors through the in RAIAR project includes those with an AR, AI and medical applications

Fatima Ezzahra Khalloufi received his master's degree in applied mathematics, from Hassan Premier University, Settat, Morocco. She is a Ph.D. student in computer research Laboratory (LaRI) at Ibn Tofail. His research interests include big data, data mining, machine and deep learning. She can be contacted at email: fatima-ezzahra.khalloufi@uit.ac .ma.

Rafalia Najat obtained three doctorates in Computer Sciences from Mohammed V University, Rabat, Morocco by collaboration with ENSEEIHT, Toulouse, France, and Ibn Tofail University, Kenitra, Morocco. Currently, she is a Professor at Department of Computer Sciences, Ibn Tofail University, Kenitra, Morocco. Her research interests are in distributed systems, multi-agent systems, concurrent and parallel programming, communication, security, big data, and cloud computing. She can be contacted at email: najat.rafalia@uit.ac.ma.

Oussama Wali holds a PhD in Computer Science and specializes in the field of artificial intelligence (AI), among other areas of expertise. With a passion for innovation and technology, Oussama has dedicated his academic and professional career to advancing the frontiers of AI, contributing to cutting-edge research and practical applications that span diverse industries. Throughout his journey, Oussama has explored various subfields within computer science, leveraging AI to solve complex problems and drive transformative solutions. His work encompasses machine learning, data analysis, and algorithm development, as well as interdisciplinary collaborations that push the boundaries of what AI can achieve. Oussama's expertise is reflected in his contributions to academic publications, conferences, and industry projects, making him a respected figure in the AI community. His ongoing research and professional endeavors continue to shape the future of AI and its impact on society, with a strong focus on ethical, efficient, and innovative solutions to real-world challenges.

Index

T

U

W

www.ingramcontent.com/pod-product-compliance
Lightning Source LLC
LaVergne TN
LVHW061546290926
849162LV00004B/925